Advanced Level
English Language

Advanced Level English Language

R. A. Banks, MA, PhD
and
F. D. A. Burns, MA, PhD

Hodder & Stoughton
LONDON SYDNEY AUCKLAND TORONTO

British Library Cataloguing in Publication Data

Banks, R A
    Advanced Level English Language
    1. English Language—Grammar—1950–
    I. Title II. Burns, F D A
    428 PE1112

ISBN 0 340 39849 3

First published 1987
Fourth impression 1991

Typeset by Macmillan India Ltd.
Printed in Great Britain for the educational publishing division of
Hodder and Stoughton Ltd, Mill Road, Dunton Green, Sevenoaks,
Kent by Page Bros (Norwich) Ltd.

For: Mary-Lou and Gwenfil Ann

Acknowledgments

The authors and publishers would like to thank the following for their kind permission to reproduce copyright materials: Times Newspapers Ltd for an extract from ' The Write Stuff ' by Peter Wilby (*Sunday Times* 3.2.85), an extract from 'The English language is not *that* important!' by Arthur Sefton (*Times Educational Supplement* 4.5.84), an extract from 'Semantic Warfare' by Bryan Silcock (*Sunday Times* 31.3.85), an extract from 'A Life in the Day of Lucy Hall' (*Sunday Times Magazine* 1984), an extract from 'The Mongrel Tongue' by John Carey (*Sunday Times* 27.1.85), and an extract from 'The Dialect of In-Speak' by Peter Wilby (*Sunday Times* 7.4.85); Guinness Superlatives for text reproduced from the *Guinness Book of Records* 1986 edition © Guinness Superlatives Ltd; the *Observer* for an article by John Silverlight (*Observer* 15.7.84); Routledge & Kegan Paul PLC for an extract from *Tales Out of School* by Roger White with David Brockingham, and for an extract from *Halliday, System and Function in Language: Selected Papers* by G. R. Kress; Hamish Hamilton for 'Jaffo the Calypsonian' by Ian McDonald from *Breaklight*; Oxford University Press for 'Rites' by Edward Kamau Braithwaite from *Islands* © Oxford University Press, for an extract from *New World* by Alan T. Dale (1967) © Oxford University Press (1967), and for an extract from *The Voice of the Past* by Paul Thompson (1978) © Oxford University Press 1978; Angela Hewins for an extract from her book *The Dillen*, published by Elm Tree Books 1981; Jon Raven and Broadside for an extract from *Tales from Aynuk's Black Country* by Jon Raven; the Post Office for their advertisement on postcodes; W & R Chambers Ltd Publishers for an extract from *Chambers Twentieth Century Dictionary*; Collins Publishers for an extract from *Collins English Dictionary*; Longman Group UK Ltd for an extract from *Roget's Thesaurus*, and for two extracts from *A Grammar of Spoken English* 3rd edition (Rev. R. Kingdom) by H. E. Palmer and F. G. Blandford; JVC for their advertisement for the JVC Ex-3 Midi System; Thistle Hotels for an extract from *Thistle Life* Autumn 1984; Wales Tourist Board for their 'What Dylan Thomas saw in Wales' advertisement; British Rail and Sealink UK Ltd for their 'European Savers' advertisement; article on car insurance claim forms by courtesy of the *Wolverhampton Express and Star* and Graham Payne Associates (*Wolverhampton Express and Star* 17.4.85); Faber & Faber Ltd for an extract from *Hot Gates* by William Golding; Sun Alliance Insurance Group for their ' This is the Girl . . . ' advertisement; Leeds University for an extract from *Child Language Survey* (Nuffield Foreign Languages Teaching Reports and Occasional Papers No. 24); Chatto & Windus and the Literary Estate of Daisy Ashford for an extract from *The Young Visiters* by Daisy Ashford; Simon & Schuster Inc. for an extract from *Television Plays* by Paddy Chayevsky © 1955 Paddy Chayevsky renewed © 1983 by Susan Chayevsky; Grafton Books for an extract from *The Boys from the Blackstuff* by Alan Bleasdale; BBC Enterprises Ltd for an extract reproduced from *Oxbridge Blues* by Frederick Raphael; Advertisement for the Porsche 924 reproduced by kind permission of Porsche Cars Great Britain Ltd; Club 18–30 Holidays for an extract from their Summer 1985 brochure; Falcon Leisure Group for an extract from the Summer 1984 Twentys Holidays brochure; Carousel Holidays for an extract from their Winter 1983/84 brochure; the Literary Estate of Isaac Rosenberg for 'Dead Man's Dump' by Isaac Rosenberg; John Farquharson on behalf of the estate of Elwyn Jones for an extract from *On Trial* by Elwyn Jones; The Society of Authors on behalf of the Estate of George Bernard Shaw for an extract from *Pygmalion* by George Bernard Shaw; The Bodley Head for an extract from *Ulysses* by James Joyce; the *Revised Standard Version* scripture quotations contained herein are from the *Revised Standard Version of the Bible*, copyrighted 1946, 1952, 1971 by the Division of Christian Education of the National Council of the Churches of Christ in the USA and are used by permission. All rights reserved; the extract taken from the Jerusalem Bible, published and copyrighted 1966, 1967 and 1968 by Darton, Longman and Todd Ltd and Doubleday and Company Inc is used by permission of the publishers; Methuen & Co. Ltd for an extract from *Our Masters' Voices* by Max Atkinson; J. M. Dent & Sons Ltd Publishers for an extract from *Put it in Writing* by John Whale; the Controller of Her Majesty's Stationery Office for an extract from *English 5–16*; *The Guardian*, Chris Nocholls, George Patterson, Rene Boote and Ronnie Parker for their contributions to the letters page of *The Guardian* (13.11.84); Martin Secker & Warburg Ltd for an extract from *Small World* by David Lodge.

We have been unable to trace copyright holders of materials not acknowledged here, and would be grateful for any information that would enable us to do so.

Contents

Introduction

This book is designed to help those students preparing for Advanced Level examinations in English Language such as those set by the University of London and the Joint Matriculation Board and those beginning language courses in colleges, polytechnics, and universities. It covers such areas as Spoken and Written English, Varieties, Style, Historical Change, Contemporary Usage, and explains the terminology students need in their discussion of language in use. There is a chapter which outlines modern approaches to grammar and there are exercises suggested of the type likely to be met in final examinations. There are some suggestions, too, as to how project work might be tackled in English Language Studies.

To come to the post-GCE (O Level) and GCSE study of the subject for the first time is somewhat daunting. The terminology alone is sufficiently baffling for many. There is a need to build on earlier close and accurate reading skills and careful thinking about how the language works in context. Advanced Level study is not merely a matter of acquiring more knowledge: it is more importantly a matter of acquiring more experience in thinking about how language works across a whole range of functions within a whole range of contexts. This book will help to provide just this knowledge and this experience.

We should like to acknowledge our indebtedness to the major writers and thinkers on the subject whose works have been milestones in the development of English Language Studies and whose ideas underlie many of those in this book. Randolph Quirk, himself one such major contributor to English Language research and teaching, acknowledged that 'all grammarians draw freely on the work of their predecessors' and, like him, we acknowledge our own debt, particularly to those whose works are listed in the Selected Bibliography, which students should find helpful in following up their own researches into the subject.

Finally, we are both grateful to our wives, Mary-Lou and Gwenfil-Ann, whose support throughout the project has been strong. Once again, Mrs Daphne Meeking has wrestled with the vagaries of our manuscripts to produce her usual immaculate typescript for us and we thank her for her care, hard work, and enthusiasm.

R. A. Banks and F. D. A. Burns

PART I

*Approaches to the
study of language*

CHAPTER 1

Observation

The study of language can be interesting, stimulating and rewarding. There is no other subject which has such direct relevance to your everyday life and whose benefits can be readily seen in the quality of your existence. You had already worked out systems of language for communicating with others, especially to get what you wanted, before you came to formal education. The fact that you said 'buyed' instead of 'bought' at the age of three was not a reflection of your incompetence, but an indication that you had already begun to work out the sound for the past tense of a verb, only to be thwarted by the nature of the English language in having so many irregular forms.

Already today, as you read this, you will have used your language in a variety of ways for a variety of purposes. You will have spoken to your friends at college in a different way from the way you spoke at breakfast time at home. If you have already had to do some written work, you will have used a different form of your language from that accepted in a group discussion. Nor does the versatility in your uses of language end there. You will know yourself that you are capable of using a variety of language structures and a range of vocabulary according to your audience and the impression you want to give and the response you want to elicit. Similarly you will have mastered how to respond to language use, whether written or spoken. You will have established for yourself, possibly intuitively, a means of assessing when a remark is to be taken seriously or humorously or when a person is being friendly or matter-of-fact or hostile. Sometimes a person you know well does not have to utter a complete statement for you to know what is meant, and conversely you may sometimes pick up a wrong signal and misunderstand a person because of a choice of word or the stress given to a syllable.

There are subtleties and complexities in the uses of language, and it is the aim of a language course to help you become aware of what is happening and why, to provide you with ways of describing what you observe, and to make you more exact in the ways you use language appropriately. In the process you are likely to want to consider the principles on which aspects of language use depend and the rules which can be deduced and how far such rules hold for every use of language.

Contexts

It may be helpful, to whet your appetite by way of introduction, to consider a variety of uses of language and the implications of each situation.

Read the following out loud in a way that makes its sense clear to you:

I should like to congratulate you on this work of art.

Did you have any difficulties? You ought to have had, for every word poses a question of interpretation. There are at least eight different ways of expressing the sentence, each bearing its own meaning. For instance, 'I' can be personal and authoritative, but it can also suggest that the person making the statement holds an opinion not held by others. Similarly, 'should' is capable of various interpretations. In speech it can be emphasised to denote pleasure, but it could also convey that a person would like to do something but cannot because of particular circumstances. It may be that 'should' should not be emphasised, being merely a form of the verb used with 'I' where 'would' would be used with 'he'. You may ask yourself if the difference between 'should' and 'would' are still relevant nowadays. What of the word 'like'? In what ways does it differ from the word 'love'? Similarly, what would be changed if 'want' had been used in place of 'should like'? You can consider 'congratulate' in a similar way. What would be gained or lost if 'compliment' or 'praise' or 'commend' were used instead, and why is 'salute' now considered inappropriate as a synonym for 'congratulate'? How do you interpret the versatile 'you'? Does it refer to one person, picked out from others, or to a group of people? What makes 'you' a more appropriate word than 'one' in this context? The word 'this' can refer to a particular item, or its use can suggest that other items are not as acceptable. As for 'work of art', does it have to be taken as an expression referring to one piece, or can the words be taken separately and given a different sense?

The statement can also be taken as a whole. Should it necessarily be expressed sincerely, or can it be uttered ironically and suggest the opposite of what the words appear to say? What features indicate that, as it stands, it represents something spoken? What conventions would need to be observed if it were to be set down in written form making the intentions of the writer readily apparent? If it were to be reported by someone, further changes would be required—'I' to 'he', 'should' to 'would', 'you' to 'him', 'her' or 'them', with the ambiguity between 'he' and 'him' being removed.

To consider the statement in yet another way, could it be changed in form and still bear some sense of the original? In what respects is 'You are to be congratulated by me on this work of art' different from what was originally stated?

It should be apparent by now that any use of words needs a context if a meaning is to be fixed, and that the observer, that is you, needs a system for describing what you observe.

To turn to another context, read the following account, taken from the *The Times* for 2nd July 1894, about the official opening of Tower Bridge in London.

THE OPENING OF THE TOWER-BRIDGE

On Saturday at noon, under a cloudless sky and as part of a pageant which delighted tens of thousands of people, the new Tower-bridge, which deserves to be reckoned among the greatest engineering triumphs of the Victorian age, was declared open for traffic by land and water by the Prince of Wales with every circumstance of pomp and splendour. The occasion was chosen, with due regard for that love of a great display of State ceremonial which is instinctive in the population of London, as an opportunity for one of those Royal processions through the streets which serve to give as many persons as possible at least a passing glimpse of Royal personages, and to keep alive that spirit of affectionate loyalty which grows, to all appearance, stronger every year in the hearts of the British people. The net result was, without doubt, a series of spectacles of striking grandeur, and few sights more imposing and majestic have ever been seen in this country than the silent and irresistible upheaval of those solid leaves of the bridge which fascinated the spectators on land and water when the Prince of Wales turned the lever which set the hydraulic machinery, gigantic in force, in motion. That is the sight which will live in the memory of those who looked upon it for years to come. It was imposing in the same sense as a great convulsion of the natural world; it was an exhibition of resistless force which held the spectators spellbound and speechless. It will be seen again many times after the 9th of July, when the bridge will really be open; it will become familiar like other wonders of engineering; but still the memory of the first occasion upon which it was exhibited will remain indelible. For the rest, let it be said that the conditions under which the pageant was carried out were faultless; Paris herself never saw a fairer sky and the Seine never shone under a brighter sun than the Thames on Saturday.

The opening of the Tower-bridge on Saturday was a picturesque and stately ceremonial, perfectly performed under the most favourable conditions. The crowds which thronged the streets and the innumerable craft upon the river were vast, orderly, and enthusiastic. The arrangements for keeping the line of the procession were designed and carried out with the skill for which the City authorities are famous. The decorations, both by land and water, were brilliant and profuse, the uniforms and robes were splendid and varied, while the glorious sunshine brought out in full relief the many beauties of the great display and of the noble river which all true Englishmen love with a proud affection as the chiefest glory of their ancient capital. The effect produced on the immense multitude of spectators by the actual opening of the movable roadway was remarkable. For a moment the great crowd were hushed in silence. Then, in a deafening shout of applause, which soared, as only a British cheer can soar, above the thunder of the Tower guns, above the ringing notes of the trumpets, and above the wild din from the sirens and whistles of the steamers, they gave vent to their admiration and delight at the marvel they had been privileged to see. They had indeed witnessed a spectacle not easily to be forgotten. The leaves of halves of the centre span of the bridge are each 115 feet long and cover between them a waterway 200 feet wide. At the touch of a silver disc small enough to be formed into the lid of a "loving cup" they rose smoothly and noiselessly under the hand of the PRINCE OF WALES. The force by which this wonderful operation was performed deserves, even at the risk of some repetition, a brief description. It is provided by hydraulic motors placed in the central piers. Each of these consists of three single-acting cylinders with a ram of 27in. stroke. The motors are supplied by accumulators constructed to provide a working pressure of 850lb. to the square inch, and the accumulators in turn are fed by pumps worked by steam engines of the horizontal-compound tandem type and of 360-horse power. In other words, the bridge is worked by hydraulic machinery, and the hydraulic power is provided by steam. In addition to the machinery for raising and lowering the movable girders or leaves of the roadway, mechanism had also to be fitted for working the hydraulic lifts which are to carry impatient passengers to the elevated footway, 140ft. above the water-level, when the waterway is open and the carriageway is closed. Access may be had to this footway by a staircase, but, as it consists of no fewer than 200 steps, it is not likely to be largely used by persons of mature years whenever the lifts are available. The machinery has been duplicated throughout in case of accident to any particular portion. While it is hoped that serious delays will be prevented in this way, great care has been taken to minimize all possible risks to life or limb in the event of any breakdown of the mechanism.

The reporters of the occasion were clearly proud of what they had observed and been part of, and equally proud to be British. In what ways does the language they use support the impression they wish to give? Two aspects are readily apparent, the choice of vocabulary and the construction of sentences. It is helpful to list the attributes—cloudless sky, pageant, engineering triumphs, pomp, splendour, state ceremonial, royal processions, spectacle of striking grandeur, and so on. The impression is given of magnificence and excellence. The adjectives reinforce this impression — brilliant, profuse, splendid, varied, glorious, noble, proud, chiefest, ancient. The sentence constructions support the impression of stateliness and grandeur. They abound with dependent clauses on dependent clauses, with the main clauses almost being submerged. At one point there is a switch to repetitive constructions—'it was imposing . . .', 'it was an exhibition . . .', 'it will be seen again . . .,' 'it will become . . .'—and again—'above the thunder of the Tower gun . . .,' 'above the ringing note of the trumpets . . .,' 'above the wild din . . .'. Throughout there is the assumption that the reader is capable of coping with the reading skills required.

Nothing is allowed to mar the occasion, not even the actual machinery which cannot be romantically presented. The reporter, at this stage, becomes obsessed with the word 'hydraulics' and also with the mechanical information. Note the number of occasions on which the report resorts to figures—27in. stroke, 850 lb to the square inch, 360 horse power—and the way in which criticism of any section of society is avoided. Towards the end of the extract there is the assumption that 'persons of mature years' are unlikely to use the footway across the Thames when the bridge is open because the staircase consists of 'no fewer than 200 steps'.

Such an extract presents some interesting features of the stylistic devices used by reporters of *The Times*. In what respects are they dated, particular to the end of the last century? It could be argued that contemporary royal events evoke a similar type of response, the most typical and recent being the wedding of Prince Andrew and Sarah Ferguson. The interest of such material in the report of the official opening of Tower Bridge is that it allows one to identify change in the uses of language and at the same time identify similar devices at work in contemporary journalism.

To move even further back in history, and to consider the relevance of a linguistic approach to the study of literature, read the following poem by Michael Drayton.

> SINCE ther's no helpe, Come let us kisse and part,
> Nay, I have done: You get no more of Me,
> And I am glad, yea glad with all my heart,
> That thus so cleanly, I my Selfe can free,
> Shake hands for ever, Cancell all our Vowes,
> And when We meet at any time againe,
> Be it not scene in either of our Browes,
> That We one jot of former Love reteyne;
> Now at the last gaspe, of Loves latest Breath,
> When his Pulse fayling, Passion speechlesse lies,
> When Faith is kneeling by his bed of Death,
> And Innocence is closing up his Eyes,
>   Now if thou would'st, when all have given him over,
>   From Death to Life, thou might'st him yet recover.

Whether you are studying language or literature, one of the first things you will notice is its length—fourteen lines—and thus you will identify it as a sonnet. The rhyme scheme will indicate what type of sonnet it is (see page 35). From rhyme it is a simple matter to move to structure—three quatrains and a final couplet. Does the poem shift in its argument as it progresses? A close examination of the language will show that, although the sonnet is technically consistent in its rhythm, there is a change in the tone established stylistically, from the first eight lines (the octave) to the final six lines (the sestet). To see what is happening, study the first eight lines more closely. The poet, writing about the end of a love relationship, uses language more appropriate to the end of a business deal. Note the idiomatic or colloquial expression of the second line—

  'Nay, I have done, you get no more of me'

with the stress falling unexpectedly on the first word 'Nay', matching the stress on 'Since', the first word of the sonnet, to be supported by the alliterative 'Shake' at the beginning of the second quatrain. Even more emphatic is the use of monosyllabic words. All but six of seventy-one words are of one syllable.

By contrast lines 9–12 present an image of personified Love/Passion on a deathbed attended by Faith and Innocence, the tableau being described in a sequence of dependent clauses, leading to the appeal or plea of the final couplet, begun by 'Now' which echoes the first word of line 9. Note how the choice of language, the order of words, the grammatical structures change, and the tone is different from that of the opening lines.

Yet a simple use of language helps to give the sonnet coherence. Did you notice the personal pronouns and adjectives? The relationship of the first eight lines, expressed through 'us', 'I', 'you', 'me' and so on, gives place to the more distant or objective 'his' of lines 9–12, which in turn is developed to 'thou' and 'him' of the final couplet. If you respond to the difference in the uses of 'you' and 'thou', you could begin to form a literary judgment that the masculine narrator of the poem, bitter but trying to be detached and controlled initially, betrays his true feelings by trying to evoke an emotional response from his loved one to a projection of the consequences of rejecting him, and ends with one final appeal to her.

This is not the place, however, for literary analysis. The intention is to show that a close study of language uses, no matter how commonplace they may seem, can prepare the ground for a sensitive response to literature.

There are, of course, other features of the language of such a sonnet that might arouse your interest—the forms of spelling, the uses of capitals, the rhymes that no longer seem to be rhymes. Any one of these could be a starting point for a study of language use and lead to generalisations about the nature of language.

These three different examples are intended to give a hint of the range of possibilities and interests in the study of language. As far as has been possible, technical terms have been so far deliberately avoided. They can be off-putting, unless or until you have a firm grasp of what is implied. Nevertheless, early in your language course, you should make a copy of your syllabus, keep it in your file for frequent reference, and begin to develop a working knowledge of the terms that it includes.

Contents

A syllabus will normally provide aims and objectives for your course and give a list of areas of particular interest and the ways in which these are to be examined. Study your syllabus carefully, and refer to the sections that follow in this book for a summary of an area and for guidance.

All syllabuses have aims which are both theoretical and practical. You will be required to show an understanding of the nature and function of English, displaying an awareness of systems underlying language and its uses, and you will be expected to display sensitivity in your response to language and in your effective use of it.

In the objectives you will be expected to reveal investigative abilities in your consideration of language, show a grasp of theoretical knowledge, particularly with reference to sound patterns, vocabulary and grammar and their relationships to meaning, and be able to analyse texts and transcripts, relating linguistic features to function and context. You may also be expected to show interpretative abilities in understanding, adapting and representing material for particular purposes and audiences, and sometimes you may be asked to demonstrate such skills by creating your own texts according to set models.

It may be helpful to cite a range of the headings you are likely to be faced with when you move on to the contents of a syllabus.

Phonology

Graphology

Grammar

Semantics

Lexis

Syntax

Dialectal and standard English

Children's and adults' speech

Language acquisition

Language change

Conversation and discourse

Spoken English

Vowel and consonants of received pronunciation

Syllable and stress, rhythm and intonation

Paralinguistic features of communication

Forms and conventions of written English

Assimilation and elision

Importance of purpose, context and register

Interpreting, adapting, editing and re-presenting source material to audiences other than those originally intended

Roman alphabet

Conventions of spelling and punctuation

Speech and writing, and the differences in acquisition, operation and use

Regional variations of speech; accents

Style in speech and writing

Style in literature

Historical change

Attitudes to contemporary usage

Stylistic features of popular media

The list may seem daunting, but it should not be if you develop skills to observe, record and consider the general implications of appropriate material.

Skills

The essential skills lie in your own talents, the sensitive uses of your eyes and ears. On a language course you need to be alert to the variety of uses of language around you at all times, and you need to develop your ability to observe what you see and listen to what you hear extremely accurately.

Moreover, you need to learn to be an accurate gatherer of material. This can take two forms—spoken and written. You need a tape recorder with a supply of tapes on which you record instances of spoken English which are of interest to you. You also need to get into the habit of collecting and storing in a file examples of printed or written English, anything of interest because of the way language is used. Access to a photocopier is ideal for your requirements. As your tape library and file grow in size, you will need to group the material into clearly marked sections, as you would your own record library.

Having gathered material, you need to be alert to its potential. For example, the exercises later in this book make specific demands or pose specific tasks, but the quoted material, which is typical of the range of material to be found in examination papers, presents other opportunities for the study of language.

Arising from this, you will find you need to develop a means of describing your observations. Here the use of terms or of systems can be helpful as a focus for your observations and ideas. Terms provide a shorthand way of focussing the attention of your reader/examiner on what is of interest to you. You must make sure that you are using terms in a precise and accurate manner that is readily identifiable by your reader, particularly when you are trying to denote sounds and structures of spoken English.

Finally, you should always show a willingness to try to make generalisations about what you observe. Is there a grammatical system which is appropriate for all uses of language? Can you detect similarities in what are different language contexts? Examiners are always looking for students prepared to grasp relationships between one language situation and another, and to draw conclusions about the nature of language.

PART II

Varieties of English

CHAPTER 2

Historical Change

Classical Latin and Ancient Greek are sometimes referred to as 'dead' languages; English, French, and German are described as 'living' languages. The distinction lies in the fact that a 'dead' language is one that has stopped developing, whereas a 'living' language is one that is continuing to change and grow.

Examine carefully the following versions of the Lord's Prayer in English and try to establish similarities between them in:
(a) vocabulary—or the words they use;
(b) word positions;
(c) phrasing; and
(d) sentence structure.
Remember that they are all in English, but the first was written before the time of the Norman Conquest and the latest in 1976. (The text of the prayer is found in *S. Matthew* VI, 9–13 and in *S. Luke* XI, 2–4).

(i) Faeder úre þu þe eart on heofonum; Si þin nama gehalgod to be cume þin ríce gewurþe ðin willa on eorðan swa swa on heofonum úrne gedaeghwamlican hlaf syle us to dæg 7 forgyf us úre gyltas swa swa we forgyfað urum gyltendum 7 ne gelæd pu us on costunge ac alys us of yfele soþlice
(*c.* 1000 AD: from a manuscript in Corpus Christi College Cambridge, MS 140 f.8ʳ)

[You will notice that this Old English (Anglo-Saxon) version uses some letters and signs no longer found in Modern English: þ = a voiceless 'th'; ð = a voiced 'th'; 7 = and; æ = a vowel pronounced like the 'a' in the Modern English word *hat* (as a short vowel) or as in *ware* (as a long vowel).]

(ii) Oure fadir that art in hevenes halowid be thi name/thi kyngdom come to/be thi wille don in er þe as in hevene/geve to us this day oure breed ovir othir substaunce*/and forgeve to us oure dettis, as we forgeven to our dettouris/and lede us not in to temptacioun: but delyver us fro yvel. Amen.
(Wycliffite Bible, 1382 AD)

[* 'ovir othir substaunce' is an attempt to translate literally the Latin *supersubstantialem* found in St Jerome's Latin version of 382 AD.]

[Look up the words *substaunce, dettis, dettouris, temptacioun,* and *delyver* in a good, modern etymological dictionary (i.e. one which gives the origins of words). What links can you find between their sources and Latin and French? Where do the other words originate?]

(iii) Our Father which art in heaven, Hallowed be thy name. Thy kingdom come. Thy will be done in earth, as it is in heaven. Give us this day our daily bread. And forgive us our debts, as we forgive our debtors. And lead us not into temptation, but deliver us from evil: Amen.

(*The Authorised Version*, 1611)

[It is interesting that *The Authorised Version*'s 'temptation' is the same as that found in the *Wycliffite Bible*, whereas the Anglo-Saxon has *costnunge* ('trial', or 'tribulation'), a rendering to which later versions return. 'Temptation' was an unfortunate translation used originally by St Jerome of the Greek *peirasmos*, which is closer in meaning to Mod. English 'trial' rather than 'temptation'. Notice particularly the differences in punctuation between this version, which follows speech rhythms, and later ones. Look up the word 'which' in a good dictionary and then look up the word 'who'; how did the Anglo-Saxon version render the relative pronoun?]

(iv) Our Father in heaven,
    thy name be revered,
    thy Reign begin,
    thy will be done
    on earth as in heaven.
    Give us to-day our bread for the morrow,
    and forgive us for debts
    as we ourselves have forgiven our debtors,
    and lead us not into temptation
    but deliver us from evil.

(Dr James Moffatt's translation,
first published in 1913, revised in 1934)

(v) Our Father in heaven,
    thy name be hallowed;
    thy kingdom come,
    thy will be done,
    on earth as in heaven.
    Give us today our daily bread.
    Forgive us the wrong we have done,
    as we have forgiven those who have wronged us.
    And do not bring us to the test,
    but save us from the evil one.

(*New English Bible*, 1961)

(vi) Our father in heaven
   May your holy name be honoured;
   may your kingdom come;
   may your will be done on earth as it is in heaven.
   Give us today the food we need.
   Forgive us the wrongs we have done, as we
   forgive the wrongs that others have done to us.
   Do not bring us to hard testing
   but keep us safe from The Evil One.

(*The Good News Bible*. Today's
English Version, British Usage
Edition, 1976)

Its birth: the origins of the English language.

English belongs to a group of languages usually referred to as Indo-European; this group contains nearly all the European languages, Iranian, and those from much of India. Indo-European languages are those which structurally have parts of speech, such as nouns, verbs, adjectives, etc.; they may have a full system of inflexions (and be described by grammarians as '**synthetic**') or have few or no inflexions (described by grammarians as '**analytic**'). The vocabulary of these languages seems to have a number of common roots. Non-Indo-European languages (e.g. Chinese, Hungarian, Finnish) do not have 'parts of speech' but build up 'phrases' and meanings by adding prefixes and suffixes to single, often monosyllabic, words.

It is conjectured that several thousand years before the Christian era, Indo-European was spoken as a language at some point in eastern or southern Europe near the border with Asia; no written forms of it are in existence. The Indo-European languages are sometimes divided into eight groups, four in the west (sometimes called the *Centum* languages) and four in the east (the *Satem* languages): in the west the group are Hellenic, Italic, Celtic and Germanic; in the east the group are Balto-Slavonic, Indo-Iranian, Armenian, and Albanian.

English belongs to the Germanic group of Indo-European languages; this group is marked by three main characteristics: the placing of the stress or emphasis on the root syllable of the word as close to its beginning as possible; the use of two main tenses, the present and the past, although these have been added to and made more sophisticated by the use of auxiliary verbs to form new ways of indicating time; the division of its verbs into two main types, the strong (which indicate their tense by a change of vowel in the main syllable e.g. *sing, sang, sung*) and the weak (which indicate their tense by adding endings—usually -d, ed, or -t, e.g. *look, looked, looked*). Some associate the endings added to the stems of weak verbs with the verb *to do*, in its earliest forms; certainly, English still uses the verb *to do* to indicate tenses of all verbs in their negative or interrogative forms; e.g. '*Did* I sing the song?' 'I *do* not look at the book'.

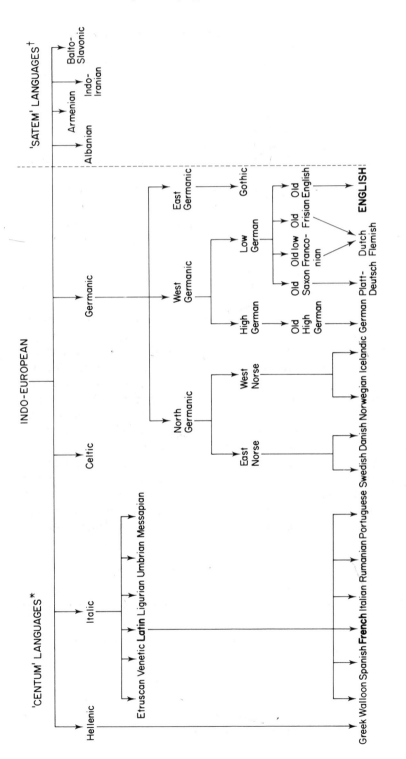

* Indo-European languages in which an original palatal consonant developed as a guttural (Latin: '*centum*' = hundred)

† Indo-European languages in which an original palatal consonant developed as a sibilant (Avestic: '*satem*' = hundred)

English in its earliest form is known as Anglo-Saxon or Old English. It is part of the Western group of Germanic languages; this group is further subdivided into **Low German** (English, Dutch, Flemish, Frisian, and 'Platt-Deutsch' spoken by some Germans in country areas) and **High German** (most Germans, especially in the southern areas and Austrians). The chart opposite shows the place of English within the Indo-European languages. It is clear from this chart that in origin English is closer to Dutch and German as languages than, say, Swedish, Danish, Norwegian, or Icelandic, but nearer to all these than, say, French, Spanish, Italian or Portuguese.

Nevertheless, English has come most strongly during its development under the infllence of:

(a) *Celtic:* when the Anglo-Saxon tribes arrived in the British Isles in the 5th and 6th centuries and during the attempts by the Celtic church to Christianise England.

(b) *Latin:* whilst the Anglo-Saxon tribes were still on the Continent in contact with European Roman civilisation (sometimes called **the Zero Period**); on their arrival in the British Isles where they met further evidence of Roman civilisation (**the First Period**); when St Augustine and his missionaries attempted to convert England to the Roman Church, AD 597 →, and later during the Benedictine Reform of the 10th century (**the Second Period**); during the late Middle Ages by the influence of the Norman Conquest, indirectly through the sources of French words, and from words borrowed directly from Latin into the language (**the Third Period**); at the time of the Renaissance, when some Latin words were re-introduced and others established for the first time in English (**the Fourth Period**). The Fourth Period was a time when Latin enriched the vocabulary of English, often by the direct way of written English set permanently in print and the growth of synonyms or words with closely related meanings. (For a full account of these 'periods' see A. C. Baugh and T. Cable, *A History of the English Language*, third edition, 1978.)

(c) *French*: largely following the Norman Conquest until the end of the so-called Middle English period (*c*. 1450 AD); the influence was at its peak from 1250 to 1400. The vocabulary was largely enriched with military, ecclesiastical, and administrative words as well as in the areas of art, fashion, learning, cooking, medicine, and social life. The French language has continued to affect the development of English, partly because of the wars between the two countries in Europe and in North America, and partly in more recent times because of closer European ties.

(d) *Scandinavian*: during the Viking invasions (8th and 9th centuries) and during the period of their settlements, especially in the north and east of England (9th and 10th centuries).

(e) *The Low Countries*: this influence occurred over a long period of time from the period of William the Conqueror (whose wife was Flemish) until the 18th century. Flemings came to England for trade, joined the English forces as mercenaries during the late Middle Ages, shared in the promising wool trade between England and the Continent, and demonstrated their skills in painting during the Renaissance period. Contact with Dutch traders and settlers, especially in Africa, has given rise to more recent borrowings such as *Boer, boorish, Hottentot, a forlorn hope* (a lost band), *nitwit* (already used in England in the 17th century), *veldt*.

The English language is living, therefore, because it is constantly changing. Chaucer recognised the fact as long ago as the 14th century, a period when it was undergoing its major transition from a medieval to a modern language:

> Ye knowe eek, that in forme of speche is chaunge
> With-inne a thousand yeer, and wordes *tho*
> That hadden *prys*, now wonder *nyce* and straunge
> Us thinketh hem; and yet they spake hem so, ...
> *(Troilus and Criseyde,* II, 22–25)

[*tho*: then; *prys:* value; *nyce*: foolish]

The language is certainly richer now than it was in Chaucer's day; yet the language used today may well need glossing if the readers of 2600 AD are to understand it.

Its growing-up: ways in which English has developed

English has changed through the centuries often through the influence of social, political, and scientific developments. The contact of the Anglo-Saxons with Roman civilisation on the Continent of Europe, their migration to Celtic Britain, the introduction of Christianity into England from Ireland and by St Augustine in 597 AD from Europe, the invasions of the Viking raiders, the Norman Conquest, the movements known now as the Reformation and the Renaissance, wars with many of our continental neighbours, world conflicts in the 20th century, emigration and immigration are but some of the factors which have led to marked changes in English from its early Germanic origins.

Wars lead to movements of peoples; economic forces bring about migration from one part of the country to another or from one land to another; better transport, travel abroad, the telephone, radio, television, communication satellites, newspapers and intermarriage destroy or at least overcome the separating and divisive effects of political frontiers.

Scientific inventions, microchip revolutions, advances in medicine or manufacturing processes, new material or geographical discoveries, developments in philosophy and experiments in literature require new expressions. All such developments alter the demands on language and its usage. Perhaps the two most dominant influences responsible for change in a language are: the emergence or development of a personal, social, political, scientific or intellectual need for a new form of expression and close contact between users of the language in communicating or expressing this need.

The changes have come about in a variety of ways. It is easiest to illustrate some of them in terms of changes in vocabulary, although there have been major changes, too, in grammar and phonology.

(a) A word common to many languages may change its meaning to suit particular conditions: e.g. words corresponding to the English word *beech* are found in many languages; in some it refers to the tree called a 'beech' in England but in others it refers to the 'oak' or the 'elder' or the 'elm'.

(b) A word with a common form in two languages may modify its meaning in one language under the influence of the other: e.g. the word 'dream' in Anglo-Saxon meant 'joy'; its modern meaning was assumed from Scandinavian (*draumr*); 'friend' in Anglo-Saxon (*freond*) carried its current English meaning but in Scandinavian it meant 'kinsman', a meaning of the word still given to it in parts of Scotland and the United States.

(c) The same word in two languages may modify its meaning in both when they come into contact with each other: e.g. the Anglo-Saxon word for a common garment '*scyrte*' became the Modern English word *shirt* but the Scandinavian word for the same article, *skyrta*, became Modern English *skirt*. The Latin word *tunic* then emerged as the word used in English to describe the original article of clothing.

(d) A word from a foreign language may oust the native word and then become the one currently used: e.g. *take* (Old Norse *taka*; Old English *niman*); *sky* (Old Norse *skȳ*—where it originally meant 'a cloud', Old English *uprodor* or *wolcen*); *egg* (Old Norse *egg*, Old English *oeg*). Caxton, as late as 1490, said in his introduction to Virgil's *Aeneid*, which he translated from a French paraphrase, that such changes in a language caused problems for him: 'What sholde a man in thyse dayes now write, *egges* or *eyren*? Certaynly it is harde to playse every man by cause of dyversite & chaunge of langage'.

(e) Sometimes a word from another language for an object, for which there was a perfectly good English word, modifies its meaning when it is adopted: e.g. English *ox*, French *beef*; English *calf*, French *veal*; English *seethe*, French *boil*.

(f)   English has been swift to use its own native method of forming new words to adapt the sense of foreign words it has borrowed: e.g. it sometimes adds native English suffixes: gentle*man*, gent*ly*, gentle*ness*; faith*ful*, faith*fully*, faith*fulness*; duke*dom*; it also uses extensively the same method with foreign prefixes it has adopted: e.g. *pre*cook, *trans*form, *super*man, *post*war, *de*frost, *tele*vision, *super*market.

(g)   At one time English was more ready than it is today to form compound words to express new ideas. Modern German has retained the facility but it is still found in English: *teenage, newsprint, Beatlemania, discotheque, footfault, typewriter, pizzaland, station wagon.*

(h)   At different times in its historical development English has adapted itself to accommodate new ideas from abroad and used the wealth of its resources to express them: e.g. *gospel* (Old English god+spel [a good story]); *Holy Ghost, lord* (Old English *hlaford* [the keeper of the bread or loaf]), *Easter* (a festival in celebration of Eostre, goddess of the dawn), *Doomsday.*

(i)   Where a foreign word could easily be anglicised English has adopted it with minor changes or left it in its original form: **from Latin**—*abbot, angel, cleric, epistle, temple, school, circle, legion, Chester* (*castra*: 'camp'), *lentil, lobster, mussel, elephant, circle*; **from Scandinavian**—*law, fellow, husband, scrap, slaughter, steak, tidings, flat, odd, rugged, scant, tight, snare, gape, die, ransack, scare, scowl, screech, thrust, tungsten*; **from French**— *table, chair, amateur, peace, government, justice, judge, jury, prison, restaurant, menu, pardon, chef, trespass, brunette, police, communion, camouflage, barrage, saint, parquet, parliament, profile, duke, baron, prince, princess* (but *king* and *queen* are Old English in origin); **from Celtic**—*Kent, Devon, York, Thames, blarney, galore, eisteddfod, sporran, brock* (a badger), *crag, coomb, loch*; **from the native languages of Australia**—*kangaroo, boomerang, wombat*; **from other languages**: *studio, confetti, stiletto, broccoli, casino, vendetta, spaghetti, ravioli, pizza* (from Italian); *rucksack, zeppelin, blitz* (from German); *robot,* (from Czech); *thug, cushy, loot* (from India); *shampoo, dinghy, tandoori, kedgeree, juggernaut* (from India); *shish-kebab* (from Turkey); *check-mate, pyjamas* (from Persia); *chop suey, kow-tow* (from Chinese); *taboo* (from Tonga), etc.

(j)   Words or new compounds are sometimes invented and/or adopted by a language to meet a new situation or describe a new invention: *computer, silicon chip, caterpillar track, steamroller, television, hoover, biro, deepfreeze, fridge, beefburger, cellophane, intelligentsia, kodak, bulldozer, commando, motorway, spaghetti junction, homeopathic, aspirin, stethoscope, penicillin, creosote, inferiority complex, parachute, bottleneck,* etc.

It is interesting, however, that some words deliberately invented failed to be adopted by the language. It was during the 16th and early 17th century that it became fashionable to enlarge the vocabulary of English by artificially inventing words. Some of the words were needed because no equivalent existed but others were unnecessary and failed to establish themselves. One of the earliest attempts to enrich the language in this way was made by Sir Thomas Elyot; in his dedication of *The Governour* to Henry VIII in 1531 he used words such as *devulgate, describe, attemptate, education, dedicate, esteme, dispraise*, some of which have survived and some of which have died. These invented words came to be known by those who opposed their introduction as **inkhorn** terms.

'. . . lyke horslaches thei can shew two tongues, I meane to mingle their writings with words sought out of strange languages as if it were alonely thyng for theim to poudre theyr bokes with **ynkehorne termes**, although perchaunce as unaptly applied as a gold rynge in a sowes nose'

Thomas Chaloner, 1549

Some of the words remained in English: *anachronism, allusion, dexterity, disability, disrespect, halo, agile, hereditary, malignant, skeleton, parasite, idiosyncrasy*, etc. Others have disappeared: *exsiccate* (to dry), *cautionate* (caution), *mansuetude* (mildness), *disadorn, exorbitate* (to stray from one's course), *temulent* (intoxicated) etc.

The living language of English is perhaps the most important language in the world. It is widely used in international commercial and political circles throughout the world; it is constantly adapting to changes and developments in society, learning, economics, and science. More people speak Chinese than English, but the position of the United States, the growth in influence of the European community, and the community of nations throughout the world where English forms a major official language, ensure for English a leading position. Its change, and therefore its life, are assured.

Dialects as a source of older or alternative historical forms of word and structure

Dialect is often described as a variant of the form of a particular language. French, German and Italian are 'languages'; the variety or form of a language peculiar to a district or class such as the vernaculars of Hampshire or Tyneside or the forms of speech used in different social strata (e.g. those of professional, unskilled workers) are dialects.

The study of dialect was, until recently, almost always *diachronic*, that is, historical in its approach, since dialects were seen as repositories of 'word hoards' from earlier times. With a more recent *synchronic* approach (i.e. one which examines features of a dialect in relation to each other at any given moment rather than through the passage of time) the emphasis in dialect study has moved out from an examination of patterns of vocabulary (i.e. *lexis*), into intonation, accents, stresses, rhythms (i.e. *phonology*). Those using diachronic approaches have often been concerned, too, with the way structures in the language have developed.

Dialect should not be confused with accent. **Standard English** is the term used to describe the dialect used by educated users of the language; **Received Pronunciation** (RP) is the accent often referred to as 'BBC English' and used by those in higher social or better educated groups and readily understood throughout the country. It is possible, therefore, for a speaker to use Standard English but to express it in a regional accent. Increasingly newsreaders and television newscasters are doing just that.

Dialects are being eroded constantly by taking in forms from neighbouring dialects or abandoning their own in favour of forms from Standard English. Attempts have been made since the end of the 19th century to establish the features of English dialects. In 1873 the English Dialect Society was set up, with W. Skeat as its first secretary, to produce an English Dialect Dictionary. Joseph Wright took up the studies where the Society left them when it closed in 1896 and produced his *English Dialect Dictionary* (1898–1905), the last part of which also included his *English Dialect Grammar*. However, Martyn F. Wakelin (*English Dialects: An Introduction*, 1972) has pointed out that 'the usefulness of the Dictionary is vitiated by the fact that its material is extracted from glossaries whose dates range over too long a period of time and that the designations of locality are far too vague: we need to know *precisely* where a word was recorded, and not merely its county or area'. In 1946 Eugen Dieth and Harold Orton planned a *Survey of English Dialects* and the basic field work for it was carried out between 1948 and 1961 and the research built up a vast collection of material, much of which was intended for a *Linguistic Atlas of England* but Dieth and Orton died with the work unfinished and funds for the project largely dried up. New methods of recording, arranging and recalling dialect material should make future work in dialects easier to handle.

The vocabulary of English dialects today certainly includes much evidence of earlier historical influences on the language. From **Celtic** the following dialect words remain: *beltane* (May I), *boggart, bugaboo*, (a hobgoblin), *crowd* (a fiddle), *ingle* (fireplace), *strath* (a valley), *tocher* (a dowry), *wheal* (a mine). From **Norse** come: *addle* (to earn), *aund* (fated), *bing* (a heap), *blayther* (idle, noisy chatter), *brisk* (to get ready), *cleck* (to hatch), *dog* (dew), *ettle* (to aim at), *gar* (to cause, make), *gilder* (a snare), *gradely* (respectable), *kittle* (to trickle), *layking* (a plaything), *lift* (air, sky), *paddock* (frog, toad), *rit* (to scratch), *spelk* (a splinter), *tarn* (a mountain pool), *wale* (to choose), etc. From **Norman French** come: *able* (rich), *afraid* (for fear that), *agreeable* (willing), *allow* (suppose), *apt* (sure), *auction* (an untidy place), etc. (See Skeat's *English Dialect Dictionary* for many hundreds of examples.)

With the help of dictionaries list native English words no longer found in Standard English, and establish the foreign origins of as many words as you can in the following passage, written by a Rev. William Hutton, Rector of Beetham in Westmoreland, 1762–1811 and edited by W. Skeat:

> Last Saturday sennet, abaut seun in the evening (twas lownd and fraaze hard) the stars twinkled, and the setting moon cast gigantic shadows. I was stalking hameward across Blackwatermosses, and whistling as I trampl'd for want of thought, when a noise struck my ear, like the crumpling of frosty murgeon; it made me stop short, and I thought I saw a strange form before me: it vanished behint a windraw; and again thare was nought in view but dreary dykes and dusky ling. An awful silence reigned araund; this was sean brokken by a skirling hullet; sure nivver did hullet, kerrensue, or miredrum, mak sic a noise before. Your minister was freetned, the hairs of his head stood an end, his blead storkened, and the haggard creature moving slawly nearer, the mirkiness of the neet shew'd her as big again as she was . . . She stoup'd and drop'd a poak, and thus began with a whining tone. 'Deary me! deary me! forgive me, good Sir, but this yance, I'll steal naar maar. This seck is elding to keep us fra starving!' (The author visits the poor woman's cottage.) She sat on a three-legg'd steal, and a dim coal smook'd within the rim of a brandreth, oor which a seety rattencreak hung dangling fra a black randletree. The walls were plaister'd with dirt, and a stee, with hardly a rung, was rear'd into a loft. Araund the woman her lile ans sprawl'd on the hearth, some whiting speals, some snottering and crying, and ya ruddy-cheek'd lad threw on a bullen to make a loww, for its mother to find her loup. By this sweal I beheld this family's poverty.

Older grammatical forms in the language have sometimes been retained in modern English dialects, whereas they have been dropped from Standard English or changed. The following descriptions give some examples of where the differences in forms can still be seen.

(a) Nouns

In Anglo-Saxon nouns were declined either by the addition of inflexions or by changes in their stem vowels: e.g. *cild* (singular), *cildru* (plural): child, children; *mus, mys*: mouse, mice; *cyning, cyningas*: king, kings; *sunu, suna*: son, sons; *mann, menn*: man, men. In order to form the possessive singular case (the genitive) some nouns added *-es*, others *-e*, and a few made no inflexional changes. Later in Standard English the normal plural of nouns was indicated by the addition of *-s*, *-es* (although there are exceptions: e.g. deer, mice, oxen, children, etc.), and the genitive singular is indicated by the addition of *-'s* (although there are exceptions: e.g. Lady day).

Dialects sometimes retain the earlier forms of the plurals and of the genitive singulars of nouns: e.g. *een* (eyes), *shoon* (shoes), *childer* (children), *kine* (cows); a cow foot, my wife father. Some dialects have run together older inflexional endings (not always the correct Anglo-Saxon ones) and *-(e)s* plural endings of nouns: e.g. *housens, childers*.

(b) Verbs

In Anglo-Saxon, verbs were conjugated according to person, number, and tense. There were two main classes of verb: strong and weak. **Strong** verbs changed their vowels from the base form to make their past tenses and past participles. They still do and are sometimes called 'irregular' verbs, e.g.

	Base	*Past tense*	*Past participle*
Anglo-Saxon:	beran (to carry) sittan (to sit) weor-eðan (to become)	bær, bǣron sæt, sǣton wearþ, wurdon	(ge) boren (ge) seten (ge) worden
Modern English:	bear sit become	bore sat became	borne sat become

Weak verbs made their past tense and past participles by adding a dental suffix to their base form. They still do and are sometimes called 'regular' verbs, e.g.

	Base	*Past tense*	*Past participle*
Anglo-Saxon:	lufian (to love) secgan (to say)	lufode, lufodon sægde, sægdon	gelufod gesægd
Modern English	love say	loved said	loved said

In Anglo-Saxon, too, the third person singular of the present tense in most dialects ended in -*eð*, which became -*eth* and remained until the 17th century and beyond, when it was replaced by -*s*: e.g. he lov*eth*, she lov*es*.

In modern English dialects, sometimes strong verbs are treated as if they were weak: *drinked, drunked*; *speaked*; *weaved*; *stoled*; *gived* (*gied*). On the other hand, some verbs which had become weak following the Anglo-Saxon period, have remained strong in some dialects today: *croppen* (*crept*); *washen* (*washed*). It is a tendency in Germanic languages for strong verbs to become weak: e.g. *dove*; *dived*; *clomb*; *climbed*. Dialects have continued the process ahead of Standard English with *knowed*; *growed*; *wored*; etc. Dialects, too, have sometimes retained the earlier -*eth* ending for the third person singular of the present tense, whereas Standard English has abandoned it: *doth*; *hath*; even *dooth*, and *wearth*.

Other dialect retentions from earlier forms include uses such as *gotten* (still common in American English); *rid* (rode); *spak* (spoke); *be* (am).

(c) *Pronouns*

Dialect forms still retain some of the early pronominal forms of English: *ich* (I); *thy* (your); *ye* (you); *tho* (those). They also show the use of *uch* instead of I; *he* (*him*); *en* (*it*); *her* (*she*). Personal pronouns often switch their subject and object forms in dialect (e.g. 'fetch they up', 'them as goes'). Sometimes, too, singular and plural forms are interchanged, especially *us* for *me:* 'give us the book', or 'gi's the book'.

(d) *Adjectives*

The most common dialect variations from Standard English occur in the comparative and superlative degrees. Standard English *normally* prefers to use *-er*, *-est* suffixes for monosyllables and *more-*, *most-* forms for polysyllabic adjectives. Dialects sometimes use the *-er*, *-est* forms for polysyllabic adjectives (*usefuller*, *usefullest*) or use unnecessary (pleonastic) more-, most-forms: *more usefuller*, *most strangest*, etc.

Anglo-Saxon normally made its comparative and superlative degrees of adjectives by adding *-ra* (*-re*), *-est* (*ost*), to the base forms.

(For further detailed discussions of retained dialect forms see also Martyn F. Wakelin, *English Dialects*: *An Introduction*, 1977, and P. Trudgill, *On Dialect*, 1983.)

CHAPTER 3

Attitudes to Contemporary Usage

Historical attempts to 'correct, improve, and ascertain the English tongue'

In 1635 Cardinal Richelieu managed to secure the founding of the French Academy which had as one of its main aims 'to give definite rules to our language, and to render it pure, eloquent, and capable of treating the arts and sciences'. It also intended to 'establish a certain usage of words' and to compile a dictionary, a grammar, a rhetoric, and a treatise on the art of poetry. This attempt to 'define', and even to 'fix', the French language has continued in France ever since and as recently as 1984 the French Academy was still resisting the introduction of words like *le hamburger* (instead of *bifteck haché*). Nevertheless, *le football, le week-end, le stress,* are Anglicisms that no rules or regulations have been able to withstand.

In England similar attempts have been made to prescribe usages of English, but once again, living languages strongly resist such attempts to confine them. In 1664 John Dryden in the dedication of *The Rival Ladies* regretted that the English did not have 'a more certain Measure' of their noble language as the French had. In December of the same year the newly founded Royal Society set up a committee of twenty-two distinguished men 'for improving the English Language' and preparing a grammar, reforms of spelling, a dictionary, and translations of classical Greek and Roman literature. In 1697 Daniel Defoe in *Essay upon Projects* proposed an English Academy, amongst whose tasks would be those of providing an 'authority for the usage of words', regulating the coinage of new words, and keeping a close supervision over translations.

In 1712 Jonathan Swift produced his work, *A Proposal for Correcting, Improving, and Ascertaining the English Tongue.* He did not propose an 'academy', as such, but he did intend a reform of the language. There was a French model to follow; grammar was defective, the vocabulary contained improprieties which were to be excluded, and some words of former periods should be 'restored on account of their energy and sound'. Above all, he wanted to 'fix' the language. His ideas received some support but opposition to the idea of an academy and fixing' the language soon grew.

John Oldmixon's *Reflections on Dr Swift's Letter to the Earl of Oxford, about the English Tongue* (1712) rejected the idea that languages could be prevented from developing, but it was Dr Johnson who finally laid the ideas to rest in the Preface to his *Dictionary* in 1755. He recognised change for what it was in language. 'Total and sudden transformations of a language seldom happen'. 'May the lexicographer be derided who shall imagine that his dictionary can embalm his language and secure it from corruption and decay and that it is in his power to change sublunary nature, or clear the world at once from folly, vanity, and affectation. With this hope, however, academies have been instituted, to guard the avenues of their languages, to retain fugitives, and repulse intruders; but their vigilance and activity have hitherto been vain; sounds are too volatile and subtile for legal restraints; to enchain syllables, and to lash the wind, are equally the undertakings of pride.' . . . 'In a race no longer barbarous, thinkers will have new ideas and knowledge.' With these new ideas would come new words, just as old words die with old customs. The real danger, Johnson thought, lay in the increasing number of translations: 'If an academy be established for the cultivation of our style, which I hope the spirit of English liberty will hinder or destroy, let them, instead of compiling grammars and dictionaries, stop the licence of translators.' He rejected totally Swift's view that there was 'no absolute necessity why any language should be perpetually changing'.

The proposal for an academy along the lines of that in France was now doomed. Thomas Sheridan (1756) and Joseph Priestley (1761) rejected it decisively.

The 18th century saw, however, a renewed interest in the grammar of English, and it was here that the greatest danger of prescription lay.

Prescriptive and descriptive approaches

In Anglo-Saxon times an interest in the study of Latin-based grammar was apparent in the *Colloquy* of AElfric who died about 1020. With the Renaissance a renewed interest in language arose and Joachim Du Bellay published his pace-making *Défense et illustration de la langue française* in 1549–50. English was stoutly defended in the 16th century by writers such as Roger Ascham (1515–68), Sir Thomas Elyot (1499?–1546), Richard Mulcaster (1530?–1611), Richard Puttenham (1520?–1601?), and Thomas Wilson (1525?–1581). These powerful writers argued for the dignity of English: 'I honour the Latin, but I worship the English.' In the 17th century, amongst others, Ben Jonson and John Milton wrote treatises on grammar. In 1653 John Wallis in *Grammatica Linguae Anglicanae* saw that Latin grammar could not be used as a sound basis for describing English grammar and in 1734 William Loughton (*Practical Grammar of the English Tongue*) attacked those who 'attempted to force our Language (contrary to its Nature) to the Method and Rules of the Latin grammar'. He even tried to dispense with terms such as 'noun', 'adjective','verb' etc., and replaced them with 'names', 'qualities', and 'affirmations'.

In 1761 Joseph Priestley produced *The Rudiments of English Grammar*; in the following year Robert Lowth wrote his *Short Introduction to English Grammar*, and found instant acclaim. Also in 1762 James Buchanan published *The British Grammar* and a simple manual of grammar appeared in 1763 with John Ash's *Grammatical Institutes*. Their aims, as A. C. Baugh and Thomas Cable (*A History of the English Language*, third edition, 1978) have shown were to: '(1) codify the principles of the language and reduce it to rule; (2) settle disputed points and decide cases of divided usage; and (3) point out common errors or what were supposed to be errors, and thus correct and improve the language.' Only Joseph Priestley showed any hesitation in **prescribing** usage.

'Prescription' was, and still is, based on three approaches: reason, etymology, and the practice of the classics. Even works like H. W. Fowler's *A Dictionary of Modern English Usage*, second edition revised by Sir Ernest Gowers, 1965, still use such justifications for their pronouncements. Logical approaches often ignore actual language usage: 'I don't want none' does *not* mean 'I want some', whatever the logical person asserts. The fact that a word or phrase is derived from a language where it had one meaning and use in English does not necessarily mean that the word or phrase has to retain its orginal meaning: 'a forlorn hope' and 'the psychological moment' are good illustrations of the point. Latin was a highly inflected language where the relationship between words in a sentence was clear, whatever their order might have been, mainly from the inflectional endings they carried; English has few such inflexions and therefore word order plays a crucial role in an English sentence to establish meaning.

Logic, etymology, and classical usage are not sufficient grounds for a **prescriptive** approach to grammar. Modern linguists are not concerned so much with what forms the language *should* or *ought to* adopt but with what forms are actually used in contexts that can be established. Theirs is a **descriptive** approach; they try to describe as accurately as they can the form of language in use within a specific context.

They are concerned, therefore, with notions of **appropriateness.** If language is used that is 'appropriate' to its context in the tightest ways possible it might be said to be 'correct'. This is quite different from arguing notions of **'correctness'** from prescriptive approaches. 'Appropriateness' as a criterion is not a lax way of accepting that 'whatever is, is right'.

Two other terms found to describe notions of approaches to contemporary usage are **acceptability** and **grammaticality**.

Acceptability is concerned with the attitudes of native users of the

English language to particular forms of usage. If one form of usage is 'acceptable' to substantial numbers of such users, then the grammatical description of the language must take that into account. For example, 'I don't want nothing' is acceptable to large numbers of people as a very emphatic statement of what somebody does not want. Such an emphatic use of double negatives must feature in a description of English grammar, although 'prescriptive' grammarians might argue that such double negatives *ought* not to be used, since they are illogical. However, the sentence 'I want don't nothing' is not acceptable to users of the language since it does not conform to the grammar of English; English structures simply do not *accept* the transposition of 'don't' and 'want' since, clearly, usage demands that the relationship between the emphatic use of the verb 'do' (or 'don't' in this example) and the base form of 'want' has to be observed. 'I don't want nothing' is, therefore, 'acceptable', whilst 'I want don't nothing' is not acceptable.

Every description of language usage has to be measured against not one or two views of what is acceptable but against what numbers of confident and experienced users will accept and recognise. The 'users' against whom a particular phrase is tested for **acceptability** ought to be what linguists describe as 'linguistically naive' in order to avoid prejudiced judgements and ought to be of the same or similar regional, social and educational backgrounds in order to eliminate disparate responses. In this way 'I don't want nothing' as a sentence might establish itself as acceptable usage amongst one band of language users but not amongst another; in that way part of the description of the usage can be determined and refined. If all users reject as 'unacceptable' 'I want don't nothing' then the sentence has to be investigated to establish what grammatical uses it has transgressed.

Ways of testing for 'acceptability' amongst users have to be more sophisticated than merely asking for an immediate response to a sentence used out of context, but the principles of 'acceptability' are embodied in the example given.

Grammaticality is concerned with the way words are formed into clauses or utterances or sentences. Grammar concerns itself with statements that are well formed and are 'acceptable'. It concerns itself with 'unacceptable' statements (e.g. 'I want don't nothing') only in so far as they help to explain and define, by looking at divergencies from normal usage, what 'acceptable' grammatical forms are. Sometimes, of course, ungrammatical sentences might be used, in poetic language for example, in order to clash words together to jar a response. However, if grammatical norms or 'rules' are drawn up from clear cases where grammaticality is beyond doubt then these rules can be applied to other statements to decide whether they are grammatical or not. D. Crystal (*Linguistics*, 1971) quotes Chomsky on this point, where the approach to **grammaticality** is succinctly put: 'as long as the theory' (or 'the rule') 'covers the clear cases, then it can be used to decide the status of the unclear cases.'

'Traditional' grammar drew up sets of rules that were prescriptive and so excluded many of the common usages of the language. For example, if it stated that prepositions should not be used to end sentences, then it would exclude hundreds of sentences where such usages clearly occur. Nevertheless, grammar which sets out to describe the relationships between elements in a sentence allows for transformations of the elements in a sentence to take place without the sentence being destroyed in terms of its grammaticality. The grammatical description must allow for the flexibility of the language to operate. For example, the following sentence is ungrammatical and its description refuses to allow the language to adjust to it:

'I want don't nothing.'

subject + infinitive without the marker 'to' + 'do' as an emphatic auxiliary + negative + direct object.

If this grammatical description were applied to form other 'sentences' then they, too, would be ungrammatical:

e.g. 'He see didn't the bus.'

Similarly, *direct object + infinitive + negative + emphatic auxiliary + subject* would also lead to ungrammaticality:

e.g. 'The bus see did not he.'

When, however, the grammatical description *subject + auxiliary + negative + infinitive + direct object* is applied an infinite number of grammatical sentences becomes possible.

e.g. 'I don't want nothing.'

'She does not understand the point.'

'They cannot read the book.'

CHAPTER 4

Directed Uses of Language

This chapter is concerned with the appropriate use of language in a given context, on a specific topic, from a clear point of view, directed towards a defined audience, for a specific purpose.

To summarize: Every use of language involves at least four aspects:

(a) **A point of view.** This is the position from which the language use emanates, the writer's or the speaker's position or stance. It is important to recognise this by taking into account such things as bias, the selection or omission of material, choice of vocabulary, and a host of stylistic features. Such a recognition is of significance in studying both literature (the 'omniscient' author, the spectator character, the participant character, the detached observer, etc.) and transactional English (personal, objective, styles; jargon; registers, etc.).

(b) **A context.** The kinds of English and their registers or levels of meaning are determined for producers of language (written and spoken) by the circumstances of their use. Legal, business, formal, informal registers are necessary for circumstance-defined uses. Native speakers are quick to recognise when 'registers' are wrongly used; sometimes, of course, to speak in the wrong 'register' is a cause of humour (e.g. See how Mak's 'posh' Southern accent is mocked by the other shepherds in *The Second Shepherd's Pageant* written by the medieval Wakefield Master).

(c) **Content.** The substance of what is said or of a piece of writing will also determine the level of language used (as well as its vocabulary, its accent, its structures, its form). Children in school quickly have to learn how the kind of writing needed to describe formally an experiment in Physics or Chemistry differs from that needed in an English 'creative-writing' exercise.

(d) **Audience.** This is a strong determining factor in language use. Every production of language, since language is concerned with communication, takes into account the person(s) for whom the utterance is intended. If the 'audience' is someone at the bar of a public house, or someone with whom a legal contract is being made, or the general reader, then the language used to convey ideas, messages, instructions, attitudes, etc., must take notice of it.

Sometimes, **the purpose** of the language being used is raised as a separate determining factor, but 'purpose' is really subsumed in the other four elements described above.

Some technical terms used by linguists to describe the stylistic features of discourse that has taken into account point of view, content and audience need to be discussed further.

Prominence

This is a term used in the discussion of spoken English to describe how one syllable of a word or one word in an utterance is given greater 'prominence' than others around it by means of such matters as *stress* (the force used in speaking), *pitch* (the relative height or depth of the voice), *rhythm* (the placing of stressed beside unstressed elements in a word or sentence) and intonation (variations in pitch). All these elements in the production of discourse will determine which elements are prominent and those which are less prominent.

Consider, for example, the use of 'prominence' in decoding the following argument in Shakespeare's *Julius Caesar*:

> (*Brutus and Cassius, two of the conspirators in the successful plot to kill Julius Caesar are quarrelling.*)
>
> *Brutus*: Let me tell you, Cassius, you yourself
> Are much condemn'd to have an itching palm;
> To sell and mart your offices for gold
> To undeservers.
> *Cassius*:   I an itching palm!
> You know that you are Brutus that speak this,
> Or, by the gods, this speech were else your last.
> *Brutus*: The name of Cassius honours this corruption,
> And chastisement doth therefore hide his head.
> *Cassius*: Chastisement!
> *Brutus*: Remember March, the ides of March remember:
> Did not great Julius bleed for justice' sake?
> What villain touch'd his body, that did stab,
> And not for justice, What! shall one of us,
> That struck the foremost man of all this world
> But for supporting robbers, shall we now
> Contaminate our fingers with base bribes,
> And sell the mighty space of our large honours
> For so much trash as may be grasped thus?
> I had rather be a dog, and bay the moon,
> Than such a Roman.

Cassius:	Brutus, bay not me;
	I'll not endure it: you forget yourself,
	To hedge me in. I am a soldier, I,
	Older in practice, abler than yourself
	To make conditions.
Brutus:	Go to; you are not, Cassius.
Cassius:	I am.
Brutus:	I say you are not.
Cassius:	Urge me no more, I shall forget myself;
	Have mind on your health; tempt me no further.
Brutus:	Away, slight man!
Cassius:	Is't possible?
Brutus:	Hear me, for I will speak. . .

Foregrounding

R. W. Chapman in *Linguistics and Literature*, 1973 has clearly described this feature of discourse:

> The word *foregrounding* is used to describe the kind of deviation which has the function of bringing some item into artistic emphasis so that it stands out from its surrounds. It is helpfully described by M. A. K. Halliday as 'prominence that is motivated'. The notion is owed to the Prague School of Linguistics* and the English word was first suggested by P. L. Garvin as a rendering of the Czech *aktualisce*. Foregrounding may be recognised in other arts as well as literature and is particularly important in the composition of a painting.

These 'deviations', as Chapman calls them, may be recognised in such things, amongst others, as syntactical variations (changes in word order, inversions) on which literary effect much depends and ellipses in grammar; the compacted pre-modifications of nouns (e.g. 'the sloeblack, slow, black, crowblack, fishingboat-bobbing sea' of Dylan Thomas's *Under Milk Wood*, quoted by Chapman); phonological deviation; lexical (or vocabulary) deviations; semantic deviations; deviations in register; deviations of historical period. (A full discussion of 'foregrounding' is found in G. N. Leech, *A Linguistic Guide to English Poetry*, 1969, Chapter 4.)

---

*

The Prague School of Linguistics refers to a group of scholars working on linguistics in the 1920s and 1930s near Prague. *The Linguistic Circle* of Prague was founded in 1926. Its main contribution lay in applying Saussure's distinction between langue and parole to phonology; they were concerned, amongst other things, with *phonemes* as the 'smallest distinctive unit operating within the network of structural relationships which constituted the sound system of a language . . . the phoneme was a concept which kept words apart. To give a specific example, it was the *difference* between *pit* and *bit*, and not the characteristics of the *p* or the *b* seen in isolation'. (See David Crystal, *Linguistics*, 1971, page 179.) The main members of this so-called 'Prague School' were Roman Jakobson, Nikolai Trubetskoy and Karl Bühler.

Foregrounding, however, may operate not through deviations but through **parallelism**, where regularities are deliberately introduced in order 'to bring some item into artistic emphasis so that it stands out from its surroundings'. (See the discussion below on metre, rhyme, alliteration, assonance, and syntactical parallelism, pages 34–9)

Phonological patterning

This includes specifically such elements as metre, rhyme, alliteration, and assonance—the elements concerned with the sounds of speech and literary discourse.

Metre is a term derived in Modern English from the Anglo-Saxon word *meter*, reinforced by the Old French word *metre*, both of which go back to the Latin *metrum*, 'measurement'. In Anglo-Saxon verse the number of syllables in a line was variable but the number and patterning of the stresses set between the two halves of each line was not. Edmund Sievers showed that this 'accentual' patterning of verse, with its six permitted variations, was carefully observed (see page 36). With influences from Italy and France, however, stresses in verse forms moved from what might be called 'accentual' to 'accentual syllabic', where the number of syllables was as important as the stresses. Since the time of Chaucer (died 1400), when applied to poetry the word *metre* refers to the regulated succession of certain groups of syllables. In Classical Literature this was seen in terms of the length of syllables. The syllables in English poetry, however, could not be measured according to their length but according to their stress. Nevertheless, the same technical descriptions have been kept to describe 'the regulated succession of certain groups of syllables' which make up verses (or lines) of poetry and stanzas (or numbers of lines or verses) of poetry. In the following summary the sign ∪ refers to unstressed syllables and the sign / refers to stressed syllables; each unit is called **a foot** and each 'foot' is made up of the following stressed (/) and unstressed (∪) patterns and contains *one* stressed syllable only:

∪ /   : *iambic* (This is the normal pattern of stress found in units of speech in Germanic languages);

/ ∪   : *trochaic* (from the Greek word *trochaios*, running, tripping);

∪ ∪ / : *anapaestic* (Greek *anapaistos*, struck back)

/ ∪ ∪ : *dactylic* (Greek *daktylos*, a finger—a finger is made up of three jointed segments, one long and two short);

/ /   : *spondaic* (the slow, solemn metre of the hymns sung at a *spondé* or 'drink-offering' in Greek times).

Verses or the lines in a stanza are described as follows according to the number of feet in them:

monometer: one foot
dimeter: two feet
trimeter: three feet
tetrameter: four feet
pentameter: five feet
hexameter: . six feet

Sometimes lines are described according to the number of syllables they contain: e.g. octosyllabic (8), hendecasyllabic (11).

When the lines are arranged in rhyming pairs they are called **couplets** and lines of unrhymed iambic pentameter are called **blank verse**. Other stanzaic forms are common in English poetry, the most common of which are:

triplet: three lines
quatrain: four lines
pentastich: five lines
sestet, sextet: six lines
heptastich: seven lines
octet, octave: eight lines

Special groupings are given special technical labels: e.g.

terza rima: 'third rhyme' used by Dante in *The Divine Comedy*; lines of iambic pentameter +one extra syllable, so rhymed that every rhyme occurs three times in alternate lines.

rhyme royal: used by Chaucer in *Troilus and Criseyde*; stanzas of seven iambic pentameters rhyming ABABBCC.

Spenserian stanzas: used by Edmund Spenser in *The Faerie Queene* and Byron in *Childe Harold*; eight iambic pentameters followed by a ninth iambic hexameter, rhyming ABABBCBCC.

Sometimes whole poems are patterned metrically. The sonnet is the best example of such 'patterned' poems: sonnets consist of fourteen lines of rhymed iambic pentameter arranged in an octave followed by a sestet. There are three main variations in English poetry:

(a) *Petrarchan*: this has a clear break in the sense/emotion between the eighth and ninth lines. The *octave* uses iambic pentameter with two rhymes only: ABBAABBA; the *sestet* uses iambic pentameter with two *or* three other rhymes so arranged that the last two lines never form a couplet, unless they also rhyme with the first line of the sestet. (Wordsworth's sonnets are Petrarchan in form.)

(b) *Miltonic*: this has a similar form to the Petrarchan sonnet, although the break in the two parts of the poem comes in the ninth line or elsewhere and not between the octave and the sestet.

(c) *Shakespearean*: this has a pause not only between the octave and the sestet but between the lines arranged as three quatrains and a final couplet; the rhyme scheme follows this patterning: each quatrain has two independent rhymes and the couplet a further rhyme: e.g. ABAB, CDCD, EFEF, GG or ABBA, CDDC, EFFE, GG.

Rhythm and metre are often contrapuntal in the way they work together in a poem. G. N. Leech (in *A Linguistic Guide to English Poetry*, 1969) quotes Yeats's comment from 'A General Introduction for My Work' which makes the point clear:

> If I repeat the first line of *Paradise Lost* so as to emphasize its five feet, I am among the folk-singers—'Of mán's first dísobédience aṅd the frúit', but speak it as I should cross it with another emphasis, that of passionate prose— 'Of mán's fiŕst disobédience and the frúit' . . . the folk-song is still there, but a ghostly voice, an unvariable possibility, an unconscious norm.

This tension between the metre of the verse and the rhythms of speech is one of the ways in which poetry controls, builds up, and releases emotion in harmony with the semantic meanings of the words themselves. Leech goes on to add a third element, that of **performance**, to the way verse is declaimed, on the stage for example, to achieve special effects, which may not be the same as metrical form or speech rhythms. Moreover, particularly in the drama of Beckett and of Pinter, **pauses** are often as important as rhythm or metre.

The 'accentual syllabic' metre of traditional verse is sometimes abandoned for **accentual** metre nearer to that of Anglo-Saxon verse. This is found where it is the number of stresses in a line and not the number of syllables which determines it. The six basic forms of 'accentual metre' in our earliest verse were as follows:

A   falling–falling $/ \cup / \cup$
B   rising–rising $\cup / \cup /$
C   clashing $\cup / / \cup$
D^1 falling by stages $/ / \backslash \cup$
D^2 broken fall $/ / \cup \backslash$
E   fall and rise $/ \backslash \cup /$

(The sign \ marks a weaker stress than /.)
Each half-line of verse carried one of these accentual patterns- in addition the first half-line carried alliteration on the two accentuated syllables and the second half-line carried a third use of alliteration on one of its accented syllables, e.g.

D^1 Ongíetan sceal gléaw hǽle hu gǽstlic bìð D^2
A   þonne ealre þisse ẃorulde wéla wéste stóndeð;   A
C   swa ńu míssenlice geond   þisne míddangeàrd D^2
A   wínde bewáune wéallas stóndaþ,   A
A   hŕime bihrórene, hrýðge þa éderas,   A
A   wóriad þa wínsalo, wáldend lícgað   A
A   dréame bidrórene.

This kind of 'accentual' metre, without the alliteration, was revived by T. S. Eliot and W. H. Auden. The 'sprung rhythm' of G. M. Hopkins is a variation of 'accentual' metre, which is seen also in the system of metrication based on stress and alliteration in early Welsh verse, that of *cynghanedd*, e.g.

And the séa flínt-fláke, blàck-bácked in the régular blów, Sitting Eástnorthéast, in cúrsed quárter, the wínd.

(See W. H. Gardner's Introduction to *Poems and Prose of Gerard Manley Hopkins*, 1953.)

Associated with the use of stress or accent in verse is the use of **enjambement,** where rhythms are allowed to run on from line to line without any end-stopping. This allows the poet or writer to defeat the expectation of the reader so that the grammatical structures overflow from one line into the next, where he or she might have expected the sense to stop by the use of a rhyme or merely by the fact that the verse unit had seemed to stop. This element of surprise in enjambement is one which poets use to good effect; in the storm scene in *King Lear*, Shakespeare uses the device to increase the tension that is threatening to tear the king apart:

> Let the great Gods,
> That keep this dreadful pudder o'er our heads,
> Find out their enemies now. Tremble, thou wretch,
> That hast within thee undivulged crimes,
> Unwhipp'd of Justice; hide thee, thou bloody hand,
> Thou perjur'd, and thou simular of virtue
> That art incestuous; caitiff, to pieces shake,
> That under covert and convenient seeming
> Has practis'd on man's life; close pent-up guilts
> Rive your concealing continents, and cry
> These dreadful summoners grace. I am a man
> More sinn'd against than sinning.

(III, ii)

Parallelism is another aspect of phonological patterning which needs describing technically, although its effect on the ear and on the eye within specific contexts is merely one of the factors that contribute to a poem's 'meaning'. Rhyme, along with **alliteration** and **assonance** (see below, pages 38–9) are examples of the function of **parallelism**. By 'parallelism' is meant the introduction of regularities rather than deviations into discourse in order to *foreground* elements in the writing. (For *foregrounding*, see above, pages 33–4.)

Metre depended on regular stressing and regular arrangement of lines, and deviations from such regularity were seen as significant. With rhyme, alliteration and assonance it is the emphasis on parallelism, or specifically introduced and emphasised regularities, which is significant.

Rhyme may be monosyllabic (sometimes called 'masculine'): run/done, blue/true; *or* two-syllabic (sometimes called 'feminine'): batter/scatter, history/mystery, pigeon/religion; *or* poly-syllabic: stationary/inflectionary, frivolity/quality. *Chambers Dictionary* defines rhyme as: 'in two or more words, identity of sound from the last stressed vowel to the end, the consonant or consonant group preceding not being the same in both (all) cases'. Where there is a complete identity of the last syllables there is no rhyme, according to the strict definition: *visible* and *invisible*, *greed* and *agreed* are not strictly rhymes.

There are a number of rhyming possibilities in English, regardless of the spelling of words, because of phonological correspondences between pairs, such as meet/seat, brought/distraught; words which have the same spellings in their terminations but not necessarily the same phonological correspondences are usually called *eye rhymes*: great/seat, wind/blind.

When a word in the middle of a line rhymes with the word at the end of the line, it is called a *medial rhyme*: e.g. writing about the fact that dates of publication of books are usually given in Roman numerals that have to be deciphered, Ogden Nash wrote:

> I am happily agog over their funerals, which are always satisfactorily followed by exhumerals,
> But I can't understand why so many of them carry their copyright lines in Roman numerals.

Ogden Nash, of course, depended heavily on invented rhymes for much of the humour in his verse.

> *The Rhinoceros*
> The rhino is a homely beast,
> For human eyes he's not a feast.
> Farewell, farewell, you old rhinoceros,
> I'll stare at something less prepoceros.

Alliteration occurs where the sounds (not necessarily the letters) at the beginnings of successive words or words in close proximity are repeated. e.g. 'He cast one longing, lingering, look behind.'

Assonance. *Chambers Dictionary* defines it as: 'a correspondence in sound: vowel rhyme, coincidence of vowels without regard to consonants, as in *mate* and *shape*, *feel* and *need*: extended to correspondence of consonants with different vowels: resemblance, correspondence.' Perhaps the best example of assonance in modern poetry occurs in Wilfred Owen's *Strange Meeting*, where assonance rather than rhyme helps to foreground the uneasiness of a nightmare:

> It seemed that out of battle I escaped
> Down some profound dull tunnel, long since scooped
> Through granites which titanic wars had groined.
> Yet also there encumbered sleepers groaned,
> Too fast in thought or death to be bestirred.
> Then, as I probed them, one sprang up, and stared
> With piteous recognition in fixed eyes,
> Lifting distressful hands as if to bless.
> And by his smile I knew that sullen hall,
> By his dead smile, I knew we stood in Hell.

Leech (op. cit. page 65) claims that 'the importance of **parallelism** as a feature of poetic language almost rivals that of deviation. He distinguishes it from mere repetition, following Roman Jakobson who had argued that in parallelism there must be a pattern of identity and of contrast. Leech quotes an example from *The Ancient Mariner* where the 'many interlocking foregrounded patterns—metre, end-rhyme, internal rhyme, alliteration and syntactic parallelism (the patterning in parallel of syntactic structures) abound:

> The fair breeze blew, the white foam flew,
> The furrow followed free;
> We were the first that ever burst
> Into that silent sea.'

Syntactic patterning, however, is not restricted to those structures where parallelism is used as a means of foregrounding.

Periodic structures: strictly, a period is any complete sentence but it is often applied to a sentence consisting of a number of clauses dependent on a main construction. These are the units that make up a discourse, 'a unit of linguistic performance which stands complete in itself.' (R. Chapman, *Linguistics and Literature*, 1973, page 100). A consideration of the sentence must play an important role in what Z. S. Harris called **discourse analysis**: 'a method of seeking in any connected discrete linear material, whether language or language-like, which contains more than one elementary sentence, some global structure characterising the whole discourse (the linear material), or large sections of it' (*Discourse Analysis Reprints*, The Hague, 1963, Monton, quoted by Chapman, op. cit., p. 101).

In discourse analysis, therefore, it is important to see the place of a single word or image within the whole context of the discourse; parallelism or deviation in structures will be significant here. The repetition of sentence structures will be of importance; consider for example the almost antiphonal, lyrical arrangement of the dialogue between Lorenzo and Jessica in *The Merchant of Venice*—'In such a night . . . In such a night . . . In such a night' (V, i) or the sermons of the 17th-century Dean of St Paul's, John Donne, whose style relies heavily on such repetitions with transformations:

> Doth not man die even in his birth? The breaking of prison is death, and what is our birth, but a breaking of prison? As soon as we were clothed by God, our very apparell was an Embleme of death. In the skins of dead beasts, he covered the skins of dying man. As soon as God set us on work, our very occupation was an Embleme of death; It was to digge the earth; not to digge pitfals for other men, but graves for our selves. Hath any man here forgot to day, that yesterday is dead? . . . We die every day, and we die all the day long; and because we are not absolutely dead, we call that an eternity, an eternity of dying: And is there comfort in that state? why, that is the state of hell it self, Eternall dying, and not dead.

The control of simple sentences here, with antithesis, rhetorical questions, climax, paradox, parallelisms foreground the central idea to which Donne returns again and again from points around the circle which he draws to show man's mortality. This is the consummate use of the period—related as it was to the sermon, image and emblem, and the spoken language delivered formally. The passage is rich and would repay close discourse analysis.

Loose sentence structure is not to be confused with sentences which oppose *acceptability* or *grammaticality* (see above, pages 28–30). There are five basic structures of a finite clause in English, each element (word, sign) of which might be 'transformed' to provide an infinite number of structures which may or may not be semantically acceptable:

(i)

SUBJECT	PREDICATE
Noun phrase, *NP*	**+ intransitive verb**, *iV* (+ adverb, *A*)
e.g. The boy (*NP*) The girl (*NP*) She (*NP*)	telephoned (*iV*) (yesterday, *A*). went (*iV*) (there, *A*). ran (*iV*) (along the street, *A*).

(ii)

SUBJECT	PREDICATE
Noun phrase, *NP*	+ to be (**or copula**) + **complement**, *C*
e.g. The clever woman (*NP*) They (*NP*) He (*NP*)	was (*TO BE*) a teacher (*C*). became (*COPULA*) ill (*C*). seemed (*COPULA*) down in the dumps (*C*).

(iii)

SUBJECT	PREDICATE
Noun phrase, *NP*	**+ transitive verb**, *tV* + **direct object**, *dO* (+ adverb, *A*).
e.g. Mary (*NP*) He (*NP*) I (*NP*)	saw (*tV*) him (*dO*) (yesterday) (*A*) wrote (*tV*) the book (*dO*) (when he could) (*A*). hit (*tV*) the nail (*dO*) (on the head) (*A*).

(iv)

SUBJECT	PREDICATE
Noun phrase, *NP*	**+transitive verb**, *tV* **+indirect object**, *iO* **+direct object**, *dO* (+adverb, *A*).
e.g. Mary (*NP*) The carpenter (*NP*)	gave (*tV*) him (*iO*) the books (*dO*) (yesterday) (*A*). made (*tV*) the customer (*iO*) a table (*dO*) (last week) (*A*).

(v)

SUBJECT	PREDICATE
Noun phrase, *NP*	**+transitive verb**, *tV* **+direct object**, *dO* **+complement**, *oC*.
e.g. The head (*NP*) The Board (*NP*) The meal (*NP*)	made (*tV*) her (*dO*) a prefect (*oC*). elected (*tV*) him (*dO*) managing director (*oC*). made (*tV*) the guest (*dO*) ill (*oC*).

Deviations from these patterns (not simply 'transformations' of these patterns in the Chomsky sense) will result in loose sentence structures. Transformations of (iii), for example, could produce an infinite number of sentences which a native speaker might never have seen before but whose grammaticality he or she would instantly recognise: e.g. 'The clumsy coal merchant smashed the ming vase in his anger'. Transformations within the pattern might produce semantic deviations which arrest the reader's attention by *foregrounding*, but they do not tolerate grammatical deviations so easily. The destruction of syntagmatic patterns is not readily tolerated without violence to the sense or to the reader's response. If this is what is intended, all well and good, but such deviations need to be judiciously used in a context that will tolerate them.

Ambiguity

In 1930 William Empson published his book *Seven Types of Ambiguity* and, at a stroke, elevated the notion of 'ambiguity' from being a stylistic weakness to a considerable stylistic strength. He defined 'ambiguity' in the very first paragraph: 'any verbal nuance, however slight, which gives room for alternative reactions to the same piece of language'.

Literary 'ambiguity' may depend on sound (**phonology**), meaning (**semantics**), or on structures (**syntax**) or on an interconnection between two or all of these features of an utterance: e.g. 'His reflexes shut the door'. Here the ambiguities abound although a context would remove most of them. *Reflexes* may be physical or emotional responses; *shut* may refer to the present or past; *the door* may be a literal door or a metaphorical door (e.g. an opportunity).

Usually, however, the 'ambiguity' arises from the use of what are called 'figures of speech', the most common of which involving 'ambiguity' are **pun**, **simile**, **metaphor**, **metonymy**, **irony**.

Pun

This is a figure in which a word is used in such a way as to suggest two or more meanings or associations simultaneously, e.g.

Epitaph on a Brewer

Here lies poor Burton;

He was both hale and stout;

Death laid him on his bitter bier.

Now in another world he hops about.

Empson describes such 'simply funny puns' as 'jumping out of their setting, yapping, and biting the Master on the ankles'. The pun makes the reader conscious of itself rather than of any deeper meaning. It is impossible to treat the pun as a superficial device, however, in a poem such as George Herbert's *The Pulley*, where the pun on the word 'Rest' is at the heart of its meaning:

The Pulley

When God at first made man,

Having a glass of blessings standing by

'Let us,' said He, 'pour on him all we can;

Let the world's wishes, which dispersed lie,

    Contract into a span.'

So Strength first made a way:

Then Beauty flow'd, then Wisdom, Honour, Pleasure.

When almost all was out, God made a stay;

Perceiving, that alone of all His treasure

    Rest in the bottom lay.

'For if I should,' said He,

'Bestow *this* jewel also on my creature,

He would adore my gifts instead of me;

And **rest** in nature, not the God of nature:—

    So both should losers be.

'Yet let him keep the **rest**;
But keep them, with repining **rest**lessness.
Let him be rich, and weary; that, at least,
If goodness lead him not, yet weariness
May toss him to my breast.'

Leech (op. cit. pages 209–11) distinguishes the two kinds of pun and calls them the *homonymic* pun and the *polysemantic* pun; the first seems to depend on an accident of language and the second on a concept of integrating the 'ambiguity' with the discourse as a whole. He goes on to distinguish also the further kinds of pun:

(i) *the repetitive pun:* e.g. in *Richard II* (IV, i)

Fitzwater: Surrey thou liest.
  Surrey: Dishonourable boy!
    That lie shall lie so heavy on my sword,
    That it shall render vengeance and revenge,
    Till then the lie-giver and that lie do lie
    In earth as quiet as thy father's skull.

(ii) *the asyntactic pun*, where its meaning does not fit easily back into the context of the syntax, e.g.

Ask for me tomorrow and you shall find me a grave man.
                                    (*Romeo and Juliet*, II, i)

(iii) *the etymological pun*, e.g.

First Clown: There is no ancient gentlemen but
                gardeners, ditchers, and grave-makers;
                they hold up Adam's profession.
Second Clown: Was he a gentleman?
First Clown. A' was the first that ever bore arms.
Second Clown. Why, he had none.
First Clown. What! art a heathen? How dost thou
                understand the Scripture? The
                Scripture says, Adam digged; could
                he dig without arms?

                                    (*Hamlet*, V, i)

(iv) *syllepsis*: a figure, a kind of pun, where a word has the same syntactical relation to two or more words but has a different sense in relation to each; a 'collapsed' pun, e.g.

A shoplifter is a shopper with the gift of grab.

Said a cat as he playfully threw
His wife down a weil in Peru,
'Relax, dearest Dora;
Please don't be angora;
I was only artesian you.'
                    (from J. S. Crosbie, *The Dictionary of Puns*, 1977)

(v) *a play on antonyms* (words of opposite meanings):

> pardon me,
> And not impute this yielding to <u>light</u> love,
> Which the <u>dark</u> night hath so discovered.
>
> (*Romeo and Juliet*, II, ii)

Simile and metaphor

A **simile** is a *direct* comparison between two or more things, fundamentally unlike, but alike in the one respect in which they are being compared; in a simile the comparison is explicit and is introduced by 'like' or 'as', e.g.

She sang like a nightingale.

He looked like a pig.

A **metaphor** is an *implied* comparison between two or more things fundamentally unlike but alike in the one respect in which they are being compared; the comparison is implicit, e.g.

He is a pig.

Allegory, *fable* and *parable* are extended forms of metaphor, since they can be taken on at least two levels of meaning: the literal and the figurative. The link with the literal provides a basis for acceptance of the comparison; it is immediately recognisable. The story of a man, for example, going on a journey from Jerusalem to Jericho or from London to Birmingham is one readily understood. The literal details of the 'parable' of the Good Samaritan (*St Luke*, XI, 30–7) are recognisable. The transference of the literal meaning to the figurative relies on 'the double meaning', implied comparison between a story and man's life and relationships one with another: in fact, on 'ambiguity', since the word means 'moving in both ways' (*ambi*, both ways, *agere*, to drive).

Metonymy

Metonymy is the term used to describe the figure of speech where there is a substitution for the name of a thing the name of an attribute of it or of something closely related to it, e.g.

'The House' for *Parliament*;

'The Crown' for *The Queen*;

'Shakespeare' for *The Works of Shakespeare*.

The word 'metonymy' is derived from a Greek word (*metonymia*) which means 'a name change'.

The figure needs to be distinguished from synecdoche, where a comprehensive term is used for a less comprehensive one or vice versa; i.e. a whole for a part or a part for the whole, e.g.

'*The school* won the cup'. (The school = the school's team.)

'Give us this day our daily bread.' (Bread = food.)

Irony

This refers to a figure of speech in which the intended meaning is the opposite of that expressed by the words actually used. It sometimes takes the form of sarcasm or ridicule couched in language that seems full of praise. For example, in Mark Antony's speech after the murder of Julius Caesar he ultimately condemns Brutus, Cassius and other conspirators by repeating again and again the idea: 'Brutus is an honourable man . . . so are they all, all honourable men'. By saying it often enough, ironically, he makes the conspirators seem to be anything but 'honourable'. In Swift's *Modest Proposal* (1729) for preventing the children of the poor from becoming a burden to their parents, the writer suggests, apparently in all seriousness, that the babes should be fattened up for the table of the rich English.

Jane Austen's opening of *Pride and Prejudice* is a superb example of literary irony:

'It is a truth universally acknowledged, that a single man in possession of a good fortune must be in want of a wife.'

PART III

Spoken and Written English

CHAPTER 5

There are marked **differences** between the spoken and the written modes of English. These differences may be grouped as follows:

(i) Spoken English is accompanied by **non-verbal** (sometimes called *paralinguistic*) features such as movements of the hands and arms, eye contact, facial expressions and even body stance which can reinforce meaning.

(ii) Written English has to devise an elaborate system of punctuation to communicate meaning. A pause in Spoken English, however, can be much more expressive than that indicated in Written English by a full stop, comma, semi-colon, question mark or explanation mark. Dialogue is marked in Spoken English by changes of accent, stress, intonation, and position.

(iii) Spoken English can constantly rephrase, repeat, annotate, and extend ideas as it proceeds in order to elicit desired responses from an audience.

(iv) Written English, in the absence of an actual audience at the time of its production, requires sophisticated techniques to adapt the language to a writer's point of view, content, context, and an audience in a way that is less immediate and less dynamic than in Spoken English which can respond at once to any variation of these elements.

(v) There are some differences in **grammar** between the two modes. Speech, for example, uses features such as contracted forms of negatives (e.g. *n't*) and of modals/auxiliaries (e.g. should've, won't've, etc.). Tag questions (e.g. . . . , didn't he? . . . . surely? etc.) are more often found in Spoken English than Written English.

(vi) Vocabulary, too, differs, often because of the association of Written English with *formal* uses, and Spoken English with *informal* uses. Colloquial English should not be confused with slang*, however.

---

*

The word 'slang' does not appear in Dr Johnson's *Dictionary* (1755) and *Chambers Twentieth Century Dictionary* says the word is of doubtful origin. Niceforo (*Le génie de l'argot*, 1912) argued that slang is used because of high spirits, the desire to appear novel or to ease social relationships, the wish to seem friendly, and the wish to be identified with one set or class of people. If slang usage becomes generally accepted it passes into colloquial English and may eventually pass into Standard English. Some of the phrases which Partridge quotes, for example, have risen from slang to acceptable colloquial speech: *down to bedrock, come up to scratch, a knock-out blow, below the belt,* etc.

Spoken English

Received Pronunciation

Received pronunciation (usually abbreviated to RP) is a convenient, rather than an accurate, term used to refer to the highest status British English accent. Most speakers in the British Isles speak Standard English but they speak it with a regional accent. RP is the accent used by radio and television broadcasters and educated people in the South; it has become the accent most readily understood throughout the country. Daniel Jones (*An Outline of English Phonetics*, ninth edition, 1962) pointed out that all speakers use more than one pronunciation and indeed might 'pronounce the same word or sequence of words differently under different circumstances. Thus in ordinary conversation the word *and* is frequently pronounced **n** when unstressed (*e.g.* in *bread and butter* **bred 'n' b** ʌ **ta**), but in serious recitation the word, even when unstressed, might often be pronounced **ænd** rhyming with *hand* **hænd**.' Jones went on to distinguish a number of pronunciations: 'rapid familiar style', 'slower colloquial style', 'the natural style used in addressing a fair-sized audience', 'the acquired style of the stage' and 'the acquired styles used in singing'.

Peter Trudgill (*On Dialect: Social and Geographical Perspectives*, 1983) has shown that the large number of people with near-RP accents frequently incorporate a number of non-RP features, 'such as northern /a/ rather than /aː/ in items such as *bath, dance* . . . The further one goes 'down' the social scale, the larger become the grammatical and lexical differences from Standard English, and the phonetic and phonological differences from RP. The largest degree of regional variation is found at the level of rural dialects, particularly as spoken by elderly people of little education' (page 187).

Vowel and consonant systems

The following tables are taken from the standard work on Spoken English, H. E. Palmer and F. G. Blandford, *A Grammar of Spoken English*, third edition, revised R. Kingdom, 1969, pages 3–4. They set out the vowel and consonant systems of Spoken English using the *Simplified System* of phonetics recommended by Daniel Jones for those beginning the serious study of the subject.

Students should examine their own regional dialect accents against these tables of the consonant and vowel systems of Received Pronunciation to see how and where differences occur. Although it is not an easy thing to do, it would be a most helpful and informative exercise to record a very short conversation between two speakers with regional accents and then to transcribe their speech phonetically. If the same conversation were then transcribed using the sound systems of RP, the differences would be immediately seen once the two transcriptions were compared.

ENGLISH VOWEL SOUNDS

No.	Symbol	Example		Short Description
				Pure Vowels
1	1ː	siː	see	Front, close
2	i	sit	sit	Front, close to half close[4]
3	e	set	set	Front, half close to half open[3]
4	a	sat	sat	Front, half open to open[3]
5	aː	faː*	far	Back, open
6	o	got	got	Back, open, rounded[3]
7	oː	soː	saw	Back, half open, rounded
8	u	fut	foot	Back, half close to close, rounded[4]
9	u	tuː	too	Back, close, rounded
10	ʌ	ʌp	up	Central, half open, unrounded[3]
11	əː	fəː*	fur	Central, half open to half close
12	ə	əgou	ago	Central, half open to half close[5]
				Falling Diphthongs
13	ei	mei	may	Narrow, front
14	ou	nou	no	Narrow, central to back
15	ai	mai	my	Wide, front
16	au	nau	now	Wide, back
17	oi	boi	boy	Wide, back to front
				Centring Diphthongs
18	iə	diə*	dear	Front, half close
19	eə	peə*	pair	Front, half open
20	oə	koə	core	Back, half open
21	uə	tuə*	tour	Back, half close[1]

* Indicates that r is added when the word is followed immediately by one beginning with a vowel or diphthong.

[1] Never occurs in initial position in native English words.

[2] Never occurs in final position and is weakened or completely elided when it occurs at the beginning of an unstressed syllable.

[3] Never occurs in final position in native English words.

[4] Never occurs in stressed final position in native English words.

[5] Never occurs stressed in native English words.

ENGLISH CONSONANT SOUNDS

Symbol	Example		Short Description
			Plosives
p	**pi:**	pea	Bilabial, voiceless
b	**bi:**	bee	Bilabial, voiced
t	**tu:**	too	Alveolar, voiceless
d	**du:**	do	Alveolar, voiced
k	**ki:**	key	Velar, voiceless
g	**gou**	go	Velar, voiced
			Nasals
m	**mai**	my	Bilabial, voiced
n	**nau**	now	Alveolar, voiced
ŋ	**siŋ**	sing	Velar, voiced[1]
			Lateral
l	**lou**	low	Alveolar, voiced
			Fricatives
f	**feə***	fair	Labio-dental, voiceless
v	**vau**	vow	Labio-dental, voiced
	in	thin	Linguo-dental, voiceless
ð	**ðen**	then	Linguo-dental, voiced
s	**soun**	sown	Alveolar, voiceless
z	**zoun**	zone	Alveolar, voiced
ʃ	**ʃou**	show	Palato-alveolar, voiceless
ʒ	**`pleʒə***	pleasure	Palato-alveolar, voiced[1]
h	**hai**	high	Laryngal, voiceless[2]
			Semi-vowels
w	**wei**	way	Bilabial and velar, voiced[3]
r	**ro:**	raw	Post-alveolar, voiced[3]
j	**ju:**	you	Palatal, voiced[3]
			Affricates
tʃ	**tʃə:tʃ**	church	Post-alveolar, voiceless
dʒ	**dʒʌdʒ**	judge	Post-alveolar, voiced

Syllable and stress in words and sentences

Stress is usually defined as the force given to one part of a word or one part of a sentence in speaking. There are graduations of stress ranging from the very weak to the very strong (although, for convenience, some grammarians reduce 'stressed' syllables to three kinds—primary, secondary, and unaccented), but it should be distinguished from: **pitch**, which is the height or depth of the voice; **prominence**, which is the making of one syllable or part of a sentence stand out (by stress, arrangement, pitch, etc.) from the others around it; **rhythm**, which is the pattern that emerges from placing stressed syllables in relation to unstressed syllables; and **intonation** (or '*tune*') which is the pattern within an expression with a significant rise and fall in pitch. Both sentence stress and intonation depend on the stressing of syllables in single words.

English words normally carry one or two main stresses but some longer ones may take more, e.g.

ˊwhether, ˊdropping, ˊregular, deˊvelop; conˊservaˊtive, ˊenterˊtain, ˊsuperimˊpose, enˊcycloˊpaediˊa, ˊextraˊordinˊary.

The stresses are not equivalent in these longer words necessarily. Notice, too, that it is customary to mark the stressed syllable with a mark preceding it. Syllables pronounced on a high pitch are usually more prominent than those on a low pitch.

The stressing of individual words, however, gives way to patterns of sentence stress when they are used in continuous utterances. Single words that, in isolation, would carry stress might emerge as unstressed elements in a sentence. For example, ˊand or ˊafter or ˊthe might lose their main stresses in sentences such as:

ˊMr *and* ˊMrs ˊBrown ˊran *after the* ˊbus.

One of the main difficulties foreigners have in learning a foreign language is to pick up the stress patterns of sentences (as well as their intonation patterns).

Questions are normally marked by a rising intonation pattern. Sentences which appear as statements may become questions if they carry this rising intonation pattern in speech or by the addition of a question mark (to indicate a rising intonation pattern) in written English, e.g.

'How many books were there?' (Direct question.)
'There were ten'. (Statement with falling intonation.)
'There were ten?' (Question with rising intonation.)

A marked feature of question construction in English which makes use of such intonation patterns is the use of a tag questions, very frequently used in conversation, e.g.

'He did it, *didn't he?*'

An affirmative statement is, therefore, followed by a negative tag; a negative statement is followed by a positive tag, e.g.

'He never did it, *did he?*'

The tag normally is used to express doubt, incredulity, sarcasm, disbelief, emphasis or even casualness about the inquiry and usually carries a falling intonation pattern. It is a useful way of indicating or recognising the attitude of a speaker or writer.

Punctuation marks in written English help to indicate some of the elements such as stress, prominence, intonation in the spoken language. Exclamation marks and question marks are particularly useful in doing this but they are not completely able to indicate such features of the language adequately. They can, however, indicate short pauses (commas), longer pauses (colons, semi-colons), and stops (full stops, question marks, exclamation marks).

Assimilation, elision and dissimilation

Consider the following two tongue-twisters:
  'Still the sinking steamer sank.'
  'I am copper-bottoming them, ma'am.'
The difficulty in saying tongue-twisters quickly arises because the spoken language is constantly trying *either* to change one sound to resemble another in close proximity to it (**assimilation**) or to change one sound to differentiate it from another in close proximity (**dissimilation**).

Assimilation makes speech more rapid and is often used in conjunction with **elision**; this refers to the situation where a vowel or group of vowels, a consonant or group of consonants is suppressed or omitted in order to speed up a spoken utterance, e.g.
  'He *could've* done it.'
  'I jus' try to do't.'
Elision in conjunction with *assimilation* is frequently used with auxiliaries (e.g. 'he's done it') or with modals (e.g. *won't, shan't, musn't, can't* or even *won', shan', musn',* or *can'*).

Other features of Spoken English

Speech is largely a matter of signalling meanings from one person to another. These signals are largely in the form of words but not entirely so. There is a range of other components in the exchange of speech which contribute to the act of communication. Such features are sometimes called **non-verbal** or even **paralinguistic.**

These features may be arbitrarily sub-divided into the **vocal** and the **non-vocal**.

Vocal signals may include sneezing, yawning, coughing, snoring, gasping, swallowing, etc., which do not depend on language but might well add to the meaning of a conversation beyond the words. *Non-vocal* signals may include nodding, gesticulating, eye contact or eye aversion, lip-pursing, smiling, frowning, eye-closing or forehead-wrinkling, body posture, etc. John Lyons in *Semantics*, I, 1977, quotes from an article by D.

Abercrombie, 'Paralanguage', *British Journal of Disorders of Communication*, **3**, 55–59):

> We speak with our vocal organs, but we converse with our whole bodies . . . Paralinguistic phenomena . . . occur alongside spoken language, interact with it, and produce together with it a total system of communication . . . The study of paralinguistic behaviour is part of the study of conversation: the conversational use of spoken language cannot be properly understood unless paralinguistic elements are taken into account.'

Lyons, himself, pointed out that conversation also depended on **modulation** and **punctuation**: *modulation* is 'the superimposing upon the utterance of a particular attitudinal colouring, indicative of the speaker's involvement in what he is saying and his desire to impress or convince the hearer'; *punctuation* is 'the marking of boundaries at the beginning and end of an utterance and at various points within the utterance to emphasize particular expressions, to segment the utterance or manageable information units, to solicit the listener's permission for the utterance to be continued, and so on.' The *ums* and the *ers* and other hesitations and self-corrections often indicate that the speaker is trying to think out meaning at the same time as signalling to the audience that the utterance is not yet ended and his indulgence to avoid intervening for the moment is being sought.

All of these features (or signs or use of semiology) are an integral part of the interpersonal activity that constitutes speech. The signalling has to be clear within the context in which the language is being used. (Lyons points out that Greek or Turkish speakers will throw their heads back to signal disagreement rather than move them from side to side; an English native speaker might, therefore, mistake disagreement for agreement with unfortunate results!)

Written English

The Roman alphabet

Germanic tribes originally wrote in runes and it seems likely that when the Anglo-Saxons migrated to the British Isles from the Continent of Europe they brought the runic alphabet with them. Runes had been adapted, many centuries before they migrated, from a North Italian variety of the Roman alphabet: the runes ᚠ and ᚱ , for example, are very close to the Roman **F** and **R**.

In Anglo-Saxon England the Christian church used a Roman-based alphabet but the letters *j*, *v* and *w* were not part of it. The Anglo-Saxons, on the other hand, did not use *q* or *z*; *q* was used more extensively by Norman scribes but *z* has always struggled in English against *s*.

The Anglo-Saxon scribes however, used five runic letters which have since been dropped from the language:

æ, Æ	(ash):	pronounced as the 'a' in Modern English *hat* (short) or *ware* (long);
ðÐ	(eth):	a voiced 'th' sound, as in Modern English *seethe*;
þ þ	(thorn):	a voiceless 'th' sound, as in Modern English *thin*;
þ þ	(wynn):	a 'w' sound as in Modern English *worthy*;
Ȝ	(yogh):	an initial palatal 'g' as in Modern English *young*.

All these letters have completely disappeared from English, with perhaps the exception of the thorn, which still survives in phrases such as '*Ye* olde tea shoppe', where the initial *y* is really an older thorn written with an open loop on the ascender. In Anglo-Saxon times spelling followed pronunciation and, therefore, the spelling found in a text provides valuable evidence of dialect pronunciations and also of the provenance of a manuscript. In fact, English spelling according to pronunciation long survived the introduction of printing (Caxton's first book in English dates from 1477) when some kind of standardised spelling might have seemed essential.

Surveys of the history and development of the **spelling and punctuation** systems of English will help to explain some current usages.

Spelling: its history and development

The British can be divided into two groups: those who can spell correctly and those who cannot; the second group is by far the bigger. The English language presents native readers and writers with immense problems, because its spelling is based partly on etymology or the way the words originated and developed. Most people do not have enough historical or linguistic knowledge to be able to relate Modern English spelling to etymology and so they fall back on trying to represent the words in writing as they sound in speech. Such an approach is often doomed before it begins, because it tends to ignore two things: first, words are not pronounced in the same way everywhere in the British Isles and the phonetic speller in Yorkshire ought, therefore, to produce the spelling for a word which is quite different from that of a phonetic speller in the West Country. Even the simple word 'gate' would produce some amazing variations in spelling throughout the country if people were to spell it exactly as they pronounced it. Secondly, words change in pronunciation over the years and English spelling would need to be in a state of constant flux from one decade to the next and one century to the next. Alexander Pope (who died in 1744) rhymed the words *obey* and *tea*, for example, but they certainly do not rhyme today; Pope spelt the rhymed syllables differently, too, since he did not base his spelling on phonetics any more than we do today. Yet rhyming in poetry is not, in itself, a sure indication of how words were pronounced; Milton (died 1674) rhymes *God* with *abode* and *load*; Dryden (died 1700) rhymes *God* with *abode*, Pope with *road*, and Gray (died 1771) with *abode*; it would seem that the word god had a pronunciation in the 17th and 18th century of [gōd]. Indeed, one writer, Price, actually said in 1668 that *God* and *goad* were pronounced alike. But the word *God* today has a short vowel, as it had in Anglo-Saxon times. The spelling of the word, whatever its pronunciation at different times and in different regions, has remained constant.

Consistency in English spelling was not, however, one of its strongest features until comparatively recent times. The scribes who produced the handwritten books for the monastic libraries in Anglo-Saxon England often spelt their English words as they pronounced them; there are even some, although fewer, variations in the way they wrote their Latin words. Variations in the spelling of English at this time have been an invaluable help to scholars who want to find out more about early regional dialects and to discover in what part of the country a particular manuscript might have been produced or even from what area a particular scribe might have originated. The spelling of words carried traces of evidence about the regional origin of the man, the book he was copying, the monastery in which he was writing, and the area in which he was working.

In about 1200 a monk, named Orm, wrote a long poem consisting of the retelling of the gospel readings for the year and some sermons based on them; the work remains unfinished but it was written somewhere in the east of England. Orm is an interesting man, for he was the first to attempt to reform English spelling; he recognised two important facts that are essential for a successful reformation of spelling: first, spelling had to be consistent—a word had to be spelt exactly the same every time it occurred; and secondly, one symbol only should be used to represent one sound. Orm doubled consonants whenever they followed short vowels (e. g. *ennglisshe, iss, inn, annd*, etc.) and used three separate symbols to represent the ways in which a 'g' could be pronounced in his time. His ideas, however, did not catch on and they died with him.

The Norman scribes who were unfamiliar with the English language and yet had to copy passages written in it introduced their own spelling variations and some of those have stayed in the language ever since. They found in English, for example, that native scribes used the symbol 'u' to represent both the long vowel [ū]: (e.g. *hūs*, house) and the short vowel [u] (e. g. *lufu*, love or *sunu*, son). They also found that English sometimes used a 'y' to represent a sound similar to that found in the French word 'juste'. There were, then, three sounds at least represented by one letter. Their task was made more difficult because a 'u' was written with two down-strokes of a quill pen and resembled an 'n' which was made in the same way; an 'm' was made with three down-strokes. In a word like *sunu*, therefore, it was not always easy to sort out whether the six down-strokes consisted of 'i's, 'u's, 'n's or 'm's. A scribal convention grew up that they would represent the long vowel 'ū' [ū]: by 'ou' (cf. O. E. *hūs*: Mod. E. *house*; O. E. *mūs*: Mod. E. *mouse*) and the short vowel 'u' [u] by an 'o', when it came before an 'm' or an 'n' or any other letter made by a down-stroke with the pen and with which it might be confused. Therefore the words *son* (O. E. *sunu*) and *monk* (O. E. *munuc*) are spelt even today with 'o's, although their pronunciation remains firmly a 'u'.

The scribes at this time were also probably responsible for another peculiarity of Modern English spelling: the 'gh' combination in many words such as *bough*, *daughter*, *might*, *rough*, *through*, etc. When they first came to grips with these words, the Norman scribes found that they bore a sound (represented in Anglo-Saxon by an 'h') which was guttural and approximated to the sound of the 'ch' in the Modern Scottish word *loch*. From the 13th century onwards this guttural sound was represented in spelling by 'gh'. At the end of the word, the sound either disappeared (cf. the Mod. E. '*bough*') or was modified with the help of the lips into an 'f' sound (cf. the Mod. E. '*rough*'). In the middle of words the sound represented by 'gh' gradually disappeared (cf. the Mod. E. *might*, *right*, *night*, etc.). For some reason the early printers retained these 'gh' spellings from manuscripts, although by the time they had begun to print their books the changes to the pronunciation of words containing the sound had already taken place. These 'gh' spellings have persisted until the present day and are often cited by those who want to reform English spelling as examples of the confusion that seems to exist in the way we spell words today. These 'gh' spellings are also quoted by foreign students who are trying to learn English as areas where they find great difficulty. They present difficulties, however, only to those who falsely think, or feel, that Modern English spelling should follow the pronunciation of words as they are spoken today. English spelling has not consistently followed the pronunciation of the language since the early medieval period. To eliminate spellings such as 'gh' from English words would be to destroy much of the historical (or 'archeological') evidence still contained in the forms our words take.

The arrival of printing in England was, perhaps, the single most important early factor in 'fixing' the spelling we use. Caxton (died 1499) returned to England in 1476, after having learnt printing probably at Cologne and practising it at Bruges, and he promptly established a press at Westminster. Between 1477 and 1491 he issued nearly eighty separate books using six founts of type. Caxton and the early English printers established the main shape of our historically phonetic spelling; their printing tended to 'fix' it. As pronunciation changed, the spelling lagged behind, set in hard printers' type. Dickens's Sam Weller thought that spelling was 'according to the taste and fancy of the speller', but printers aimed (not always successfully) at consistency. The word in a book was generally spelt in the same way throughout the book; its spelling was historically phonetic but it took little account in practice of regional variation and no account of where the book was to be read. Printing gave an air of authority to the spelling used but variations occurred widely, even so, until the late part of the 18th century.

About one hundred years after the introduction of printing into England, the attempts to reform and regulate English spelling got under way. In 1568, Sir Thomas Smith, a Secretary of State to Queen Elizabeth I, published a dialogue in Latin between himself and a pupil called Quintus about the way English was written. (Dialogues, modelled on Plato, had been popular in the West during the Middle Ages. The Anglo-Saxon writer, Ælfric, for example, wrote a dialogue (*a Colloquy*) between himself as master and his pupil who was learning Latin.) He called the work *De recta & emendata linguae Anglicae scriptione, dialogus* (A Dialogue about the Correct and Corrected Writing of the English Language); it was part of the times that it seemed appropriate to discuss the English language in another tongue altogether! In this dialogue Smith commented upon the apparent inconsistencies and absurdities in English spelling and proposed an English extended alphabet of some thirty-four symbols supplemented by accents and signs in an attempt to put the matter right. The attempt failed.

In 1569, a year later, John Hart wrote *An Orthographie conteyning the due order and reason, howe to write or paint thimage of mannes voice, most like to the life or nature.* At least he thought it proper to discuss English in English. Some, he argued, 'maintain our abused English writing' because they want to show the orgins of the words. He had his own elaborate system to reform English spelling; it never became popular.

The schoolmasters now took up the fight. In 1580 William Bullokar wrote *Bullokar's Booke at large, for the Amendment of Orthographie for English Speech: wherein, a most perfect supplie is made, for the wantes and double sounde of letters in the olde Orthographie, with Examples for the same, with the easie conference and use of both Orthographies.*

He saw as the basic problem of English spelling 'the want of concord in the eye, voice, and ear'. His proposed reform was complicated, with an elaborate system of 'marks, strikes, and accents'. The cure seemed worse than the illness; it was not taken up.

Richard Mulcaster's book *Elementarie* was published in 1582. This was an important book in the Renaissance discussion of language and grammar. He wanted to bring together Sound, Custom, and Reason in his reform. He was wary of those who 'appeall to sound' and 'fly to innovations'; the principles which should underlie our spelling were Rule, Proportion (Analogy), Enfranchisement (adapting foreign words to English usage), Composition, Derivation, Distinction, and Prerogative. His use of analogy in spelling is especially interesting: he justifies the spelling of *where* by comparing it with *here* and *there*, for example, although such an explanation is historically inaccurate. It was during the Renaissance, too, that analogy with Latin introduced a silent 'b' into *doubt* and *debt* (*dubitum, debitum*) whereas the words had been introduced originally from French where no 'b' existed. Similarly 'gh' was introduced wrongly by analogy with *light* and *night* into words similarly pronounced, such as *delight* and *tight*. Other false analogies resulted during the late Middle Ages and early Renaissance in spellings such as *fault* (cf. Latin *fallere* French *fautè*) and *perfect* (cf. Latin *perfectum*, French *parf(a)it*). Dr Johnson introduced the 'p' into the word *receipt* (Latin *receptum*) although he inconsistently omitted it from *conceit* and *deceit* when he composed his *Dictionary* in 1755. Other examples of the introduction of strange letters into English borrowed words by false analogy may be found in *isle, island* (cf. Latin *insula* but French *île* from which the English word came), in *foreign* (cf. Latin *foris*) and in *sovereign* (French *souverain*) by analogy with *reign* (properly derived from French *regner*), and in *admiral* (cf. Latin *admirabilis*, although the English word was derived from French *amiral* or Arabic *amir-al-bahr*, lord of the sea).

'Orthography' was popular during Shakespeare's lifetime, although Shakespeare himself cannot refrain from using it for humour. In *Much Ado about Nothing* Benedick scorns the newly fallen-in-love Claudio:

> He was wont to speak plain and to the purpose, like an honest man and a soldier; and now is he turned orthographer; his words are a very fantastical banquet, just so many strange dishes.

The new fashion for spelling correctly occurs—for humorous purposes in *Twelfth Night*. Malvolio has been tricked by Sir Toby, Fabian, Sir Andrew, and Maria and has found a letter which includes the letters M O A I. Try as he might he cannot make them spell Malvolio:

> M—but then there is no consonancy in the sequel, that suffers under probation: A should follow, but O does.

In 1621 Alexander Gill, the High Master of St Paul's School, wrote a Latin treatise on orthography entitled *Linguae Anglicae Logonomia*. He believed that spelling should follow the sound of the spoken language, but he conceded that some other influences might also operate: etymology, difference of meaning, accepted usage, and dialect. Charles Butler in 1634 wrote *The English Grammar or the Institution of Letters, Syllables, and Words in the English Tung* in which he made some detailed suggestions for reforming the alphabet to make it conform with English sounds. The industry of spelling reform continued unabated with Simon Daines's book in 1640: *Orthoepia Anglicana: or the First Principall Part of the English Grammar: Teaching the Art of right speaking and pronouncing English, with certain exact rules of Orthograpy, and rules of spelling or combining of Syllables, and directions for keeping of stops or points between sentence and sentence.* This book is interesting for it reveals some of the changes that Daines observed taking place in the pronunciation of English in the 17th century.

Three years later, in 1643, Richard Hodges wrote a book called *A Special*

Help to Orthographie or the True-writing of English. He discusses the relation of symbol to sound and uses the phonetic approach to spelling reform. He it was who made the point that 'howsoever wee use to Write thus *leadeth* it, *maketh* it, *noteth* it, *raketh* it, per-*fumeth* it, &c. Yet in our ordinary speech (which is best to be understood) wee say, *leads* it, *makes* it, *notes* it, *rakes* it, per-*fumes* it.' The final *-s* seems to have become the usual third-person present-tense singular ending of verbs in common, spoken English during the early part of the 17th century.

In 1668 John Wilkins read a treatise to the recently formed Royal Society: *An Essay Towards a Real Character and a Philosophical Language*. He admits that in spite of the efforts of Smith, Hart, Bullokar and Gill 'so invincible is custom that still we retain the same errors and incongruities in writing which our Forefathers taught us'.

It was at this time that dictionaries began to develop. Glossaries of words, giving both Latin and their English equivalents, had been in existence from the time of the Middle Ages. Now the dictionaries sought to define the words taken into the language from foreign tongues. Edward Phillips's *The New World of Words or Universal English Dictionary* appeared in 1658, Nathaniel Bailey's *A More Compleat Universal Etymological Dictionary* in 1721, Benjamin Martin's *English Dictionary* in 1749 and John Wesley's *Complete English Dictionary* in 1753. Alongside the development of dictionaries there were published tables of English words, *Thesauruses*, and *Etymologies* (e.g. Stephen Skinner's in 1667 and Francis Junius's in 1677).

The written forms of English words were hardening as these dictionaries appeared. One of the most important books in English appeared at this time: Dr Samuel Johnson's *Dictionary of the English Language* (1755). It rapidly became the standard book for English spelling and developed Nathaniel Bailey's technique of illustrating the meanings of words by giving quotations from selected writers—a technique still followed in the standard English dictionary, *A New English Dictionary on Historical Principles* (usually referred to as 'The Oxford Dictionary'). Dr Johnson's *Dictionary* has affected English spelling since its publication. Boswell spoke of his friend as 'the man who had conferred stability on the language of his country'. Sheridan in 1756 wrote, 'If our language should ever be fixed, he must be considered by all posterity as the founder, and his dictionary as the corner stone'. Only a few of our spelling conventions differ from those instituted by Dr Johnson; we no longer retain the final *-k* in the ending *-ic(k)* of some of our nouns and adjectives (e.g. *panic, academic, music*, etc.) although British English has been inconsistent in retaining or dropping the *-u-* in the ending *-our* to some nouns (e.g. *honour, labour, favour*, but *terror, author, horror*).

Spelling reform waned as an activity for a long time after Dr Johnson's definitive work. By the mid-19th century new movements began. Sir Isaac Pitman (1813–47) introduced a method of shorthand based on phonetic principles and the consistency he sought between sounds and symbols for his shorthand showed up anew the inconsistencies in English spelling. His associate Alexander Ellis produced two periodicals *Fonetic Friend* (1849) and *Spelling Reformer* (1849–50) in an attempt to change the shape of English words.

Pitman's work led to new interest in spelling reform and there followed the formation of The Simplified Spelling Society, which has been supported by a number of distinguished philologists, amongst whom were Skeat, Gilbert Murray, Lloyd James and Daniel Jones. Spelling has also been the concern of The Society for Pure English, with a learned body of members. Henry Bradley, Sir William Craigie and Robert Bridges, at one time the Poet Laureate, have also made contributions to the debate on spelling reform. Bernard Shaw advocated the development of a completely new alphabet and left a considerable sum of money which was to be used for this purpose: he refused 'the innumerable schemes for spelling English phonetically with the old ABC, repeating the same stale arguments and proposing the same changes'. He advocated an alphabet of forty or fifty new letters to be taught side by side with the old one to see which of the two would prove the fittest to survive. Since then there has been a major move in the 1960s to popularise in schools the Initial Teaching Alphabet (ITA), which set out to simplify the relationships between sounds and spelling so that children, at least in the early years of their schooling, could learn to read more quickly. Problems arose, however, when the pupils had to switch from the scheme they used in primary schools to the conventional system of spelling in the secondary schools.

Today the person who cannot spell accurately according to the conventions set up by printers and maintained by dictionary compilers is considered illiterate. It would take some strong arguments, however, to sweep away at a stroke the evidence of some 800 years of the development of our language contained in our spelling. So far English has rejected all such attempts.

Spelling 'rules'

So-called 'rules' for language always seem to carry a list of exceptions; nevertheless, it is often useful to observe the patterns of usage of a language. The 'exceptions' provide the tests against which the 'rules' can be measured; linguists sometimes refer to the exceptions as 'elsewhere words' since they show that 'elsewhere' a usage is adopted different from the 'rule'.

Plural of nouns
(i) Regularly nouns in the plural are spelt by adding an -*s* to the singular form: e.g. dog, *dogs*; book, *books*; song, *songs*. [This final -*s* arose from a contracted inflectional ending of masculine nouns, -*as*, in old English.]
(ii) Some nouns, because of their forms earlier in the language, make their plurals in other ways:

(a) by adding -*en*; e.g. ox, *oxen*; brother, *brethren* (in a religious context: otherwise, *brothers*). N.B. The word 'children' is interesting since it carries a double plural ending. At one time the plural of 'child' was *childer* (O.E. *cild, cildru*). To the plural *childer* was added a further plural ending and the -*er* syllable was contracted, and so *children* resulted as the plural.

(b) The following nouns ending in -*f*, or -*fe* change the 'f' into 'v' and add a final-(e)s to form their plurals: e.g. calf, *calves*; elf, *elves*; half, *halves*; hoof, *hooves*; knife, *knives*; leaf, *leaves*; loaf, *loaves*; life, *lives*; self, *selves*; scarf, *scarves*; shelf, *shelves*; thief, *thieves*; wharf, *wharves*; wife, *wives*.

Other words ending in -f are regular, i.e. they take '-*s*' to form their plurals: e.g. cliff, cliffs, proof, proofs; N.B. handkerchief, *handkerchiefs*; roof, *roofs* (although with these two latter words the pronunciation of their plural endings may be either *fs* or *vz*.

(c) Some nouns change the medial vowel of the singular to form the plural: e.g. man, *men*; woman, *women*; postman, *postmen*; fireman, *firemen*; gentleman, *gentlemen*; (but note, German, *Germans*; Roman, *Romans*); foot, *feet*; tooth, *teeth*; mouse, *mice*; louse, *lice*; goose, *geese*.

(d) Singular nouns ending in *a consonant* + *y*, change the '*y*' to an '*i*' and add '-*es*' to form the plural: e.g. baby, *babies*; lady, *ladies*; penny, *pennies* (although this word also has the plural form *pence*).

(e) Singular nouns ending in a *vowel* +*y* form their plurals by adding a final -*s*: e.g. chimney, *chimneys*; monkey, *monkeys*.

(f) Singular nouns ending in -*ch*, -*s*, -*sh*, and -*x* add -*es* to form the plural: e.g. church, *churches*; bus, *buses*; bush, *bushes*; box, *boxes*; tax, *taxes*.

(g) Some nouns carry the same form in both singular and plural: e.g. sheep, *sheep*; deer, *deer*; salmon, *salmon*; trout, *trout*; grouse, *grouse*; mackerel, *mackerel*; plaice, *plaice*.

(h) Singular nouns ending in -*o* often take a final -*es* to form the plural: e.g. potato, *potatoes*; tomato, *tomatoes*; hero, *heroes*; echo, *echoes*. **But** the following form their plurals merely by adding a final -*s*: bamboo, *bamboos*; embryo, *embryos*; folio, *folios*; kangaroo, *kangaroos*; radio, *radios*; zoo, *zoos*; kilo, *kilos*; photo, *photos*; piano, *pianos*; solo, *solos*; soprano, *sopranos*; Eskimo, *Eskimos*; dynamo, *dynamos*.

(iii) Words that end in a final -*s* in the singular provide special problems:

(a) Some of them seem to have a plural form but are used only with a singular verb: *news, physics, measles*, and—when they refer to a specific science as a subject—*linguistics, mathematics, politics, statistics*; (when these do not refer directly to a science they may take a plural verb).

(b) Some, however, with a seemingly plural form, may be used with either a singular or a plural verb, according to the context and sense; *athletics; bellows; gallows; headquarters; innings; kennels; series; species.*

(c) Some with a plural form are used only with plural verbs: e.g. *alms; binoculars; braces; eaves; glasses; knickers; pants; pliers; pyjamas; scales; scissors; shorts; spectacles; tights; tongs; tweezers; arrears; belongings; clothes; earnings; looks; odds; proceeds; remains; riches; surroundings; thanks; wages;* etc.

(iv) Nouns derived from classical languages and retaining their recognisable classical forms in the singular:

(a) sometimes retain their classical plural forms: e.g. radius, *radii*; stimulus, *stimuli*; fungus, *fungi*; nucleus, *nuclei*; tumulus, *tumuli*; genus, *genera*; antenna, *antennae*; medium, *media*; bacterium, *bacteria*; curriculum, *curricula*; larva, *larvae*.

(b) sometimes take either the classical plural ending or add a new native English ending: e.g. formula, *formulae*, or *formulas*; terminus, *termini* or *terminuses*; (N.B. the plural of 'genius' is usually *geniuses*); radius, *radii* or *radiuses*;

(c) sometimes end in *-is* (singular) but *-es* (plural): e.g. basis, *bases*; crisis, *crises*; diagnosis, *diagnoses*; hypothesis, *hypotheses*; oasis, *oases*; neurosis, *neuroses*; thesis, *theses*;

(d) sometimes have a singular form ending *-on* but a plural form ending *-a*: e.g. phenomenon, *phenomena*; criterion, *criteria*;

(e) sometimes have a singular form ending *-ix* but a plural form ending *-ices*: e.g. appendix, *appendices*; index, *indices*.

(v) Some words recently borrowed from foreign languages retain their own foreign singular and plural forms: bureau, *bureaux*; plateau, *plateaux.*

It is often useful to examine a word to see how it can be divided into syllables and to isolate its prefixes and suffixes. To establish what is the prefix or the suffix frequently helps correct spelling.

Prefixes

(i) Sometimes the prefix is 'assimilated' with the next syllable: i.e. the last consonant of the prefix is 'made similar' to the first consonant of the next syllable:

(a) *ad-* (cf. *adumbrate*) becomes *ac-* : *ac*/cident; *ac*/cord;
(Latin: 'to')   *af-* : *af*-fect; *af*/ford;
     ag- : *ag*/gression;
     al- : *al*/literation; *al*/low;
     an- : *an*/nihilate; *an*/nounce;
     ap- : *ap*/proximate; *ap*/peal
     ar- : *ar*/rive; *ar*/range;
     as- : *as*/similate; *as*/semble;
     at- : *at*/tract; *at*/tack.

dis- (cf. *dis*/affect) becomes *dif-* : *dif*/fer; *dif*/ficult;
(Latin: 'in two'; 'apart') *dif*/fuse;

com- (cf. *com*/memorate) becomes *col-* : *col*/late; *col*/lect;
(Latin: cum : with) *con-* : *con*/nive; *con*/nect;
cor- : *cor*/respond; *cor*/rect;

in- (cf. *in*/ability; becomes *il-* : *il*/logical; *il*/legible;
in/nocent) *il*/legal
(Latin: used to form
negative) *im-* : *im*/mortal; *im*/mobile;
im/moderate; *im*/modest
ir- : *ir*/regular; *ir*/relevant;
ir/reparable

sub- (cf. *sub*/marine) becomes *suf-* : *suf*/focate; *suf*/fix;
(Latin: 'under') *suf*/fer
sug- : *sug*/gest;

(b) *dis-* *dis*/agree; *dis*/appear; *dis*/appoint; *dis*/able;
(Latin: 'in two' *dis*/solve; *dis*/satisfied; *dis*/arm;
'apart') *dis*/colour; *dis*/oblige; *dis*/service;
dis/ease; *dis*/sociate; *dis*/solve;
dis/sect.

(c) *inter-* *inter*/act; *inter*/cede; *inter*/change;
(Latin: 'between') *inter*/est; *inter*/regnum;
inter/rogation;
inter/relation; *inter*/rupt;

(d) *re-* *re*/act; *re*/cur; *re*/occur; *re*/quite;
(Latin: 'again' 'back') *re*/produce.

Inflexional endings and suffixes

(i) Additions to ends of words as inflexions to indicate tense, or as markers
to show whether a word is an adjective, adverb, or participle very
frequently baffle those who find English spelling difficult. There are
some general 'rules' which will help, however:

(a) Before inflexions (e.g. *-ed*, *-ing*), or suffixes (e.g. *-er*) beginning with
a vowel a final consonant in the base form of the word is doubled
provided the vowel in front of it is stressed and spelt with a single
letter, e.g.

be/gin, beginning
re/fer, referred, referring
oc/cur, occurred, occurring
/sad, sadder.

N.B.[1] Where the vowel is not stressed, the final consonant is not
doubled before the inflexional ending is added, e.g.

/enter, entered, entering
/offer, offered, offering
/alter, altered, altering
/differ, differed, differing.

N.B.[2] Where the vowel sound (stressed or unstressed) in the base
form is spelt with a double letter, the final consonant is not
doubled before the inflexional ending is added, e.g.

/dream, dreamed, dreaming
enter/tain, entertained, entertaining.

EXCEPTIONS

(a) When the base form of the word ends in a vowel spelt with a single
letter + a single *c*, *g*, *l*, *m*, or *p*, the final consonant is doubled in
British English—even if the vowel in front of it is *not* stressed—
before the inflexion is added, e.g.

panic, panicked, panicking ('ck' = cc)
debug, debugged, debugging
travel, travelled, travelling
tunnel, tunnelled, tunnelling
im peril, imperilled, imperilling
be dim, bedimmed, bedimming
worship, worshipped, worshipping.

(b) Where the base form of a word ends in *a consonant* + *y*, the *y* is
changed to an *i* before an inflexion or a suffix not beginning with an
'*i*' (e.g. *-ed*) is added, e.g.

marry, married, marriage
carry, carried, carriage
ally, allied, alliance
hurry, hurried.

Where the ending begins with an *i*, however, (e.g. *-ing*), the 'y' in
the base form is left unchanged, e.g.

carry, carrying.
hurry, hurrying.

(c) *y* is retained in words ending in *a vowel* + *y* if the inflexional ending
or suffix begins with a vowel: e.g.

delay, delayed, delaying
volley, volleyed, volleying
convey, conveying, conveyance
play, playing, player
annoy, annoyed, annoyance.

(d) Three verbs which end in *a vowel* + *y* change the 'y' to an *i* before
adding the inflexion *-d*, although they keep the *-y* before adding the
inflexion *-ing:* e.g.

say, said, saying
lay, laid, laying
pay, paid, paying.

(e) Some verbs which end in *-ie* change these letters to a *-y* before
adding the inflexional ending *-ing*, although they retain the *-ie* form
before adding *-d*: e.g.

die, died, dying
tie, tied, tying
vie, vied, vying.

A few others, however, which end in *a consonant* + *y*, change the *-y* to an *-i* before adding the inflexional ending *-ed*, although they retain the *-y* before adding *-ing*.

(f) Words which end in *-e* sometimes provide difficulties of spelling when inflexional endings are added. Usually the final *-e* is dropped before the inflexional ending is added, e.g.

save, saved, saving
live, lived, living
pine, pined, pining.

If the words end in *-ee*, *-ye*, *-oe* and sometimes *-ge*, however, they drop the final *-e* before adding the inflexional ending *-ed*, but retain the final *-e* before adding the inflexional ending *-ing*, e.g.

agree, agreed, agreeing
decree, decreed, decreeing
dye, dyed, dyeing (to distinguish the word from 'dying', perhaps)
hoe, hoed, hoeing
singe, singed, singeing (to indicate the palatal pronunciation of the 'g' in order to distinguish the word from 'singing', perhaps)
(*but cringe, cringed, cringing*).

(g) Words which end in a single *-e* usually drop this final *-e* before adding the suffixes *-able, -ment*, e.g.

love, lovable
move, movable
save, savable
judge, judgment (also *judgement*)
acknowledge, acknowledgment (also *acknowledgement*)
value, valuable
desire, desirable
abridge, abridgment (also *abridgement*)
like, likable (also *likeable*).

(h) It is difficult sometimes to be certain about the suffixes *-er* or *-or* or *-ar* to denote agents, or those who carry out an action.
The *-er* ending is of French origin (from earlier Latin *-arius*) but it is added to words of both French and native English origin, e.g.

grocer, officer, baker, driver, propeller

The *-or* ending is from Latin *-ornis* but often it has been changed to *-er* by analogy with other words, e.g.

actor, supervisor; but *convener* as well as *convenor*

The *-ar* ending (Latin *-arius*) has all but been dropped from the language, e.g.

beggar, burnar, pedlar

The pronunciation of the vowels in all three suffixes (*-er, -or, -ar*) has been reduced to a neutral, unstressed vowel (**a**).

(i) This reduction of vowel sound in suffixes has led to problems, too, with words ending in *-ance, -ence, -ant, -ent*, e.g.

repentance,   existence,   abundance
repentant,   existent,   abundant

(j) Similarly, the endings *-ary, -ory, -ery*, e.g.

ordinary,   satisfactory,   monastery

(k) Again, the endings *-able, -ible* cause difficulties, e.g.

capable, audible
rely, relied, relying
caddy, caddied, caddying
deny, denied, denying.

(l) The spellings *-or, -or-, -our, -our-,* provide special problems. Here the history of the English language explains, even if it does not justify, what happened.

Because of the influence of French the Latin ending *-or* was often spelt *-our* in the late Middle Ages. During the Renaissance, which delighted in tracing classical origins, the Latin spelling *-or* was given new currency (and American English has retained this form). During the 18th century Dr Johnson approved of words such as *terrour, horrour, authour.* Modern British English is, however, inconsistent; it has: *honour, humour, vapour, colour, vigour,* but *mirror, horror, stupor.*

When this syllable occurs medially (in the middle of the word) it sometimes retains the 'u' and sometimes drops it:

honourable, honorary
colourful, coloration (also *colouration)*
humourless, humorous
vapoury, vaporise.

(m) There is often an active discussion about the distinction between the use of the suffixes *-ise, -ize.*

Some publishers seem to prefer the *-ize* form, irrespective of the origins of the suffixes, in many verbs but Fowler (*Modern English Usage*) suggests that the following words always prefer the following forms:

advertise, chastise, circumcise, comprise, compromise, demise, despise, devise, disfranchise, disguise, enfranchise, enterprise, excise, exercise, improvise, incise, premise, supervise, surmise, surprise.

The origin of the *-ize* form is usually attributed to the Greek *-izo*; it does not seem to matter whether the verb with which it is to be used is derived from a Greek stem or not, for Modern English. The Oxford University Press publishers of the *Oxford English Dictionary*), Cambridge University Press (publishers of *The Encyclopaedia Britannica*) and *The Times* prefer the spelling *-ize* for most words. Modern French has standardised its verbal endings for such words as *-iser* but *The Oxford English Dictionary* argues that 'there is no reason why in English the special French spelling should be followed.'

(n)   For some reason writers of English still confuse the order of *i*'s and *e*'s. The rule that 'i' comes before 'e' except after 'c' to make the sound '*ee*' [$\bar{e}$] works well:

      achieve, relieve, niece;

but (*after c*) *receive, deceive, ceiling, conceive.*

There are two exceptions: *counterfeit, seize.*

N.B. Words such as *their, neighbour, leisure, reign, foreign, weird, heir*, etc., do not bear the pronunciation [$\bar{e}$].

(o)   There are some pairs of words which vary their spelling according to their function as either verb or noun:

      (verbs):   *advise, practise, license, prophesy*

      (nouns):   *advice, practice, licence, prophecy.*

(p)   *-all, -full, -fill, -well* sometimes drop one of the *l*'s when used in combinations (as prefixes or suffixes) with other words:

      overal/overall (as noun, adverb, or adjective), *almost, already, altogether/all together, almighty; fulfil; fulness/fullness, spoonful, hopeful, beautiful, welcome, welfare.*

Punctuation

The punctuation of Modern English is based on syntax—i.e. it follows the grammatical structures of the language and indicates meaning by pointing to the relationships between parts of a sentence and between sentences themselves.

Until about 1600 English punctuation was based not on syntax but on how a piece of writing was to be read aloud; it served as a guide to the pauses of various lengths that a reader was expected to make. George Puttenham in *The Arte of English Poesie* (1589) and Simon Daines in *Orthoepia Anglicana* (1640) went so far as to set out a system which used a comma for a pause of one unit, a semi-colon for a pause of two units, and a colon for a pause of three units. A glance at the work of John Donne or Richard Hooker or at Shakespeare's plays or even at the much later *Pilgrim's Progress* (1678) will show that the punctuation is intended to indicate how the texts should be read aloud. Consider, for example, the punctuation in the following passage from the *Authorised Version of the Bible* (1611):

Give ear, O my people, to my law: incline your ears to the words of my mouth.

I will open my mouth in a parable: I will utter dark sayings of old;

Which we have heard and known, and our fathers have told us.

(Psalm LXXVIII, 1–3)

It was Ben Jonson in his English Grammar (written about 1617 but published posthumously in 1640) who first recommended a system of punctuation for English based on syntax. Francis Bacon's *Essayes* (1625) followed such a system and from then onwards English punctuation became syntactical rather than rhetorical. By the 18th century writers began to use punctuation marks excessively and sprinkled commas liberally but it was the publication of *The King's English* in 1906 by H. W. and F. G. Fowler which helped to establish firmly the present practice of using punctuation marks economically, where the grammatical structures (syntax) dictated it.

The punctuation marks themselves

Ancient Greek inscriptions before the 5th century BC were normally written continuously, but occasionally phrases were marked off from each other by a vertical row of two or three points. Aristotle mentioned only one punctuation mark in his writings—the *paragraphos*, a mark placed under the first word at the beginning of a line introducing a new topic. Aristophanes, the librarian at Alexandria (*c.* 200 BC), suggested a system of signs, accents and breathings. To mark the end of a short section (a *comma*) he suggested a point after the middle of the last letter. The end of a longer section (a *colon*) might be marked by a point after the bottom of the last letter and the longest section of all (a *period*) might be concluded with a point after the top of the last letter.

   Roman inscriptions often used points to separate individual words and when writing was transferred to papyrus sheets the same system was used. The scribes introduced a way of marking the beginning of a new section by allowing the first letter or two to project into the margin—the opposite of the modern way of indenting paragraphs. Sometimes the ends of sentences were shown by gaps left between words and occasionally by the use of enlarged initial letters to indicate where the next sentence began. St Jerome (*c.* 340–420 AD) devised a system of punctuation *per cola et commata* (i. e. by phrases) to help the reading aloud of his new translation of the Scriptures (*The Vulgate*) and of liturgical texts, a method based on rhetoric and partially derived from the writings of Demosthenes and Cicero, two famous orators from classical times. St Jerome's insistence that religious texts should be punctuated so that they might be read accurately was taken up enthusiastically during the reign of Charlemagne (742–814 AD). At the Carolingian court an Englishman, Alcuin of York, worked from 782 until 796 to introduce a number of educational reforms and a new, beautiful, rounded script was developed and used for copying manuscripts at Aachen and at Corbie. The new form of handwriting spread quickly through Europe and with it came the *Carolingian system of punctuation*:

   The point (or *punctus*) continued to be used to mark off phrases and groups of points indicated the ends of sentences.

Two signs from the musical notation (*neums*) used to sing Gregorian chants were later added to show an intonation pattern and make it clear where the voice was to be raised or lowered—the raised point (*punctus elevatus*) marked a light point and the interrogatory point (*punctus interrogativus*) indicated that the voice was to turn upwards to form a question. As the system developed, another point the *punctus circumflexus* (7) was introduced to show that a subordinate clause had ended but that the main statement still had to be completed.

During the period from the 12th to the 14th century the *virgule* (,) was used to mark a light pause in reading; after about 1450 the *virgule* slipped down on to the line and developed a curve to avoid the letters on the line below and so became the *modern comma*. The use of brackets (*parentheses*) came in before 1500 and they marked an interpolation in much the same manner as they do today.

A printer in Venice, Aldus Manitius (died 1515), realised that books were permanent and that the wealthy would wish to buy them for their own private use. The need for a punctuation system to help reading aloud diminished and he concentrated on adapting the earlier medieval system based on rhetoric to one that was based on grammatical structures. His grandson, Aldo Manuzio, formulated it in this book *Orthographiae Ratio (A System of Orthography)* published in 1566. By the end of the 17th century in England the names we now use (comma, colon, semi-colon, full stop, etc.) had become established and quotation marks, exclamation marks and dashes had made their way into the written language.

Speech and Writing

Two basic views are taken of the relationship between **speech** and **writing**, the two mediums for language:
  (i) Writing is not simply a way of recording speech; both are distinct and distinguishable mediums for language. (See W. R. O'Donnell and L. Todd, *Variety in Contemporary English*, 1980.)
 (ii) Writing, 'a recent development in mankind's linguistic behaviour', is a secondary medium, parasitic on speech, the primary medium with which linguists should concern themselves. (L. Bloomfield, *Language*, 1933.)

O'Donnell and Todd justify their view by showing that 'the substances of the two mediums differ from one another in every important particular': the substance of speech is sound which does not last and which is effective for only relatively short distances; writing is organised in space rather than time, is more laborious than speech, is relatively permanent, and is effective over great distances of space and time. The two substances are linked however: what is written down can be spoken, and what is spoken can be written down.

Not all written language, they demonstrate, is based on the sounds of the spoken medium. Chinese relies on symbols and English uses numerals rather than spellings sometimes as signs in the written medium. Spoken English has an immediate audience and relies on paralinguistic features (see above, pages 54–5) to reinforce meaning. Written English has 'an absent addressee', has not necessarily an intention to create an immediate effect and so can be planned, and it can be re-drafted and revised. This last point, of course, means that its grammar will be ordered and its syntax free from hesitations, self-correction, and so-called 'fillers' (e.g. . . . *er* . . . *um* . . . , etc.).

The differences between the two mediums result not only in syntactical and grammatical differences but *essential differences in uses* to which they are put, writing being used for the recording and communicating of knowledge in a permanent form; it also provides the major vehicle for teaching and learning, as a result.

O'Donnell and Todd go further: these are *differences in the ways the two mediums are acquired.* 'Speech comes first in the individual as in the species. It is acquired early and unconsciously.' The way we speak is gradually modified as we learn the second of the mediums: 'When educated people speak Standard English they are speaking a variety of English which originated and was propagated largely in writing . . . The acquisition of writing demands a relatively high level of abstraction.' It comes later than speech and may be acquired by a 'phonic' method—using the alphabet as signs representing sounds, or a modified alphabet which has at its root a simplification of the representation of the sound system of English—or on a method of recognising words individually or as elements in a sequence. A. C. Gimson 'The Transmission of Language', in R. Quirk, *The Use of English*, 1962, Supplement 1, has an excellent set of illustrations showing how an understanding of what is written depends to a large extent on the appearance of the words on the page in recognisable patterns.

The two works by A. C. Gimson and by O'Donnell and Todd are important to a consideration of the relationship between the written and spoken mediums of English.

Direct and indirect (reported) speech

Direct speech quotes the actual words used by a speaker, e.g.
    He said, 'I am ill.'
The words actually used are placed in inverted commas. The introductory words *he said* may precede or follow the words directly used, e.g.
    'I am ill,' he said.

Indirect speech (sometimes called *reported speech*) reports the words said without actually using the words originally spoken, e.g.
    He said (that) he was ill.
Inverted commas are not used with indirect speech. Notice that the clause

following *He said* stands in the relationship of a direct object (dO) to the verb 'said', e.g.

He said *it*. (dO)

He said *(that) he was ill*. (dO)

(N. B. The relative pronoun may be included or omitted in such indirect statements.)

Indirect speech may report either a statement, or a question, or an exclamation or a command, e.g.

He asked, '*Where are you going?*' (Direct question)

He asked *where he (she, they) was/were going*. (Indirect question)

He asked her, '*Can you come with me?*' (Direct question)

He asked her *whether she could come with him*. (Indirect question)

He exclaimed, '*How well you look!*' (Direct exclamation)

He exclaimed *how well he (she, they) looked*. (Indirect exclamation)

He shouted, '*Stop it!*' (Direct command)

He shouted *at him (her, them) to stop it*. (Indirect command)

N. B. Indirect commands, since they contain no finite verb (i.e. a verb with its own subject) but use an infinitive, must be used with *either* an indirect object (iO) *or* a prepositional phrase, e.g.

He told *him* (iO) to stop it.

He shouted *at them* (prepositional phrase) to stop it.

In changing direct speech to indirect speech a number of changes have to be made (with some minor exceptions). The distancing or *back-shift* needs always to be made carefully with regard to the sense.

(i) **Change of pronouns**

Subject	Object
I > he, she	me > him, her
we > they	us > them
you > he, she, they	you > him, her, them

e.g. '*I* am ill,' he said. (Direct)
He was ill, he said. (Indirect)

He commanded the pupil, 'Give *me* the book!' (Direct)
He commanded the pupil to give *him* the book. (Indirect)

He said, '*We* are keen to attend.' (Direct)
He said *they* were keen to attend. (Indirect)

He said, 'The girl saw *us* get on the bus.' (Direct)
He said (that) the girl had seen *them* get on the bus. (Indirect)

He said, 'You never kept your promise.' (Direct)
He said he (she, they) had never kept his (her, their) promise. (Indirect)

(ii) **Change of verbs**

(a) Verbs will all be used in the third person (singular or plural) in indirect statements, questions, or exclamations or in the infinitive form in indirect commands, e.g.

He said, 'I *am* ill.' (Direct statement)
He said he *was* ill. (Indirect statement)

He commanded the guards, 'Quick march!'
(Direct command)
He commanded the guards to quick march.
(Indirect command)

(b) The *tenses* of verbs also change

A. *Direct speech*		*Indirect speech*
Present	>	Past
Present perfect		
Past simple	>	Past perfect
Past perfect		

e.g. He said, 'I *am* ill.' (Direct: present)
He said he *was* ill. (Indirect: past)

He said, 'I *have been* ill.' (Direct: present perfect)
He said he *had been* ill. (Indirect: past perfect)

He said, 'I *came* two days ago.' (Direct: past simple)

He said he *had come* two days before. (Indirect: past perfect)

He said, 'I *had been* ill.' (Direct: past perfect)

He said he *had been* ill. (Indirect: past perfect)

B. The modal auxiliaries will normally also shift backwards in time:

can   > could
shall > should/would
should > should
will   > would
may   > might

e.g. He said, 'I can do it.' (Direct)
He said he could do it. (Indirect)

He said, 'I shall do it.' (Direct)
He said he would do it. (Indirect)

N.B. The difference in meaning between:
He said he would do it. (Indirect)

He said I should do it. (Indirect:
here *I* does not refer back to *He* in *He said*)

He said I should do it. (Indirect)
He said, 'You shall do it.' (Direct)
or He said, 'You should do it.' (Direct)

He said, 'The girl will do it.' (Direct)
He said the girl would do it. (Indirect)

He said, 'I may do it.' (Direct)
He said he might do it. (Indirect)

(iii) **Change of *this/these* to *that/those***

Sometimes the back-shift involved in reported speech necessitates the change of this > that and these > those. The meaning, however, will determine whether this change is necessary, e.g.

He said, 'I like this book.' (Direct)

He said that he liked this book. (Indirect)

He said that he liked that book. (Indirect)

Great care is needed to see that ambiguity does not creep into the indirect statement if a change is made. The change should **not** be made automatically.

(iv) **Change of some adverbs**

Again, the back-shift of adverbs needs to be used very cautiously in changing direct to indirect statements. Consider the difference in meanings, for example, in the following:

He said, 'I can come *tomorrow.*' (Direct)
He said, 'I can come *the next day.*' (Direct)
He said he could come *tomorrow.* (Indirect)
He said he could come *the next day.* (Indirect)

or He said, 'I can be *here* with her.' (Direct)
He said, 'I can be *there* with her.' (Direct)
He said he could be *here* with her. (Indirect)
He said he could be *there* with her. (Indirect)

or He said, 'I came two days ago.' (Direct)
He said, 'I came two days before.' (Direct)
He said he had come two days ago. (Indirect)
He said he had come two days before. (Indirect)

PART IV

Terminology

CHAPTER 6

Language

'*Language*' carries a multiplicity of meanings. Since the time of Ferdinand de Saussure (*Cours de linguistique générale*, 1915) it was seen as a system in which each item was defined in terms of its relationship with others, rather like a piece on a chessboard during a game of chess. In 1933 L. Bloomfield (*Language*) set out to describe language in terms of the way its items were arranged in structures and his method gave rise to the work on descriptive analysis in language studies. In 1957 Noam Chomsky (*Syntactic Structures*) showed the difficulties in trying to extract perfect descriptions of a language according to Bloomfield's methods and argued that it should be possible to describe quite explicitly the rules or sets of statements which show what structures can be generated, and which could not be generated, within a language. This store of control over potential grammatical structures Chomsky referred to as **competence**; how an individual generated structures from this store he called **performance**. From Chomsky's statements the description of language in terms of *transformational-generative grammar* (*TGE* or *TG*) arose.

Chomsky's work took account of Saussure's earlier distinctions:

language: human speech as a whole developed within communities as part of human 'behaviour';

langue: the store of a language's elements (e.g. grammar, vocabulary, pronunciation) belonging to a specific community and available for individuals in that community to use but not necessarily to change (loosely, Chomsky's *competence*);

parole: the utterance by one individual in one community at a given time in a specific context in a specific community, following the elements of the language available to him (*langue*) (loosely, Chomsky's *performance*).

Dialect

Dialect is the language system used by a smaller community than that used to define *langue*. (See also above, pages 21–5.)

Idiolect refers to the total control over his language by one individual in one community, e.g. a word such as 'metonymy' is part of the English *langue* but it is not necessarily part of every Englishman's *idiolect*.

Accent

Accent refers to the sounds of speech distinctive of a specific regional or social group of speakers. It can also refer to the sounds of speech made by one individual but which could also have been made by other members of the same group, e.g. 'she spoke with a French accent'; 'he had a strong Yorkshire accent'. Its specific qualities (particularly those of vowels and consonant clusters) can be described by close and careful observation.

Standard English

This is a term normally used to describe an 'ideal' form of the language used by one writer (it is usually used to describe the written medium) to communicate with members of a wider community. Randolph Quirk (*The Use of English*, 1962) attempted a definition of it:

> Standard English is . . . 'normal English': that kind of English which draws least attention to itself over the widest area and through the widest range of usage . . . This norm is a complex function of vocabulary, grammar and transmission, most clearly established in one of the means of transmission (spelling), and least clearly established in the other means of transmission (pronunciation).

'Formal' and 'informal' English

These words describe the kinds of English appropriate for particular contexts used by particular individuals. The terms should not be confused with notions of 'correctness'; they are used to describe the levels of language appropriate to one situation rather than another. Again, 'informal' English should not be confused with 'slang' or with 'debased' uses of the language. A letter to a solicitor, for example, is likely to use a more formal level of language than that found in a letter to a close friend. It should be seen that there are not just *two* kinds of language, the 'formal' and the 'informal'; the levels of language use run along a continuum from one to the other and draw on a number of different levels to suit immediate contexts, rather than remaining on one only. Even a letter to a solicitor is likely to use a number of these levels (once called **registers**) to describe, express anger or worry, ask for clarification or help, etc.

Slang (see above, page 49)

It is not easy to distinguish 'colloquial' English from 'slang'; Quirk (*The Use of English*) made a distinction: 'Describing a usage as "colloquial" means only that it tends not to be used on *formal* occasions, though perfectly polite and acceptable in informal conversation. A slang usage, on the other hand, is not generally introduced into informal conversation unless the speakers are on very intimate terms . . .' Some slang words become accepted, even, into formal uses of the language; until 1900 *carouse* (German *gar aus*, quite out: i.e. empty the glass), *hoax* (Latin *hocus-pocus*), and *nincompoop* (from *non compos mentis?*) were listed as slang words.

Jargon

Jargon is a term sometimes used with the same sense as 'slang'; *Chambers Twentieth Century Dictionary* gives this sense as one of its main meanings. However, the word *jargon* properly refers to a trade dialect. Lawyers, doctors, teachers, car mechanics—and the members of any profession or trade—use vocabulary peculiar to their craft; it is far from careless, imprecise, or slovenly language but is economical and accurate. (See Eric Partridge, *Slang Today and Yesterday*, third edition, 1950.)

Spoken English

Received pronunciation (RP)

This has already been discussed (see above, page 50).

Vowels

Daniel Jones (*An Outline of English Phonetics*, ninth edition, revised, 1962) defined a vowel as 'a voiced sound in forming which the air issues in a continuous stream through the pharynx and mouth, there being no obstruction and no narrowing such as would cause audible friction'.

Consonants include all other sounds: (i) all sounds which are not voiced (e.g. **p, s, S**); (ii) all sounds in the production of which the air has an impeded passage through the mouth (e.g. **b, l,** rolled **r**); (iii) all sounds in the production of which the air does not pass through the mouth (e.g. **m**); (iv) all sounds in which there is audible friction (e.g. **f, v, s, h**) (D. Jones, op. cit.).

Diphthongs (N.B. the spelling: *di-*, (twice) + *phthongos* (sounding)) are 'independent vowel glides each not containing within itself either a "peak" or "trough" of prominence. By a vowel glide we mean that the speech-organs start in the position of one vowel and move in the direction of another vowel. By "independent" we mean that the glide is expressly made and is not merely an unavoidable concomitant of sounds preceding and following' (D. Jones, op. cit.). Diphthongs consist of one syllable and one end of a diphthong is normally more prominent than the other, and so may be termed *rising* (or *centring*) or *falling*. (In phonetics the mark ˘ is placed above the less prominent part: e.g. **oŭ, aĭ, aŭ,** etc.).

Intonation, stress, rhythm (see above, page 53)

Syllables

Daniel Jones in *An Outline of English Phonetics* (ninth edition, revised, 1962) says, 'A syllable consists of a sequence of sounds containing one peak of prominence . . . Each sound which constitutes a peak of prominence is said to be *syllabic*, and the word or phrase is said to contain as many *syllables* as there are peaks of prominence', e.g. *roller-skate* has three syllables, *roly-poly* has four.

Written English

Read carefully the section on **Written English** above (pages 55–71) which discusses at length **alphabet, spelling** and **punctuation**.

Letter

Strictly, this is a conventional mark used to express a sound of speech, or a piece of printing type used to represent a sound of speech.

Digraph

This is the use of *two* letters to express *one* sound; e.g. the 'ph' in the word 'digra**ph**'. It should not be confused with a **ligature**, which is a term used by printers to describe a piece of type which consists of two or more letters joined together: e.g. **ff**.

Vocabulary and Word Meaning

The form of a word presented in a dictionary is known as its **lexical** form. Most dictionaries present words alphabetically and indicate for each entry the part of speech a word can be, e.g.

level:	*n.*	an instrument for testing horizontality: a horizontal position: a horizontal plan or time: height: the thing aimed at;
	adj.	horizontal: even: smooth: uniform: well-balanced;
	adv.	in a level manner: point-blank;
	v.t.	to make horizontal: to make flat or smooth: to raze: to aim;
	v.i.	to make things level: to aim: to make one word, form, the same as another.

(See *Chambers Twentieth Century Dictionary*, p. 756)
The entry in an etymological dictionary also gives the origin of a word, usually at the end of the definition and within brackets, e.g.

    level: (O. Fr. *livel, liveau* (Fr. niveau)—L. *libella*, a plummet, dim. of *libra*, a balance).

Synonyms and antonyms

Words which have the same, or very similar meanings are termed synonyms. A living language will not tolerate exact synonyms, words with exactly the same meanings, for long. Usually one of three developments will take place:

(i) One of the words will slightly change its meaning, e.g.

n.	*work*:	*labour*;
v.i.	*toil*:	*travail*;
adj.	*nice*:	*foolish*.

(N.B. Both Chaucer and Shakespeare use the word 'nice' in the sense of 'foolish'.)

(ii) Both words will change their meaning and the original sense will be conveyed by a newly introduced third word, e.g.

Old English	*scyrte*	shirt
Old Norse	*skyrte*	skirt
New Word (Latin)	—	*tunic*

(iii) One of the words will fall from the language leaving the other alive, e.g.

Old English *niman*: Mod. English *take* (from Old Norse)
Old English *torn*: Mod. English *anger* (from Old Norse)
Old English *wolcen*: Mod. English *sky* (from Old Norse)
Old English *weorpan*: Mod. English *cast* (from Old Norse)

Strict synonyms do not remain in the language long as synonyms, therefore. A glance at a book which sets out lists of synonyms and antonyms (words with opposite meanings) will, show just how refined meanings of synonymous words have become, e.g.

LOVE v.: *love, like, fancy, care for, favour, become enamoured, fall or be in love with; revere, take to, make much of, hold dear, prize, hug, cling to, cherish, pet; adore, idolize, love to distraction, dote on, desire; throw oneself at, lose or give one's heart to.* Slang: *go for, fall for, be sweet on, be nuts about, go steady with, spoon with;*

(A book which lists words in this fashion is usually known as a *Thesaurus*; the most famous of such collections is *Roget's Thesaurus*, first published in 1852 by an English doctor, but revised several times since.)

Words of opposite meaning are termed **antonyms**, but strict antonyms, like strict synonyms, are rare. For example, the antonym of *increase* may be *contract, lessen, shorten, diminish, shrivel*, etc. as well as *decrease*. In a similar way the antonym of *silent* may be: *loud, noisy, deafening, ear-splitting, sonorous*, etc.

Homonyms, homographs, and homophones

Words with the same spelling and sound but with different meanings or use are termed **homonyms**, e.g.

```
 bear  = an animal
       = to carry
  lie  = to tell an untruth
       = to assume a horizontal position
 fair  = light-coloured
       = an entertainment
```

Words written in the same form but with different meanings and possibly pronunciations are termed **homographs**, e.g.

```
  lead  = to show the way
        = a metal
  tear  = to split apart
        = water from the eye
 wound  = a hurt
        = past tense of 'to wind'
```

Words with the same pronunciation but with different spellings and meanings are termed **homophones**, e.g.

```
 { read  = past tense of the verb 'to read'
 { red   = a colour
 { read  = present tense of the verb 'to read'
 { reed  = a marsh grass
 { bear  = to carry; an animal
 { bare  = naked
```

(cf. *to/too/two*; *write, right, rite*; *their, there*; *quay, key*; *heir, air*).

It is worth noting that some words have become confused in their usage because of their similarity in pronunciation, e.g.

Practice (a noun)/*practise* (a verb)
licence (a noun)/*license* (a verb)
principal (= main; head)/*principle* (= a fundamental quality).

Introduction of new words into English

This is an area where the 'living' nature of the English language is clearly and immediately seen.

(i) During the middle of the 16th century there was a conscious attempt to enrich the vocabulary of English, mainly with words invented or derived consciously from Latin and Greek. This period in English history, the Renaissance, was marked by new activity in science, art, religion, and politics; moreover, there was new interest in translating works of classical French and Italian writers into English. New words were needed and invented. Sir Thomas Elyot, the author of an influential book *The Governour* (1531), apologised:

> Wherfore I am constrained to usurpe a latine word . . ., which worde, though it be strange and dark, yet . . . ones brought in custome, shall be facile to understand as other wordes late Commen out of Italy and France.

These 'invented' or deliberately borrowed and Anglicised words are now termed **inkhorn words** or **inkhorns**, because they were drawn from the inkpot rather than from popular usage. The term was an attempt originally to ridicule them. (See also above, page 21.)

The words, however, were often obscure and by 1601 words such as *obstupefact, turgidous, lubrical* were under attack. Some of the inkhorn words have survived, nevertheless, into Modern English, e.g.

reciprocal, spurious, method, figurative, atmosphere, anachronism, conspicuous, malignant, dogma, emphasis, pneumonia.

(ii)   Some words have remained in the language, although they were deliberately and artificially introduced, because of **the standing of the person** who introduced them, e.g.

Sir Thomas More (1478–1535) introduced *denunciation, exasperate, monopoly, pretext* and many others; *sandwich* (after the fourth Earl of Sandwich 1718–92, who invented the idea to avoid having to leave the gaming table for dinner); *iron curtain* (Sir W. Churchill).

(iii) Words from Italian and French were thought '**fashionable**' during the Renaissance and words such as *balcony, design, violin,* and *volcano* came from Italian, and *battalion, brusque, frigate,* and *infantry* from French . . . Words from Spanish and Portuguese also found favour during the Renaissance: *alligator, barricade, hurricane, potato,* etc.

(iv) Some words were re-formed to come into line with a supposed classical origin. For example, *debt* (Latin *debitum*, French *dette*); *doubt* (Latin *dubitum*, French *doute*)—words still pronounced according to their French rather than their Latin origins.

Some words current in Modern English have been abbreviated from longer words. Jonathan Swift objected in 1710 to such abbreviations but today many words exist mainly in abbreviated form: *cab, phone, tele, car, mob, TV, ad, disco, burger,* etc.

(v) **New inventions** demand new words and the process of introducing *new words* or *new compounds* or *adapting old* words to describe them is still a vital part of living English, e.g.

computer, hardware, software; transistor, bleeper; videotape, teleprinter, telex; shuttle, lift-off; sci-fi, SF; Sunday supplement; anti-biotic; degradable, etc.

From earlier periods words such as the following arrived permanently:

aeroplane, helicopter, telephone, turntable, photography, deep-freeze, dishwasher, prefabricated, junkie, video(-recorder).

(vi) **New borrowings** have played a major role in the development of English. Closer connections with the Continent of Europe and with the Far East, Africa, and the West Indies, the Middle East and Scandinavia have popularised a number of words: *blitz; doodlebug; cruise; Sputnik; aperitive; chauffeur* (originally the man who kept the boiler going); *robot* (a Czech word *robota,* from a 1920 Karel Capek play where the word referred to labour conscripted by law); *chapati, loot, thug* (Hindi words); *pop(p) adum* (from Malaysia); *curry* (a Tamil word); *UDI* (Unilateral Declaration of Independence), *mau-mau; zebra* (Bantu); *anorak* (Eskimo); *sherbet* (Arabic); *tycoon* (Japanese 'taikun', a great prince); *pyjamas* (Persian); *ukelele* (Hawaian); *yoghurt* (Turkish), etc.

(vii) **The formation of new compounds** is a convenient method of describing new ideas, fashions, and inventions, e.g.

hitchhike, teenager, typewriter, lipstick, caterpillar-tractor, teleprinter, golf-ball typewriter, word-processor, ball-point, water bed, double-glazing, wind tunnel, laser beam, moonwalk, search-and-destroy, knee-capping, arms-limitation, iron-curtain, drop-out, fall-out, motorway, etc.

(viii) Some current words in English have been retained in the language with new **up-dated meanings**: e.g. *skyline* (formerly = 'horizon' but cf. 'the London skyline'); *radiator; record; tape; chauffeur; film; barrage; cope; choke; broadcast; transformer; evacuate; fox-hole; commando* (originally S. African from Portuguese: 'a military party'); *ceiling; bottle-neck; maquis* (from French, where the word originally referred to the thick shrub formations found on the Mediterranean coasts).

(ix) Some words have entered the language permanently from their **associations with manufactured products carrying trade names or the names of their inventors**: *hoover, frigidaire, kodak, zipper* (a word registered by the B. F. Goodrich company in 1925), *bic, bakelite* (after L. A. Baekeland, the inventor), *shrapnel* (after a British general); *colt* (a gun, invented by Samuel Colt, 1814–62); *mackintosh* (after Charles Macintosh, 1766–1843, a Glasgow chemist); *boycott* (after Captain Boycott of County Mayo who was 'boycotted' by his neighbours in December, 1880); *lynch* (after Captain William Lynch of Virginia, about 1776); *quisling* (a Norwegian collaborator with the Germans during the Second World War, Vidkun Quisling); *tarmac* (after John Loudon McAdam, 1756–1836, the inventor); *bowler* (after the name of the hatter thought to have invented it in 1850); etc.

(x) **The media and advertising** have introduced many new words into English, e.g.

pinta (from 'Drinka pinta milka day'); *back* (a horse); *comb* (the countryside); *caught napping* (from baseball); *SDP; a page-three girl; telecaster; Watergate; containerise* (to pack goods for transport in bulk).

These forces have also been blamed for the so-called 'degeneration' of the meaning of such words as *amazing, colossal, sensational, stupendous* through 'over-exposure' (one of their own coinages!).

Prefixes, suffixes, affixes, inflections compounds, word class

Prefixes and **suffixes** are used in English to form words by modifying the 'base' form, e.g. *form* (base), *reform* (prefix + base), *formation* (base + suffix), *reformation* (prefix + base + suffix). **Affixes** is the term used to refer to any elements added to base forms which may or may not change their **word class** or part of speech (e.g. a noun becoming an adjective becoming a noun: *truth* >*truthful* > *truthfulness*). **Affixation** (sometimes called 'zero-affixation') should not be confused with **conversion**—where a 'base' is given another word class without the addition of an affix and without changing its form: e.g. *cost* (verb), *cost* (noun); *divorced* (adjective), *divorced* (noun, the divorced)—or with **compounding**—where two bases are brought together to form a new word: e.g. *goalpost, blackhead.*

Prefixes are sometimes 'assimilated' with the next syllable, i.e. the last consonant of the last syllable of the prefix is 'made similar' to the first consonant of the base form:

ad- (Latin 'to') becomes *ac-*: *ac*/cident; *ac*/cord;

af-: *af*/fect; *af*/ford;

dis- (Latin 'in two', 'apart') becomes *dif-*: *dif*/fer; *dif*/ficult;

com- (Latin 'with') becomes *col-*: *col*/late; *col*/lect;

con-: *con*/nive; *con*/nect;

cor-: *cor*/respond; *cor*/rect;

sub- (Latin 'under') becomes *suf-* : *suf* /focate; *suf* /fix;

sug- : *sug*/gest.

Inflexions added to the ends of words indicate tenses (without changing the word class) or function as markers to show whether a word is an adjective, adverb, or noun (i.e. changing the word class from the base form):

refer, *referred* (tense)

entertain, *entertainment* (verb/noun).

(See also above, pages 64–9.)

Denotation, connotation, reference, semantics

John Lyons in his important work *Semantics I, II*, 1977, acknowledges the confusion of **denotation** with **reference:** 'the term "denotation" is employed by many authors for what we are calling reference; conversely, "reference" has frequently been used for what we will in this section distinguish as denotation.' P. T. Geach (*Reference and Generality*, 1962), as Lyons pointed out, even argued that 'so battered and defaced a coin as *denotation* should be withdrawn from philosophical currency'.

The terms 'denotation' ('reference') and 'connotation' are employed in the study of meaning known as **semantics** (from the Greek *sema*, 'a sign' or 'a signal'). It is concerned with why some grammatical constructions are semantically acceptable in a language and why other similar grammatical constructions are not acceptable, e.g.

The choir sang the oratorio. (Acceptable)

The choir composed the oratorio.(Acceptable)

The choir bought the oratorio. (Acceptable)

The choir painted the oratorio. (Unacceptable)

What is there in the word 'painted' or in its relation to its context which makes this verb unacceptable, whilst the other verbs ('sang', 'composed', 'bought'), as different as they are, might be acceptable semantically? The syntactical structures of all four examples above are similar—noun phrase (subject) + transitive verb + noun phrase (direct object).

The answer to the question lies in the 'lexical' meaning of the word *painted*, the meanings you might find for the word in a dictionary; other words similar in a lexical sense to 'painting' might have functioned perfectly well, however, semantically: e.g. *rendered, elaborated, designed*.

It is clear that the meaning of a word emerges only from the lexical structure in which it is being used; every lexical item in such a structure contributes its own meaning to the structure: e.g. notice the differences in meaning between

'the *tabby* cat sat on the *sofa*'

'the *black* cat sat on the *cupboard* '.

The words in italics here refer to quite specific meanings within the contexts of their sentences; each indicates which cat sat in which specifically described place—and, it might be argued, there were two cats involved but only one 'sofa' and only one 'cupboard'.

Other lexical items, however, in acceptable semantic structures bring to their contexts wider, 'ambiguous' (see above, pages 41–2) meanings. Words such as 'feminism' or 'democracy' or words selected by poets for particular contexts often carry connotations which are embraced within their immediate, precise, but total lexical definitions. Compare for example, the following:

'Joan is a *spinster*.'

'Mary is more of a *spinster* than Joan.'

Consider the 'denotative' and 'connotative' meanings of the word 'spinster' in these contexts. Other constructions might be added:

'Joan, as a *spinster*, could not ·understand Sarah's marital problems.'

'Mary, the *spinster*, soon alienated her feminist sisters.'

The terms *denotative* and *connotative* are more complex than this over-simplified account might suggest.

R. A. Waldron (*Sense and Sense Development*, 1967, page 78) pointed out John Stuart Mill's 'distinction (in his *System of Logic*) between the *denotation* of a word—that is the collection of entities which the word may legitimately denote (the sum of all its true referents)—and its *connotation* — that is the set of criteria by virtue of which anything is judged to belong to the class in question'. John Lyons (*Semantics I*, 1977, pages 176–7) showed, however, that this distinction between *denotation* and *connotation* is a philosophical one and that in one usage 'the *connotation* of a word is thought of as an emotive or effective component additional to its central meaning. The reader should be on his guard whenever he meets the term "connotation" in semantics. If it is explicitly contrasted with "denotation", it will normally have its philosophical sense; but authors do not always make it clear in which of the two senses it is to be taken.'

The matter becomes more intricate when it is linked with notions of **collocation,** a term used by J. R. Firth (*Papers in Linguistics, 1934–1951*, 1957), but discussed by John Lyons (op. cit., 2, pages 612–3) who suggested that Firth's meaning of 'collocability was never made clear' but Lyons helped, however, to bring out part of its sense by showing that one of the meanings of 'night' depends on its collocability with 'dark', with which it often exists in context. An excellent example of this (where Shakespeare uses this 'collocability' for fun, too) occurs in the play of Pyramus and Thisbe in *A Midsummer Night's Dream.*

> *Pyramus*: O grim-look'd night! O night with hue so black!
> O night, which ever art when day is not!
> O night! O night!

Syntax

The word 'syntax' refers to grammatical structure. Clearly, control over the use of a language depends on the control over its syntax. For this reason many books on learning a foreign language devote much of their time to describing grammatical structure. It is impossible, for example, to learn how to speak German without mastering the syntactical construction of subordinate clauses and the placing of verbs within them. In order to describe the syntax of the language it is essential to have devised an adequate description of its grammatical structure. (See Chapter 7, pages 97–106, for an explanation of some of the problems and solutions in evolving such a description for English.) It is not the purpose of this book to describe English syntax; that has been done elsewhere (R. Quirk and S. Greenbaum, *A University Grammar of English*, 1973, and R. A. Close, *A Reference Grammar for Students of English*, 1975). Some terms, however, may be usefully mentioned specifically here.

Syntactic patterning, period structures, sentence patterns

These have been discussed earlier in this book (see pages 39–41).

Gender

Gender in English affects:

(*i*) the form of some nouns: -*ess* (actress, mistress); -*ine* (heroine); -*ix* (executrix); -man/-woman (chairman, chairwoman—although some users have recently come to prefer 'chairperson' or even 'chair' to avoid overt sex specification!);

(ii) personal, possessive, reflexive, and emphatic pronouns: *he, him, she, her, it; his, hers, its; himself, herself, itself;*

(iii) possessive adjectives: *his, her, its.*

It does not affect the forms of verbs.

The use of *he/him* in the third person singular as an equivalent to the impersonal *one* is still widely current and avoids the clumsiness of using *he and she* or *him and her* etc., which some advocate.

Gender in grammar often carries with it, however, some sexual connotations—as in the uses outlined above. But the use of terms such as 'masculine' or 'feminine' (and sometimes 'neuter') to describe the classification of nouns usually carries no sexual significance but merely denotes the terms used to label categories that might equally well have been called 1, 2, 3 or A, B, C. In a few cases gender has become conventionally used to describe a ship as 'she' (or even a ship's hooter: there *she* blows!).

Count and non-count nouns, noun phrases

Some modern grammarians categorise nouns in a way which runs across some of the traditional categories (e.g. common, collective, abstract, etc.). They make two broad classes for both grammatical and semantic reasons:

(i) *Count nouns*: these are nouns which are used to refer to individual and countable units; objects or entities; e.g. consider the use of the word *experience* in the following sentences:

A: 'I had a strange *experience.*'

B: 'The explanation was based on *experience.*'

In A, *experience* refers to an individual incident which can be counted (cf. I faced many *difficulties*); in B, *experience* refers to an un-differentiated or uncountable series of events which have produced an effect (cf. 'I had *difficulty* in understanding the point').

(ii) *Non-count (or mass) nouns:* these are nouns which are used to refer to undifferentiated mass: e.g. consider the use of *paper* in the following sentences:

A: 'The audience listened to the *paper* read by the professor.'

B: 'I wrapped the fish in *paper.*'

In A, *paper* refers to a single, identifiable object and is a count-noun; in B, *paper* refers to a mass of substance and is a non-count noun.

(iii) *Count nouns* (and some nouns are always count nouns such as 'desk' or 'friend') can be preceded by *a, an,* or *one* and may have a plural form preceded by *two, three, many*, etc., or words which allow them to be counted. *Non-count nouns* (e.g. cotton, cooking, safety) cannot be preceded as nouns by *a, an,* or *one,* do not have a plural form, but may be preceded by words which indicate mass, such as *much, a lot of , a small quantity of,* etc.

(iv) Whilst some nouns are always count nouns and others always non-count nouns, many nouns may be one or the other according to their meaning and usage; for example compare the following:

A: 'The boy picked up a *stone*.' (Count noun)

B: 'The statue was made of *stone*.' (Non-count noun)

A: 'He switched on the *light*.' (Count noun)

B: 'He was dazzled by the *light* as he emerged from the cave.' (Non-count noun)

It is commonly the case that the traditional classification of nouns also needs to go much further when noun usage is examined within English grammatical structures (such as phrases or sentences). For example, nouns are often said to act as subjects, objects or complements:

'The *man* felt happy.' (Subject)

'The soldier shot the *man*.' (Direct object)

'The child became the *man*.' (Complement)

Subjects, objects, and complements, however, may not contain the traditional categories of nouns but may consist of phrases or clauses functioning as noun equivalents, e.g.

'*What he was* appalled me.' (Subject)

'I did not like *what he was*.' (Direct Object)

'The thief was *what he was*.' (Complement)

(i) The **noun phrase** or clause which functions as the subject, direct object or complement of a sentence usually, however, does contain a main noun (known as the 'head' word) which may be modified by articles, adjectives, adjectival phrases (or **modifiers**, sometimes known as **determiners**). At this point it will be sufficient to illustrate the elements found in a noun phrase and the functions of the noun phrase within English sentences. Take the noun phrases (with the head word in italics):

A: The *book;*

B: The big *book;*

C: The big *book* on the table;

D: The big *book* which is on the table.

The head word *book* is here modified by the definite article (A), the definite article + adjective (B), the definite article + adjective (as premodifiers) + a prepositional phrase (as a post-modifier) (C), and by the definite article + adjective (as premodifier) + adjectival clause (as a postmodifier) (D).

(ii) Each of these noun phrases might be replaced by the single pronoun *it* and the grammatical function of *it* and the noun phrase would remain the same:

As subject

A: *The book*

B: *The big book*

C: *The big book on the table*

D: *The big book which is on the table*

E: *It*

is bound in leather.

As direct object

A: { *the book.*
B: { *the big book.*
C: He saw { *the big book on the table.*
D: { *the big book which is on the table.*
E: { *it.*

As complement

A: { *the book.*
B: { *the big book.*
C: That seems to be { *the book on the table.*
D: { *the book which is on the table.*
E: { *it.*

Co-ordination, subordination (*parataxis, hypotaxis*)

English syntactical patterns rely on either **parataxis** or **hypotaxis**:

Parataxis: the arrangement of statements simply beside each other. Often the statements are not joined by any conjunctions at all but are separated by full stops or semi-colons; sometimes they are simply joined by co-ordinating conjunctions (*and, but, or*).

Hypotaxis: the arrangement of statements so that they are inter-dependent. They are often joined by subordinating conjunctions (e.g. when, because, so that, until, on condition that, etc.

Children often use paratactic structures to narrate events:

> I got up and went downstairs. I had my breakfast and then had a wash. I got dressed and went to school. I was late and my teacher told me off.

Books of instructions and some scientific textbooks use *parataxis* in order to make the processes seem simple:

> Weigh a small dry test-tube. Introduce a small piece of marble and weigh again. Set up the apparatus. Weigh the whole apparatus. Then loosen the cork. The small tube will then slip down.

This is hardly elegant writing but it is clear and appropriate. Sometimes, however, writers deliberately choose a paratactic style, perhaps to suggest strong emotions, drama, direct experience or simple, deeply felt reactions. For example, examine the following 'paratactic' passage which describes the experience of a short-sighted boy as he emerges from an optician's shop and sees the world for the first time through his new pair of spectacles:

> The lamplight! I looked in wonder at the diminishing crystals of gas-flame strung down the hill. Clapham was hung with necklaces of light, and the

horses pulling the omnibuses struck the granite road with hooves of iron and ebony. I could see the skeletons inside the flesh and blood of the Saturday-night shoppers. The garments they wore were made of separate threads.

(R.Church, *Over the Bridge*)

This is writing that is clear, appropriate, and elegant.

Embedding

This is the technical term used by linguists to describe the insertion or addition of one sentence-like structure in to another; e.g.

This house, *the one which Jack built*, is falling apart. The italicised words are 'embedded' into the sentence. 'This house is falling apart'. The 'embedding' process can move on to include other 'embedding' in the embedded' clause:

This house, the one which Jack, *when he was much younger,* built, is falling apart.

Here the italicised words are embedded in the clause 'the one which Jack built', which in its turn is embedded in 'This house is falling apart'.

Embedding, subordination and co-ordination allow an English sentence to be of indefinite length. Nevertheless, the English sentence, with or without such inserted or additional structures, will be of one of the *five* kinds outlined above (see pages 40–1).

Cohesion—including reference, substitution, ellipsis et alia

The ways in which meanings develop in a language are complex. (A very clear and helpful analysis of some of the processes involved is to be found in R. A. Waldron's *Sense and Sense Development,* 1967.) English is dominated by a number of forces which try constantly to regulate it and make it 'cohere' or hang together.

Amongst these forces listed by Gustaf Stern (*Meaning and Change of Meaning,* 1931) and quoted by Waldron are:

Analogy:	by form, etymology, sound, or spelling.
Substitution:	brought about by changes outside linguistics; e.g. see how the word 'democracy' has changed its meaning through the ages by looking up the *Oxford English Dictionary.*
Ellipsis:	marked by the omission of a word or words which the reader or hearer will be able to supply easily within a sentence, e.g. 'Coffee?' (*'Do you want coffee?'*).
Nomination:	occasioned by the need to invent new words for new ideas and inventions or to use old words for new purposes, e.g. *television, polytechnic,* etc.
Transfer:	Similar to nomination, but occurring especially where words are carried across from one meaning to another to suit new situations: e.g. *satellite, shuttle, computer,* etc.

Permutation: defined by Stern as 'a shift in the point of view concerning a detail of a total situation, or detail of a phrase referent, the same word being retained to denote it', e.g. the word 'boon' once meant a request or a prayer and then became the thing itself requested.

Adequation: resulting from the situation when 'the original reason for the choice of a particular name gets forgotten or disregarded'. Waldron points out that Stern gave as his main example the way the word *horn* evolved in its meaning from a part of an animal to 'an instrument for producing a certain kind of sound'.

Reference is clearly discussed as a term by John Lyons in *Semantics I*, 1977, pages 174–97. It is concerned with 'the relationship which holds between an expression and what that expression stands for on particular occasions of its utterance'. Linguists have used the term to distinguish 'cognitive or descriptive' meaning (referential) from 'affective or emotional' meaning. Lyons reminds his reader that 'the terms "reference" or "referential meaning" are now fairly well established in the literature of linguistic semantics and stylistics in the sense of "cognitive meaning" or "descriptive meaning" '. He cites the example used by C. K. Ogden and I. A. Richards (*The Meaning of Meaning*, 1923) to exemplify the point: 'two words . . . might have the same referential meaning, but differ in emotive meaning e.g. "horse" and "steed" '.

'Cognitive or descriptive' (referential) meanings are, however, dependent on how the expressions containing them are said or the contexts in which they are used. Statements which seem to contain some illogicality, omission, ambiguity, or lack of definition in isolation can carry definite cognitive or descriptive meanings when they have 'reference'. For example, the simple question, 'Coffee?' has to be totally context-or utterance-linked before it can convey much meaning; once the reference is established, the meaning becomes definite.

(Lyons (*op. cit.*) correctly concludes his discussion of 'reference' by asserting, 'it should be clear that some understanding of how reference operates in language-behaviour is essential for the analysis of actual texts whether written or spoken'; students should examine his discussion of 'reference' in the context of logic, philosophy, and semantics, and particularly his distinction between 'sense' and reference.)

PART V

Grammar

CHAPTER 7

Which grammar?

At the beginning of the 20th century English Grammar was **prescriptive** and **Latin-based**; it set out to lay down or prescribe rules for the language according to those of another language only distantly related in the Indo-Germanic family (see the chart on page 16). Now grammar attempts to be **descriptive** and is moving much more strongly towards discovering a **universal** grammar; it is seeking to describe adequately the essential properties which make up language. The way to do this seems through the study of *a* language (for example, English), to uncover its essential elements, to test whether the description accounts exhaustively for all its elements and does not allow faulty (or non-acceptable) constructions, and to ensure that the account contains no inherent self-contradictions. The description must aim to be simple and yet comprehensive. As it is being developed for one language, the description can be tested against others; if there is a clash, the clash needs to be justified or the description needs to be amended.

English grammar is, therefore, still in the state of being developed. In the 1960s and 1970s some notable strides were taken and the description took on new directions. A survey of the major grammatical approaches, with their advantages and shortcomings, will help to highlight the problems and show where some of the possible solutions may lie. In the meantime English, as a living language, continues its inexorable development.

Traditional grammar

The 19th century took an essential diachronic view of language; it concerned itself with the way languages changed throughout history. The approach is certainly not an unfruitful one since it may (i) explain current forms, and (ii) reveal some of the processes which lead to change.

For example, the 19th century explained why some nouns in English changed their stem vowels to form their plurals (e.g. men, geese) whilst others added -en, and the majority added an -s termination. In order to do this the philologists went back to the earliest forms of the language extant (Anglo-Saxon) and, with the help of comparative philology, postulated earlier forms. They suggested that the development of the plural of 'man' would have been:

mann (singular), *mannis (plural) menn.

The presence of the 'i' in the reconstructed plural (indicated by an asterisk) would have 'fronted' the preceding back vowel (a) to a front vowel (e). The same 'fronting' of vowels in stressed syllables caused by the presence of an 'i' or 'j' in a following syllable could be seen at work in such nouns as gōs, gēs (geese), bōc, bēc (books), mūs, mys (mice), cū, cȳ (cows).

Similarly it was possible to explain why the Latin word *hostis* had an equivalent Gothic form *gasts*, an early English form *gastis*, an Anglo-Saxon form ȝiest, and a Modern English form *guest* by examining the relationship between the vowels *o* and *a* in stressed syllables and the relationship between guttural and palatal consonants (h/g/ȝ) in Indo-European languages.

Such early studies in Germanic philology led to satisfactory explanations of the way the sound systems of the inter-related languages in the newly defined Indo-European group had developed; the explanations accounted for many of the existing forms of words in modern European languages.

This attempt to see a development of the major languages of the Western world across a wide front led on inevitably from an examination of phonology to a study of syntax. One Indo-European language, Latin, had received constant attention by scholars and philologists from the Middle Ages onwards. Anglo-Saxon scholars even had the use of a Latin primer to encourage accurate mastery of Latin (Ælfric's *Colloquy*). In view of the demonstrable link phonologically between Latin and early forms of Germanic languages, it was not unreasonable, perhaps, to want to see links between the grammar of English and the grammar of Latin. The one problem, however, was that Latin had ceased to develop as a language in its own right and was effectively 'dead' (although the so-called 'Romance' languages of Italian, French, Spanish, etc., were still actively growing) but English had undergone major changes particularly in the last thousand years (see Chapter 2). These changes had affected phonology and syntax as well as vocabulary and grammatical description, to cover exhaustively every variety of the language and to exclude all non-forms of the language, had to take account of such development.

The diachronic study of English, which had begun as long ago as 27 September 1786, when Sir William Jones pointed out in a lecture to the Royal Asiatic Society in Calcutta that Sanskrit showed marked structural similarities with Latin, Greek, Celtic and Germanic, gathered momentum and Darwin's view in the mid-19th century about the origin of the species encouraged an evolutionary view of the world, and language was seen as part of that process. English was a major feature in the development of

Indo-European (the earliest life form of language that could be postulated). Historical linguistics, however, began to raise new problems. For example, if it could be observed that a sound change occurred in a given set of phonological conditions, it ought to occur every time that these conditions were met—in whatever language or in whatever dialect it appeared. In this way the emergence of 'laws' or 'rules' of language became acceptable and once these had been accepted prescriptions about how languages *ought* to behave rather than descriptions of how they *actually* behaved became equally acceptable.

Prescriptive grammar, then, based on a diachronic view of English became the order of the day. 'Traditional' grammars, as they have become known, were taught until recently in many schools and textbooks still abound on English grammar based on Latin structures, inadequate as such descriptions have been shown to be. Such views of English have stressed 'correctness' rather than "appropriateness' but linguists acknowledge that whatever is accepted by most educated speakers of the language is Standard English. (For a discussion of correctness/appropriateness, see pages 28–9.)

Moreover, traditional grammarians have tended to assume that the written mode of the language, because it will stay still long enough to be dissected, is the primary one to study and the battleground in which the fight for 'correctness' is to be waged. Modern linguists, however, prefer to acknowledge that their first study should be of the spoken language, since this was both the earliest form and the latest. Although records of the earliest form clearly do not exist, technological advances do allow the current latest forms to be recorded for detailed analysis.

Traditional grammar based on Latin, however, has been shown to be an unsatisfactory way of describing Modern English since English today retains few inflexional endings for its nouns, does not 'conjugate' its verbs to any marked extent, has different syntactical patterns from those of Latin, refuses to be bound by Latin 'categories' such as ablatives and datives, has much more sophisticated tenses (including continuous and progressive tenses) than the simple past, present, and future of Latin, and constructs its subordinate clauses differently. There is no reason whatsoever that the structure of Modern English should be reduced or forced into the pattern of any other language, particularly into the framework of a language which effectively ceased to develop 1500 years or so ago, belongs to another line of historical progression, and has demonstrably pronounced structural differences.

A much more productive approach to Modern English is to describe what is actually there, particularly in the spoken mode, to use a **synchronic** approach which sees one variety of the language with its own other co-existent varieties, and to work towards the identification of a universal grammar which will explain language structures rather than force one later language into the framework of another earlier language for purely arbitrary reasons. No single person, of course, has enough knowledge of enough languages to produce such a grammar single-handedly. Linguists today are still moving towards finding a way of describing language, providing a framework of description which can be applied to particular languages; Latin on its own is clearly not that framework.

Immediate constituent (IC) analysis

Leonard Bloomfield, Professor of Germanic Philosophy in the University of Chicago, introduced the term in his influential book *Language* in 1933.

He recognised the inherent weakness in the traditional approaches to grammatical description:

> The term *parts of speech* is traditionally applied to the most inclusive and fundamental word-classes of a language, and then . . . the syntactic form-classes are described in terms of the parts of speech that appear in them. However, it is impossible to set up a fully consistent scheme of parts of speech, because the word-classes overlap and cross each other.

He re-examined the use of nouns and rapidly found he had moved into a consideration of noun expressions. 'Milk' is a noun, 'fresh milk' is a noun phrase, and both forms are noun expressions. When the meaning of 'milk' is 'determined' by the addition of one attribute ('fresh') or by several ('this good, sweet, fresh milk') it remains a noun expression capable of further expansion until an 'attribute' (adjective) such as 'all' is added and the construction becomes closed.

Bloomfield's systematic approach led on from traditional grammar's classification of nouns to include: **Names** (proper nouns) always singular, definite, and without a determiner (e.g. John, Chicago); **Common nouns** may be *definite* or *indefinite* (e.g. the houses, houses), *bounded* (e.g. the house, a house), *unbounded*, *mass* nouns, or *abstract* nouns.

To describe how constituents in a sentence related to each other Bloomfield began by breaking down the sentence, *Poor John ran away*:

> Any English-speaking person who concerns himself with this matter is sure to tell us that the *immediate constituents* of *Poor John ran away* are the two forms *Poor John* and *ran away*; that each of these is, in turn, a complex form; that the immediate constituents of *ran away* are *ran*, a morpheme*, and *away*, a complex form, whose constituents are the morphemes *a-* and *way*; and that the constituents of *poor John* are the morphemes poor and John.

---

*

Morpheme: a linguistic unit (word or part of a word) that has meaning (*Chambers Twentieth Century Dictionary*).

To describe each constituent, however, would not be enough—to say that *John* is a noun, *poor* an adjective, *ran* a verb, and *away* a particle. Take, for example, the sentence *John hit Bill*, where *John* is a noun, *hit* is a verb, and *Bill* is a noun. If the sentence changed its order to *Bill hit John*, the constituents would bear the same descriptions but the sense had radically changed. Therefore, Bloomfield concluded, 'the meaningful arrangements of forms in a language constitute its *grammar*' (page 163). He went on to attempt to describe this arranging of linguistic forms. Clearly, therefore, the breaking down of the constituents in *Poor John ran away* needs a further description to add to the adjective–noun–verb–particle breakdown; that of *subject and predicate*.

David Crystal (*Linguistics*, 1971) has claimed that IC analysis, although having some similarities to the parsing of sentences advocated by traditional grammarians, 'forced the analyst to be far more explicit about his reasons for analysing the data in a given way' and recognised that constituents in a construction could be expanded in an infinite number of ways. He pointed out, on the other hand, that IC analysis sometimes failed to provide clear lines where the constituents could be divided, or more relevantly, should be divided. He gives as an example, *That nice, efficient, old-fashioned secretary is here* to illustrate the problem: how are the adjectives to be divided, if at all? Moreover, and much more importantly, Crystal demonstrated that IC analysis failed to describe some important grammatical relationships, say, for example, between the active and passive statements of the same idea. 'Its essential weakness was that it did not take fully into account the very strong case . . . for saying that the whole of language is a network of mutually defining structural relationships'. Meaning played an insignificant role in comparison to the description of the elements analysed, whereas the prime function of language is seen by most users to be that of communicating meaning.

Structural grammars

The approach and the emphasis from IC analysis methods led in the 1950s to a formalised approach to grammar through structure. Zellig Harris wrote *Methods in Structural Linguistics* (1951) and Charles Carpenter Fries *The Structure of English* (1952). Essentially, structural grammarians tried to break down utterances into their smallest possible units and then to examine their relationships to each other. They insisted that this examination should take into account phonology, morphology and syntax or the sounds of the language, its single units of meaning and its complex arrangement of morphemes into structures.

The structural grammarians, as Jeanne H. Herndon has shown (*A Survey of Modern Grammars*, second edition, 1976), broke down English syntax into form-class words and function words: 'There are four categories of form-class words: nouns, verbs, adjectives, and adverbs. Pronouns are usually considered a subcategory of nouns. Function words are categorised on the basis of their use with certain form-class words and their use in sentence patterns. The principal categories are determiners, auxiliary verbs, qualifiers, prepositions, conjunctions, sub-ordinators, and interrogatives.'

These structural grammarians, sometimes called 'the post-Bloomfieldian school', were not all of the same kind. Whilst some used Bloomfield's IC system of analysis others devised their own systems of setting out their descriptions of language. **The emphasis remained, however, on structure and classification rather than on meaning.**

Post-structural grammars: tagmemic, systemic, stratificational

In order to relate description of structure and meaning, it became clear that a system which took account of the semantic differences between, as Chomsky pointed out,

John is eager to please.

John is easy to please.

would need to be found. Jeanne Herndon quotes two further examples where IC analysis runs into considerable difficulty:

Flying planes can be dangerous.

Visiting relatives can be tiresome.

Traditional grammarians would have spotted immediately that the real problem lay in the -ing form in English which can function here either as an adjective or as a 'gerund'; IC analysis, however, would need to establish what are the true subjects of *can* in both sentences, which their reduction to immediate constituents would not make immediately obvious.

Kenneth Pike (*Language in Relation to a Unified Theory of the Structure of Human Behaviour*, 1954) doubted whether the three levels of phonology, morphology and syntax of the structural grammarians could remain separated in analysis and took up and developed a notion found in Bloomfield, that of the **tagmeme**: 'the smallest meaningful unit of grammatical form' (*Language*, page 166). David Crystal has described Pike's view of the tagmeme as 'a Janus-faced construct: it tries to combine into one conceptual unit two ideas which had previously been quite dis-associated, the ideas of class and function'. *Poor John ran away* would not be analysed as four 'bits' each described by its class (IC analysis) but as a series of tagmemes, each related to others in the structure as a whole. Tagmemic grammar set out to describe structure and function simultaneously by using somewhat complicated matrices. Nevertheless, the development towards relating structure, function, and meaning had at least set down some of the areas in which grammarians needed to work.

Systemic grammar is largely associated with the work of Michael Halliday. Like tagmemic grammar it began by looking once again at traditional grammar's splitting of the parts of an utterance: sentence, clause, phrase, word, morpheme. Each part had a level or 'rank' within the utterance. Halliday proposed four **categories**: *class* (e.g. verb, noun); *unit* (e.g. clause, phrase or 'group' as it was called); *structure* (e.g. subject, predicate); *system* (sets of tenses, aspects). Each category was related to others and each group of related categories could be 'ranked' or 'scaled'. For this reason this view of grammar was known as **scale and category grammar**. (For a discussion of 'rank' and 'scale' see D. J. Allerton, *Essentials of Grammatical Theory*, 1979, pages 183–209.) This kind of grammar is expounded in M. A. K. Halliday, A. McIntosh, and Peter Strevens, *The Linguistic Sciences and Language Teaching*, 1964.

Systemic grammar is a development from the earlier *scale and category grammar*. It takes as its starting point the notion that language has systems which interrelate with each other in a context and which in their turn can be broken down into smaller units. For example, a clause could be broken down into 'groups' (phrases), and groups into smaller units still. Each unit can be identified and described in its own right but it will interrelate with others in the structure by its function. The idea of 'function within context' as a definition of meaning was one that both Firth and Malinowski had stressed ('The Problem of Meaning in Primitive Languages' in C. K. Ogden and I. A. Richards, *The Meaning of Meaning*, 1923). Moreover, language was multi-functional, Malinowski had argued, and had social as well as personal contextual connotations. Malinowski had categorised the language used by the people of Polynesia, and Whorf, too, in exploring what would now be called 'deep' structures (see page 105), had propounded a theory of overt categories and covert categories of languages use; his system of categorising led him on to seeing 'types' of language (e.g. Standard Average European).

From J. R. Firth came the view that system in a language was the enumerated set of choices available to a user within a specific context. A useful summary of Halliday's position is found in G. R. Kress's Introduction to *Halliday: System and Function in Language: Selected Papers*, edited by G. R. Kress, 1976:

> This then is the theory. Language is a social activity. It has developed as it has, both in the functions it serves, and in the structures which express these functions, in response to the demands made by society and as a reflection of these demands . . . Halliday's position would be that the statement of the totality of all systems in one language would differ from that of another language: the search for universals is then best conducted through a comparison of the full systemic potential of different languages.

David Crystal (*Linguistics*, 1971) has also summarised the importance of the systemic model of grammar (pages 215–6):

this approach . . . tries very hard to integrate information about structure with information about classification in a single model. In the hierarchy of units, for instance, each unit has a particular structure and belongs to a particular class, and thus has a range of functions. As such, there is an important development here from previous grammatical approaches of the constituent analysis type.

Stratificational grammar saw the simultaneous interrelation of at least three levels or *strata* of a language in an utterance: semiology, grammar, and phonology, each of which could be subdivided into strata within their own categories. Sydney Lamb's *Outline of Stratificational Grammar*, 1966, set out the main approaches to this model; in the Introduction, Lamb acknowledged his debt to, amongst others, Halliday. The opening paragraph to this Introduction outlines Lamb's approach:

> The system presented here is called stratificational because one of its chief features is its treatment of linguistic structure as comprising several structural layers or strata. A language, by its nature, relates sounds (or graphs, i.e. marks on paper or the like) to meanings; the relationship turns out to be a very complex one, which can be analysed in terms of a series of code-like systems each of which has a structure analagous to that which some earlier linguistic theories ascribed to language as a whole . . . a linguistic structure as a whole has a series of tactic components rather than just one. These several systems may be called **stratal systems**, and each may be said to be associated with a **stratum** of linguistic structure.

Lamb says that all 'natural' languages have at least four strata and English has six: *semiology*—related to meaning, *phonology* to speech—and *grammar*—intermediate between the two; each of these three has two stratal systems; he ranked the six resultant strata, from lowest to highest, as follows: hypophonemic (phonetic), phonemic, morphemic, lexemic, sememic, hypersememic (or semantic). In representing the relationships between these strata Lamb devised an elaborate system of diagrams or graphs to use notational devices rather than words to describe the complexity of the strata.

Transformational-generative grammar

The complexities of tagmemic, systemic and stratificational grammars are such that Crystal concludes, 'I doubt whether there is any linguist alive capable of giving a *detailed* account of all three'; it is not clear whether Crystal was suggesting implicitly that attempting to do so had resulted in a number of dead linguists!* For a student coming to the serious study of

---

*

'So, with the throttling hands of death at strife,
Ground (they) at grammar.' (Robert Browning, *A Grammarian's Funeral*)

language, however, the importance of these three ways of moving on the study of grammar from traditional to IC approaches lies in their discussions about units of language, contexts, function, the complexity within language structures and their interrelationships, levels, and the need to find an accurate and unambiguous way of describing them. These movements in grammar also provide the setting for the views of grammar currently being explored.

Noam Chomsky considered attempts to classify and name the elements in grammar 'taxonomic'. (The word is derived from the Greek word for a division in the army (the group of soldiers from a *phyle*, or tribe of people.) The word taxonomy is defined in *Chambers Twentieth Century Dictionary* as 'classification or its principles', particularly of plants or animals.) In *Syntactic Structures*, 1957, Chomsky argued that such taxonomic principles could deal only with 'surface' structures and not with 'deep' structures of meaning, but it must be remembered that he was writing before both Halliday and Lamb had produced their work on systemic and stratificational grammars, both of which do take into account 'surface' and 'deep' structure meanings. Chomsky explored some of the differences between 'surface' and 'deep' structures further in *Aspects of the Theory of Syntax* in 1965. Deep structures were seen to appear only indirectly in the IC analysis of sentences such as: 'Flying planes can be dangerous', Chomsky's own example. The sentence can mean *at least* two things and grammatical description should be able to distinguish the meanings. Even if the traditional grammarian's two possible accounts of *flying* here (present participle being used adjectivally/gerund governing 'planes' as its object) are accepted, IC analysis would still leave the division of the sentence into 'flying+planes, can, be, dangerous'; J. Lyons has discussed the analysis of this sentence in *Semantics*, 2, page 402 within the context of *ambiguity* in relation to generative grammars.

Transformational grammars acknowledge that sentences which may seem superficially different may be generated from a simple 'base' structure, e.g.

John ate the bananas.

John did not eat the bananas. (Negative transformation)

Did John eat the bananas? (Interrogative transformation)

Did John not eat the bananas? (Interrogative/negative transformations)

The bananas were eaten by John. (Passive transformation).

They also acknowledge that superficially similar (or identical) sentences may be derived from different deep structures, e.g.

Flying planes can be dangerous.

('Planes which are in flight can be dangerous'; the flying of planes can be dangerous.)

To explain the differences or similarities in the surface structures of these two sets of examples is immediately to involve oneself in a consideration of deep structures. It is within these areas that transformational grammars operate.

A language has the ability to 'generate' an infinite number of sentences from basic items such as 'base strings', 'kernel' sentences, negatives, passives, interrogatives, etc. Chomsky uses two terms to explain the *potential* that lies in a structure that a person can use for transformation/ generation (**competence**) and what sentences actually are used (**performance**). Chomsky thought that grammar should largely be concerned with the study of 'competence' and, in this way, moved a step further on from what had in earlier times been seen by some as 'functional grammar', the examination of actual utterances in order to establish fundamental rules.

Chomsky's work has developed since the publication of *Syntactic Structures* in 1957. Students wishing to study in detail this development should look particularly at *Aspects of the Theory of Syntax*, 1965, *Topics in the Theory of Generative Grammar*, 1966, *Language and Mind*, second (enlarged) edition (New York) 1972, *Studies on Semantics in Generative Grammar*, 1972, and *Rules and Representations*, 1980. Discussions of Chomsky's ideas are helpful in David Crystal's *Linguistics*, 1971, John Lyons's *Semantics, 1 and 2*, 1977, and Ian Robinson's *The New Grammarian's Funeral: A Critique of Noam Chomsky's Linguistics*, 1975. A simpler but very lucid account with which to begin is to be found in Jean Aitchison's *Linguistics* ('Teach Yourself Books'), second edition, 1978.

The development has by no means ended.

English grammar

In 1972 Randolph Quirk, Sidney Greenbaum, Geoffrey Leech, and Jan Svartvik published *A Grammar of Contemporary English*. It aimed at 'comprehensiveness and depth in treating English irrespective of frontiers' and its field was 'the grammar of educated English current in the second half of the twentieth century in the world's major English-speaking communities'. It drew 'both on the long-established tradition and on the insights of several contemporary schools of linguistics' without getting involved in a detailed discussion of the theoretical issues. It acknowledged that, although many linguistic theories have stimulated thinking about grammar, 'none, however, seems yet adequate for all linguistic phenomena, and recent trends suggest that our own compromise position is a fair reflection of the way in which the major theories are responding to the influence from others' (the Introduction).

This work rapidly established itself as the reference grammar of contemporary English. In 1973, a shorter version of the book appeared, produced by Randolph Quirk and Sidney Greenbaum: *A University Grammar of English*.

PART VI

Exercises

The next three chapters contain exercises on your study of the language, as follows:

Chapter 8 (Exercises 1–32)
Exercises demanding close attention to particular features of language study.

> First read the question and the text carefully. Once you have made your observations, refer to the appropriate section about language earlier in the book. (You will find the index at the end helpful for this.) You should have a dictionary handy, and you should also be able to refer to other books about language.

Chapter 9 (Exercises 33–52)
Exercises requiring not only detailed observations but also general comments, changes in texts and, at times, the creation of new texts.

> Note that the exercises are typical of the scrutiny you need to give to language uses. You will find it valuable and interesting to supplement the work with your own examples of texts.

Chapter 10 (Exercise 53–70)
Exercises calling for general assumptions to be made about aspects of language.

> You will be required to theorise about a number of assumptions, and you will find it helpful at all times to refer to general works on language.

CHAPTER 8

Exercise 1

Comment on the following uses of language:

(a) I campaign   You intrigue   He conspires
(b) I am a traveller   You are a visitor   He is a tripper
(c) I am a freedom fighter   You are an urban guerilla
     He is a terrorist

Exercise 2

All the following words can be used as characteristics of a person. Write a sentence for each word in the following pairs of words which shows clearly the meaning and use of the word, and then comment briefly on the differences between the words in each pair:

(a) resolute   inflexible
(b) single-minded   narrow-minded
(c) pragmatic   expedient
(d) moderate   weak
(e) amenable   answerable
(f) determined   stubborn

Exercise 3

Discuss the use of the following in present-day spoken English:

(a) wireless   radio
(b) railway station   train station

Exercise 4

Comment on the differences in the meaning and use in each of the following.

(a) a loudspeaker   a loud speaker
(b) a briefcase   a brief case
(c) a greenhouse   a green house

Exercise 5

Comment on the following and their uses in spoken English.

at the end of the day
in point of fact
to cut a long story short
actually
you know

Exercise 6

Comment on the verbs and particles in the following groups of sentences.

(a) The woman took the book up to her bedroom.
    The old man took up gardening as a hobby.
    The lawyer took up the case of the injured passenger.
    The mother took up the hem of her daughter's dress.
    The sportsman took up the challenge from his rival.
    The student took up French where she had left off.
    The person who was early for the interview took up time by walking slowly.
    The member of the audience took the speaker up on two of his remarks.
    The girl took her friend up on her invitation to stay for the weekend.
    The dissatisfied customer took up the fault with the firm.
    The young person took up with friends his parents did not approve of.

(b) The handle broke off the cup in my hands.
    The child broke a piece off the bar of chocolate.
    The girl broke off her engagement.
    The statesman broke off the negotiations.
    The speaker broke off in mid-sentence.

(c) He put on a coat.
    He put on an act.
    He put on a play.
    He put on weight.
    He put on fifty runs in an hour.

He put ten pounds on the favourite.
He put the spinner on to bowl.
He put a tax on cars.
He put the police on to the criminal.
He dialled the number and then put his partner on the line.

Exercise 7

Comment on the italicised words, and the ways in which they are formed, in the following:

(a) From a letter by the poet William Shenstone to his friend Richard Jago commenting on the death of their friend William Somervile, July 1742:

Whatever the world may esteem in poor Somervile, I really find, upon critical enquiry, that I loved him for nothing so much as his *flocci-nauci-nihili-pili-fication* of money.

(b) From a lecture by Mr Cranium, a character in Thomas Love Peacock's humorous novel *Headlong Hall*, 1816:

I invite you, when you have sufficiently restored, replenished, refreshed, and exhilarated that *osteosarchaematosplanchnoch-ondroneureomuelous*, or to employ a more intelligible term, *osseocarnisanguineoviscericartilaginonervomedullary*, compages, or shell, the body . . .

(c) From Webster's *Third International Dictionary*, giving the plural of a lung disease contracted by some miners:

pneumonoultramicroscopicsilicovolcanoconiosises.

(d) A title of a song in the film *Mary Poppins*:

Supercalifragilisticexpialidocious.

(e) From an advertisement:

Lipsmackinthirstquenchinacetastinmotivatingoodbuzzincooltalkinhighwalkin-fastlivinnevergivincoolfizzin-PEPSI

Exercise 8

The following notice was found in a room in a Spanish hotel. What can you deduce from it about the similarities and differences of different languages? Comment on any other features of the language that are of interest to you.

AGUA NO POTABLE
LEIDINGSWATER IS NIET DRINKBAAR
L'EAU N'EST PAS POTABLE
WE ADVISE YOU THAT THE WATER IN THE ROOMS IS
NOT DRINK WATER
WASSER IM ZIMMER IST NICHT ZU DRINKEN

Exercise 9

Comment on the language of the following:

Please note that we do not accept responsibility for any injury, loss or damage of whatever nature and howsoever caused arising either directly or indirectly out of the use of this machine or these premises.

Exercise 10

Comment on the wording of the following notice inserted in a local newspaper.

Public Notices

NOTICE IS HEREBY GIVEN pursuant to Section 27 of the Trustees Act 1925, that any person having claims against or any interest in the estate of any of the deceased persons, whose names and addresses and descriptions are set out below, are hereby required to send particulars in writing of his claim or interest of the person in relation to the deceased person concerned before the date specified, after which date the estate of the deceased will be distributed by the personal representatives among the persons entitled hereto, having regard only to the claims and interest of which they have had notice and they will not as respect and property distributed be liable to any person whose claims they shall not have had notice.

SMITH (John), late of 29 Shakespeare Court, Putney, London, who died 16 March 1986. Particulars to Martin Jones & Co., 1 Brown Square, London, by 31 July 1986.

Exercise 11

(a) Comment on the spellings and mis-spellings of the following words.

saucer	sauser	sacuere
said	sed	siad
very	verry	verery
there	their	therr
played	plade	palyed
daughter	dorter	dagfa

(b) The following observation is taken from a newspaper. Comment on the types of spelling errors, offer reasons why they may have occurred, and suggest ways in which the student might learn to eliminate them.

SHE HAD spent 'houres' over her essay but she had no 'apptitude' and no 'flare' for spelling. Even after a 'brake' for lunch, it was still 'suprisingly' bad, though you could tell what she 'ment'. An 'independant' girl, she did not find it 'forefilling'. Despite 'baring' a good 'refrencence' and a respectable 'adress', her hopes of college 'enterance' were dashed because she was not 'apreciated'.

All those spelling mistakes are taken from an essay written by an 18-year-old student of A-level English literature. She failed the exam, but she seemed to have no idea why.

(c) The writer implies that the mis-spellings contributed considerably to the failure of the student in the examination. Give your views about this, commenting in particular on the importance of accurate spelling in an English examination.

Exercise 12

(a) Comment on the uses of *that* in the following:

    (i) When I started that job that I had looked forward to doing, I realised that that that I had to do was more difficult than it looked.

    (ii) The town is not that far away.

    (iii) The matter is not that important.

(b) '*That* is just about the most remarkable word in the English language.' Dicuss this comment by considering the different modern uses of the word *that*.

Exercise 13

Imagine that you are a teacher and wish to give an instruction to your class. Comment on the implications of the following, and then provide your own form of instruction, with a brief explanation of why you have chosen it.

(a) Open your books at page twenty-two.
(b) I should like you to open your books at page twenty-two.
(c) Would you open your books at page twenty-two?
(d) We can continue our work by turning to page twenty-two.

Exercise 14

The *Guinness Book of Records* has the following entry:

> The most over-worked word in English is the word *set* which has 58 noun uses, 126 verbal uses and 10 as a participial adjective.

Imagine that you are the compiler of a dictionary and have to provide an entry for the word *set*.

(a) Give as many uses as you can for the word *set*, supporting each use with an illustrative example.

(b) Organise your information about the word *set* as an entry for a dictionary intended for those for whom English is not a first language.

(c) Compare what you have done with the entries in two standard dictionaries. Comment on any differences in the organisation and presentation.

Exercise 15

Comment on the following:

> By far the commonest meaning of *see* in contemporary English is to understand or follow, as in 'I see what you mean'.
> The most frequent meaning of *keep* is not to retain ownership, but to continue or maintain, as in 'keep warm' or 'keep smiling'.
> We are most likely to use *give* not in connection with gifts, but as mere verbal padding, as in 'give a look' or 'give a report'.

Exercise 16

Read the following short article on the use of the word 'onto'.

> ONTO: Mr C. F. Scott, of Solihull, in Warwickshire, writes: 'Into, unto, upon—why not onto?' It's a word I have never been certain about so I went to the OED to find that not only does it exist but is rather interesting. In Old English 'on' used to mean both 'upon', when it took the dative, and 'on' implying motion, when it took the accusative. Then case endings disap-

peared and ambiguity crept in. 'But,' the entry goes on, while "in to, into" was in use by 900, the need for "on to, onto" appears not to have been felt before the sixteenth century, while its written recognition as a combination is still quite recent [entry ready for publication in 1903] and limited. Yet in the sense in which it corresponds to "into," "onto" is in speech a real compound, the "n" being shortened by its rapid passage into the allied mute "t", while in "on to" as two words, the "n" is long and does not glide into the "t".' Recognition of 'onto' is still limited. Fowler, in a tetchy little article (carried unchanged by Sir Ernest Gowers in the 1965 revision), questions the need for 'onto' at all; the implication seems to be that 'on' will usually do by itself. The 'house style' of the Oxford University Press forbids its use and the Concise Oxford does not even give it a separate entry (nor does Chambers). Collins, however, notes that it 'is now generally accepted as a word in its own right.' About time too. In this OED example dated 1881, 'On a cliff there were men trying to send a rope out onto the ship,' I would not substitute either 'on' or 'on to'.

John Silverlight

(a) Summarise the argument of the article and discuss whether or not you would consider the use of 'onto' as one word acceptable.

(b) With detailed reference to a variety of dictionaries and other works on English usage, compose a short article considering whether or not the use of 'alright' as one word can now be considered acceptable.

Exercise 17

Here are some well-known children's jokes. Discuss the ways in which the humour depends on the use of language.

(a) 'Come on, Charles. I'll take you to the zoo.'
'If the zoo wants me, let them come and get me!'

(b) 'Dad, what are those holes in the new fence?'
'They're knot-holes.'
'That's strange. I can put my finger into them.'

(c) 'Susan, what are you doing out there in the rain?'
'Getting wet.'

(d) 'John, name two pronouns.'
'Who, me?'
'That's right.'

(e) 'How long will the next bus be?'
'About ten metres.'

(f) Teacher: Who spilt that paint on the floor?
Pupil: I done it.
Teacher: Where's your grammar?
Pupil: At home.

(g) 'Will this path take me to the main road?'
   'No, you'll have to go by yourself.'

(h) Two lorries, one carrying red paint and one purple paint, collided on a
   desert island. The drivers are now marooned.

(i) 'Is it difficult to become a professor?'
   'No, you do it by degrees.'

Exercise 18

The following reports are taken from newspapers and record similar
incidents separated by a hundred years. Comment on the differences in the
uses and features of the language which are of interest to you.

FATAL FIRE

A fire attended with fatal consequences was discovered at a quarter to 9 o'clock yesterday morning at Clapham-park-road, S. W., in a large private house tenanted by a Mrs. Lydia James, a maiden lady 67 years of age, of very retired and eccentric habits. The fire broke out, from some cause which is at present unascertained, in the front room in the basement, which was blazing furiously when the firemen from Clapham-common, called up by the ringing of the fire alarm, arrived on the scene. A stand-pipe was got to work, and the house was saved from complete destruction, but the lower part of the premises was burnt out, and serious damage caused to the rest of the house and the contents. On the firemen entering the premises, the charred remains of the occupant were found in the basement, among the ruins of an armchair, which, it is stated, had formed her bedstead for the two years during which she has occupied the house. In the remaining rooms of the house the furniture was found scattered about exactly where it had been placed when it was moved in.

Smoker died in blazing armchair

An elderly Birmingham widow who was a heavy smoker died in an armchair in a fire at her home. City coroner Dr Richard Whittington recorded a verdict of accidental death on Mrs Edith Green, of Spider Road, Stechford, who died two days before her 89th birthday. He said careless use of a cigarette must have led to her death. She may have fallen asleep and her clothing caught fire. The charred body of Mrs Green was found by firemen in the early hours of June 20. There were a large number of cigarette ends and packets around the room. Social worker Mrs Ethel Joiner said that Mrs Green had been warned regularly to be careful about her smoking.
Mrs Green, who was said to be confused, was taken to a day centre most days of the week and had regular visits from social services and a daily home help.

Exercise 19

Rewrite in modern English the following report of a drowning at Worcester over two hundred years ago. Comment on the changes you have made.

> Thomas Bromfield, a Boy about Ten Years of Age, bathing in our river Severn at the Top of Pitchcroft in Worcester, was forced out of his Depth, and unfortunately drowned; and though his body was taken up within ten Minutes after, yet the Means used for his Recovery by an eminent Surgeon, who humanely gave him immediate assistance, were ineffectual.

Exercise 20

The following exercises are taken from a textbook used in schools over 100 years ago. Discuss the linguistic assumptions in what was set, in particular in the choice of material and in what the omissions indicate about what was being tested.

SUPPLY THE WORDS OMITTED IN THE FOLLOWING STORIES.

(a)   *The Mexican Youths*

After the death of Montezuma, the Mexicans——possession of a high tower in the great temple——overlooked the Spanish quarters, and ——there a garrison of their principal——.
Not a Spaniard could—— without being exposed to the missiles of the Mexicans. From this post it was——to dislodge them at any——. A Spanish officer thrice made the——, but was——. Cortes, the Spanish commander,——that not only the reputation, but the safety of his army,——on the success of this assault,——a buckler to be——to his arm, as he could not——it with his wounded hand. Animated by the——of their general, the Spaniards returned to the charge with such——that they gradually—— their way up the steps of the tower, and——the Mexicans to the top. There a——carnage began, when two young Mexicans of high rank, seeing Cortes encourage his soldiers by his voice and example,——to sacrifice their own lives in order to cut off the author of all the——that desolated their country. They—— him in a suppliant posture, as if they——to lay down their weapons; and——him in their arms, hurried him towards the walls, over—— they threw themselves headlong with the——of dragging him along with them. But Cortes, by his strength and agility,——loose from their——, and the gallant youths——in the generous attempt to—— their country.

(b)   *The Swallow and other Birds*

A swallow, observing a farmer―― in sowing hemp, called the little
birds together,――them what the farmer was――, and, telling
them――hemp was the material――which the nets, so fatal to the
feathered――, were constructed――them to join in picking it up, in
order to――the consequences. The birds,――not believing his information, or neglecting his――, gave themselves no――about the
matter. In a――time, the hemp appeared――ground. The friendly
swallow, again addressing――to the birds, told them that it was not yet
too――, provided they would set about the work――the seeds had
taken too deep――. But they still――his advice, he――their society,
――for safety to towns and cities, and there――his habitation and
――his residence. One day,――he was skimming along the street, he
――to see a number of these very birds――in a cage on the shoulders
of a bird-catcher. 'Unhappy wretches,' said he, 'you now――the
punishment of your neglect.' Thus, those who have no foresight of
their own, and who――the wholesome admonitions of their friends,
――the mischiefs which their own obstinacy or negligence――upon
their heads.

Exercise 21

Here are some observations by students about teachers they remember.
Discuss what you find interesting about the different ways they express
their opinions. What features of the language indicate that they were
giving their views orally?
A good teacher is...

(a) Teachers should know that they're not going into a job but a way of
    life—and they're doing it through their own choice. That's the
    difference between them and kids. Kids are there because they've got
    to be; teachers are there because they want to be. If they appreciate
    that, they'll know that they've got to be understanding and be
    superhumanly patient.

                    Kerry Parkes, aged 21, Great Barr, Birmingham

(b) School is about learning and you can't get away from it. But there's
    different ways tae teach. Some teachers just put it over really good and
    make you learn things without you realising you're learning. We went
    tae a dairy culture farm recently, and there was a girl there with young
    kids and it was amazing how she kept their attention, and was teaching
    them at the same time. She didnae say, 'This is a cow and it has so
    many udders,' or, 'This is a milking machine.' She'd say, 'This is a
    cow, would you like tae feel it? Come and touch it, this is where the
    milk comes from.' The way she kept their attention was brilliant; she

was really good with kids. That's the way you've got tae do it in schools.

Jayne Harper, aged 16, Edinburgh

(c) A good teacher is someone with a lot of patience, who tries to show no favouritism at all and who is prepared to listen to your point of view. When you reach fourteen or fifteen you develop your own opinions. I think the trouble with a lot of teachers is that they aren't prepared to listen to young people's ideas. If teachers were to hold more discussions in the classroom, rather than tell you points, the teacher–pupil relationship could improve a great deal.

Helen Ashworth, aged 19, Sutton Coldfield, West Midlands

(d) A good teacher is one with a sense of humour, but who is quite strict so you can't go too far. Some teachers have a way so that they can control the class without having to use the belt. I've had the belt three times. Twice was by a really pathetic Latin teacher who would line six of you up and belt you and it just didn't hurt at all; it was hysterical. The other was by this man for forgetting my jotter three times. He absolutely walloped me, and I didn't like him after that—but he was a good teacher. Being able to control classes is an ability some teachers have and some don't. Some can control the class but are absolutely hopeless teachers. Yet other teachers who can't control the class are really good teachers and the ones who want to learn come round to them.

Yvonne Gray, aged 19, Marchment, Edinburgh

(e) The best teachers are those who aren't trying to project their authority all the time—who feel secure in allowing you to go so far and no further.

Nicola Northway, aged 16, Longbenton, Newcastle-upon-Tyne

(f) The worst teachers were the oldest teachers—the ones who said, 'We fought the war for people like you.' If I was there I'd have fought it myself. It wasn't my fault I wasn't born then.

Mark Baker, aged 19, Bretton, Peterborough

(g) Once, when we went away on a rugby trip to play a team in Beverley, Yorkshire, they took along a teacher we didn't like in school. But we got on well with him at the weekend 'cos he was different. We found that he was human. But he became the same person again when he got back to school. We'd say, 'hello' in the corridor and he'd just reply with, 'Where are *you* going? Get out!'—that sort of thing.

Andrew Seal, aged 19, Great Barr, Birmingham

'The way teachers start lessons is important'
(h) The best teacher taught us maths for a double period on Monday morning. He'd start off by saying 'Had a nice weekend everyone?' and

he'd ask people what they'd done and sometimes we'd all fold up on the floor with laughter. He'd even come out with jokes himself. Then he'd say, 'Let's get on with some work, take your books out' and that was it.

John Smith, aged 17, Essex

(i) My favourite teacher was Mr McIntosh who taught us physics. He did nae treat you quite so childishly. He didnae belt you and he didnae hand out lines just because you hadnae done your homework. He would listen tae your answer for it, and then he'd tell you tae do it, and explain if you didnae do it it was your own fault. That's different tae saying, 'You must do it, or you'll get three of the belt.'

We could call him Tosh and he didnae mind and I didnae lose any respect for him. I really don't see why teachers and pupils can't be on first name terms. Tosh did a lot of things that other teachers didnae. We could go and sit on his desk and talk tae him or he would come and sit on our desks. We used tae sit in a circle so that everyone could talk across the classroom, rather than sitting in rows facing the teacher.

Mary Seath, aged 17, Edinburgh

Exercise 22

Comment on the language of the following poems:

(a) The first is written by James Berry:

IN A BRIXTAN MARKIT

I walk in a Brixtan markit
believin I a respectable man
you know. An wha happn? Policeman
come straight up an search mi bag! Man
—straight to mi, like them did a-wait fi
mi. Come search mi bag, man. Fi mi
bag. An wha them si in deh? Two piece
a yam, a dasheen, a han a banana, a
piece a pork, an mi lates' Bob Marley.
Man all a suddn I feel me head nah fi
mi. This ya now is when man kill
somody, nah! 'Tony,' I sey, 'hol on.
Hol on Tony. Dohn shove. Dohn
shove. Dohn mover neidda fis', tongue
nor emotion. Battn down Tony. Battn
down.' An, man, Tony win.

(b) The second is by Edward Brathwaite:

RITES
(an extract from the poem)

Many a time I have seen him savin'
the side (the tailor was saying
as he sat and sewed in his shop).

You remember that tourney wid Brandon?
What-he-name-now
that big-able water policeman –

de one in charge o' de Harbour Patrol . . .
You mean Hop-
a-long Cass? Is because a cow

give he mother a kick before he did born
that he foot come out so.
Yes, I know

but is not what I talkin' about. Ol'
Hoppy was bowlin' that day
as if he was hurricane father.

Lambert went in, play-
in' he know all about it as us'al
an' *swoosh!* there he go fan-

nin' outside the off-stump an'
is *click!*
he snick

de ball straight into de slips.
'Well boys it look like we lossin'
this match', says the skipper,

writin' nought in the exercise book
he was keepin' the score in; 'you think
we could chance it an' sen' Gullstone in

before Charlie or Spooks?'
So Gullstone went in.
You could see he face whitenin'

under he tan an' you know
that that saga-boy frighten: bat
tappin', feet walkin' 'bout like they talkin'

wid ants; had was to stop meself axin'
meself if he ever play cricket on Brown's beach before.
An' I tole him,

I tole him over an' over
agen: *watch de ball, man,* watch
de ball like it hook to you eye

when you first goes in an' you doan know de pitch
Uh doan mean to *poke*
but you jes got to *watch what you doin'*:

this isn't no time for playin'
the fool nor makin' no sport; this is cricket!
But Gullstone too deaf:

mudder doan clean out de wax in'e ear!
Firs' ball from Cass an' he fishin';
secon' ball an' he missin', swishin'

he bat like he wishin'
to catch butterfly; though the all Gullstone ever could catch
pun dis beach was a cole!

But is always the trouble wid we:
too fraid an' too frighten.
Is all very well when it rosy an' sweet,

but leh murder start an' *bruggalungdung!*
you cahn fine a man to hole up de side.

Look wha' happen las' week at de O-
val!

At de Oval?
Wha' happen las' week at de Oval?

You mean to say that you come
in here wid dat lime-skin cone

that you callin' a hat
pun you head, an' them slip slop shoe strap

on to you foot like a touris';
you sprawl you ass

all over my chair widdout askin'me please leave nor licence,

wastin' muh time when you know very well that uh cahn fine
enough to finish these zoot suits

'fore Christmas; an' on top
o' all this, you could wine up de nerve to stop

me cool cool cool in de middle
o' all me needle

an' t'read; make me prick me hand in me haste;
an' tell me broad an' bole to me face
THAT YOU DOAN REALLY KNOW WHA' HAPPEN
at Kensington Oval?

We was *only* playin' de MCC, man;
M-C-C
who come all de way out from Inglan.

We was battin', you see;
score wasn't too bad; one
hurren an'ninety

seven fuh three
The openers out, Tae Worrell out,
Everton Weekes jus glide two foh fifty

an'jack, is de GIANT to come!
Feller name Wardle
was bowlin'; tossin'it up

sweet sweet slow-medium syrup.
Firs' ball . . .
'N . . . o . . . o . . .'

back down de wicket to Wardle.
Secon' ball . . .
'N . . . o . . . o . . .'

back down de wicket to Wardle.
Third ball comin'up
an' we know wha' goin' happen to syrup:

Clyde back pun he back
foot an' *prax!*
is through extra cover an' four red runs all de way.

'You see dat shot?' the people was shoutin';
'Jesus, Chrise, man, wunna see dat shot?'
All over de groun' fellers shakin' hands wid each other

as if was *they* wheelin' de willow
as if was *them* had the power;
one man run out pun de field wid a red fowl cock

goin' quawk quawk quawk in' e han';
would' a give it to Clyde right then an' right there
if a police hadn't stop' e!

An' in front o' where I was sittin',
one ball-headed sceptic snatch hat off he head
as if he did crazy

an' pointin' he finger at Wardle,
he jump up an' down
like a sun-shatter daisy an' bawl

out: 'B . . . L . . . O . . . O . . . D, B . . . I . . . G . . . B . . . O . . . Y . . .
bring me he B . . . L . . . O . . . O . . . D'
Who would'a think that for twenty-

five years he was standin' up there
in them Post Office cages, lickin' gloy
pun de Gover'ment stamps.

If uh wasn't there to see fuh meself,
I would'a never believe it,
I would'a never believe it.

But I say it once an' I say it agen:
when things goin' good, you cahn touch
we; but leh murder start an' you cahn fine a man to hold up de side.

(c) The third is by Ian McDonald:

JAFFO, THE CALYPSONIAN

Jaffo was a great calypsonian; a fire ate up his soul to sing and
    play calypso iron music.
Even when he was small, he made many-coloured ping-pong
    drums, and searched them for the island music,
drums of beaten oil-barrel iron, daubed in triangles with stolen
    paint from a harbour warehouse.
Now, he seized the sorrow and the bawdy farce in metal-harsh
    beat and his own thick voice.
He was not famous in the tents; he went there once, and not a
    stone clapped; and he was afraid of respectable eyes;
the white-suited or gay-shirted lines of buinessmen or tourists
    muffled his deep urge;
but he went back to the Indian tailor's shop and sang well, and
    to the Chinese sweet-and-sweepstake shop and sang well,
unsponsored calypsoes; and in the scrap lots near the Dry
    River, lit by one pitchoil lamp or two,
he would pound his ping-pong, and sing his hoarse voice out for
    ragged still-eyed men.
But, in the rum-shop, he was best; drinking the heavy sweet
    molasses rum, he was better than any other calypso man.
In front of the rows of dark red bottles, in the cane-scented
    rooms, his clogged throat rang and rang with staccato shouts.
Drunk, then, he was best; easier in pain from the cancer in his
    throat but holding the memory of it.
On the rough floors of the rum-shops, strewn with bottle-tops
    and silver-headed corks and broken green bottle-glass,
he was released from pain into remembered pain, and his thick
    voice rose and grated in brassy fear and fierce jokes.
His voice beat with bitterness and fun, as if he told of old
    things, hurt ancestral pride, and great slave humour.
He would get a rum, if he sang well; so perhaps there was that
    to it too.
He was always the best, though; he *was* the best; the ragged
    men said so, and the old men.
One month before he died, his voice thickened to a hard final
    silence.
The look of unsung calypsoes stared in his eyes, a terrible thing
    to watch in the rat-trap rum-shops.

When he could not stand for pain, he was taken to the public
    ward of the Colonial Hospital.
Rafeeq, the Indian man who in Marine Square watches the
    birds all day long for his God, was there also.
Later, he told about Jaffo in a long mad chant to the rum-shop
    men. They laughed at the story:
until the end, Jaffo stole spoons from the harried nurses to beat
    out rhythms on his iron bedposts.

Exercise 23

A parody is a comic or satirical imitation of an original work which
exaggerates its subject matter and style.

(a) Here is a Divine Song by Isaac Watts (1674–1748) and a parody by
'Lewis Carroll' (Charles Dodgson 1832–98). Comment on the differences in the texts and the effect these have upon the tone of the
parody.

Against Idleness and Mischief	*How Doth . . .*
How doth the little busy Bee	How doth the little crocodile
Improve each shining Hour,	Improve his shining tail,
And gather Honey all the Day	And pour the waters of the Nile
From ev'ry op'ning Flow'r!	On every golden scale!
How skilfully she builds her Cell!	How cheerfully he seems to grin,
How neat she spreads the Wax!	How neatly spreads his claws,
And labours hard to store it well	And welcomes little fishes in
With the sweet Food she makes.	With gently smiling jaws!
In Works of Labour or of Skill	
I would be busy too:	
For *Satan* finds some Mischief still	
For idle Hands to do.	
In books, or Work, or healthful Play,	
Let my first Years be past,	
That I may give for every Day	
Some good Account as last.	

(b) Now find a well known poem which you believe can be considered less
seriously than was originally intended and try to write a parody of it.

Exercise 24

The following extract is taken from *The Dillen* (1983) and represents the
language of George Hewins who lived at Stratford on Avon early this
century. Comment on the features of the language, particularly where they
deviate from what is considered 'normal English'.

Who should I bump into but Mr Doonan the postmaster. 'Ullo George! Could you manage time off for the day?'

I tried not to look too keen.

'Somebody's gettin wed at Clopton House, the Reverend Hodgsons's.'

I said: 'What's it a telegram?'

He said: '*Sixpence!*'

I couldn't believe my luck: they was nobility, there was *bound* to be a lot o' telegrams! So—I runned backwards and forwards, backwards and forwards, from the Post Office in Sheep Street to Clopton House, back down to Stratford, up again to Clopton. I must a-runned about eighteen miles that day.

Then Doonan says to me: 'Our caretaker's packed up. Would you like to take the job till you starts work again?'

I said: 'Yes, I would!'

I took the job on, sweeping the Post Office up. I took the keys home with me at night, the front door keys, and unlocked it early morning, did all the cleaning and the dusting and the polishing. The first morning I was there I was a-dusting where they stood to write telegrams out. There was a ten-bob note under the wadding.

I said to myself: The bugger! Well, I shan't 'ave it!

I went to the postmaster and I said: 'There was this ten-shillin note under the waddin pad.'

'Oh!' he said. 'Somebody's writ a telegram an left it be'ind! They'll come back for it, sure to.'

That's all he'd say. There never was another. They set all sorts o' traps for you, at that time o'day.

They got me doing the last train. They took the truck up for me and I walked to the station and fetched a truckload back, about eight bags o' mail. If anybody got off at Stratford, a couple for the weeksend and the bloke said with a wink—'Could you recommend me to a hotel?' I directed them to the 'Shakespeare'. 'Just ask for Miss Justins. Er's very obligin.'

One night it was past twelve afore the train came. The next day I seen the copper. He says: 'Late last night, weren't you?'

I says: 'Ah. The train were late—where was you?'

He says: 'We watched you unlock the Post Office, put your bags in, put the keys through the letter box!'

'Well,' I said, 'I'm more happy now I *knows* I'm being watched— cos I used to get nervy, unlocking that gate,' I said, 'and goin right up that back. That's relieved me a good lot, I can tell you.'

'Ah,' he says, 'we watches!'

Exercise 25

Here are three humorous tales about two characters, Enoch and Eli. The effect of the tales depends on the way the dialect of the characters is expressed.

(a) Comment on the ways the representation of dialect contributes to the effect of the tales.

AYNUK AND AYLI

(i) Aynuk on return from his first visit to the seaside, told Ayli that he had 'sid an iron boat sairlin' on the say'.

Ayli: 'Doh be daft, Aynuk, it 'ud sink'.

Aynuk: 'I tell yo it day sink'.

So when he got home and to prove whether Aynuk was right or wrong, Ayli throws the iron bedstead into the cut—and, of course, it sinks.

Next day, Ayli sees Aynuk and said 'I thort yo told me that an iron boat day sink. I've chucked t' ode bedstead into the cut and it went straight to the bottom.'

Aynuk: 'Goo on, thee fule. Dusta know yo gorrave salt wairter?'

(ii) After a long spell on the 'dole' Aynuk got a job at the brickworks. But after three weeks pushing, shoving and heaving, he went to the gaffer and asked for his cards.

'What's the matter?' he asked. 'Aren't the wages right? They're the standard union rate.'

Replied Aynuk, 'No gaffer, it ay that. The wages am orrite. But I cor goo on much longer like this. I lies awake at night worrying, becos I'm kipping a 'oss out of a job.'

(iii) Young Aynuk was wooing his sweetheart by the side of Baggeridge pool.

'Lizzie', he sighed, 'yo con see that pool, cor yer?'

'Ar I con', answered Liz.

'Well, if that was beer an' yo promised me a kiss ah'd swim in it wi' me mouth closed.'

(b) Now gather tales in dialect from the locality where you live and comment on the features of the language.

Exercise 26

Write a 'translation' of the following dialect poem. Then comment on the changes you have made and what you have discovered about the pronunciation of words in the dialect of the poem.

"DOH THEY SLIP UP"!

SUM PRETEND TER BE WOT THEY BAY
BUT THEY ALLUZ GI' THE SHOW AWAY
PRAPS A BIGGER 'OUSE UN NEWER CAR
UN SUM ULL GOO ALL "LA-DI-DAH"
IT'S ALL A PROPER LOOD UV BULL
SOO STUFF YER EARS WI' COTTON WOOL . . .

... "BLACK COUNTRY TORK" THEY WANT TER FORGET
BUT THEY COR DEW IT DOH YER FRET
THE "CONVERSERSHUN" CUD'NT BE DULLER
WOT WI' TEW T.Vs ... UV CORSE IN CULLER
YET IT ONY TEKS ONE WERD TER SLIP
THEY FEEL THEY WANT TER BITE THE LIP

THEY BOOK THE "MEALS" AT SUM "POSH PLERCE"
WHEER "COMMON FOLKS" DOH SHOW THE FERCE
THEY DOH WANT TER KNOW THE "FERTHER" OR
"MUTHER"
THEY'M NEITHER ONE THING NOR ANUTHER
WOT THEY BIN IS ARF UN ARF
NO GUD FER A LOFF NO GUD FOR "A LARF"

"CONVERSERSHUN" BECUMS A BIND
IF YOH COR SAY WOT YO'DE AMIND
UN IF YOH SAY WOT YOH DOH MEAN
YO'VE BECUM A LUMP UV PLASTERSEEN
UN DOH 'JUST FLASH A RING OR TEW
TER IMPRESS THEM WI' NO "I.Q." ...

... THE GENUINE FOLKS ... THEER'S SUM AROUND
KEEP THE FEET DAHN ON THE GROUND
THEY SMILE AT THESE INVERTED SNOBS
OOH TRY TER ACT LIKE REAL "TOP KNOBS"
YOH FEEL SORRY FER 'EM AH SHUD SAY
CUS THE SLIP UPS GI' THEIR "SHOW" AWAY!

Harry Harrison

Exercise 27

The following was written by a seventeen year old student as part of an article about a day at school published in a colour magazine. It was intentionally chatty and humorous. Describe and comment on features of the language of the text.

Break eventually arrives after three periods of the best years of our lives—French, English, German or Italian. I'm on break duty so I pile along to the appointed exit with a mug of coffee (the sign of a senior), looking down my nose and repeating in suitably bored but polite tones, 'Could you go outside, please?', 'Would you mind going out of this door?', 'Get outside, you little horror!', to the first-years who are scared of us. You soon recognise the trouble-makers: uniform subtly scruffier, nose screwed to one side, a pout, and shifty eyes. Then you nobble 'em.

Break is over too soon, but only two periods until dinnertime. Power again! I, like most prefects, am a megalomaniac and thoroughly enjoy withering first-years with a carefully aimed eyebrow. Dinner duty means hovering over the lunch queues (armed with a cup of coffee), ready to pounce on them what's talking. 'I didn't do it, honest. It was 'er wot said it . . .', 'Well you were pushing her.', 'I wasn't! She kicked over my bag, so I had to bend over and she . . .' They're quite intelligent, most of them, but you really wouldn't believe it at times.

If you're a sports maniac, like friend Kate, you are given a completely free rein at lunchtimes. Cross country is not my scene, although everyone in the school is driven around the field for the appointed number of times once a year. (Note—all PE teachers are sadists.)

I could go to hockey, but it is a lethal game; not suited to those of a nervous disposition and only useful for finishing off undesirables with a slip of the hockey stick . . . Athletics are out at this time of year, but anyway they are merely forms of forcing your body to do what it can't and won't do. Swimming—green water (water? liquid ice!), with the temperature optimistically put at 76, then on with the moth-eaten black costume and emerald green hat to dive into the murky depths . . . I could also go to choir, orchestra (a fate worse than death), library, bookshop, or go 'Up Town'—which I usually choose to do.

Only the sixth form is supposed to cross the hallowed school border, but half the school is there to mingle with the fray of the Grammar School. Oh, those black uniforms with the yellow striped ties will remain in my heart for ever. Perhaps not when I remember the spotty, greasy, stammering contents . . .

Exercise 28

Here is a part of a leaflet issued by the Post Office to explain the use of the postcode.

Discuss the features of the text, noting in particular the choice of vocabulary and grammar, the relationship of the text to the layout, and the appropriateness to the type of reader intended.

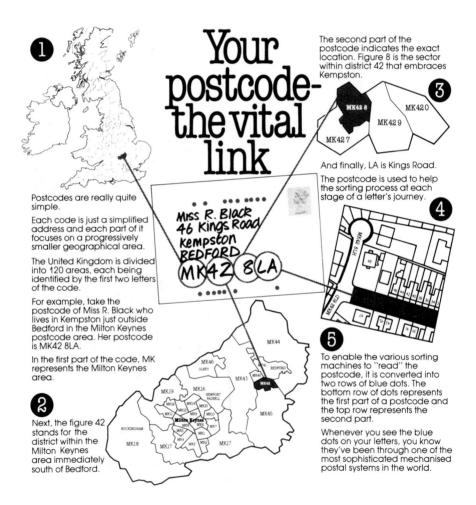

1

Your postcode- the vital link

The second part of the postcode indicates the exact location. Figure 8 is the sector within district 42 that embraces Kempston.

3

And finally, LA is Kings Road.

The postcode is used to help the sorting process at each stage of a letter's journey.

4

Postcodes are really quite simple.

Each code is just a simplified address and each part of it focuses on a progressively smaller geographical area.

The United Kingdom is divided into 120 areas, each being identified by the first two letters of the code.

For example, take the postcode of Miss R. Black who lives in Kempston just outside Bedford in the Milton Keynes postcode area. Her postcode is MK42 8LA.

In the first part of the code, MK represents the Milton Keynes area.

2

Next, the figure 42 stands for the district within the Milton Keynes area immediately south of Bedford.

Miss R. Black
46 Kings Road
Kempston
BEDFORD
MK42 8LA

5

To enable the various sorting machines to "read" the postcode, it is converted into two rows of blue dots. The bottom row of dots represents the first part of a postcode and the top row represents the second part.

Whenever you see the blue dots on your letters, you know they've been through one of the most sophisticated mechanised postal systems in the world.

Exercise 29

Compilers of dictionaries have to make decisions about the information they want to include about any word and the ways of setting this out.

(a) Make your own list of the information you would want to find about any word if you were consulting a dictionary.

(b) Here are entries from two modern dictionaries for the word 'speed'. Comment, with precise references, on the differences you find between the entries in the dictionaries.

(i) **speed,** *spēd, n. (arch.)* success : a help to success : quickness, velocity.—*v.i. (arch.)* to succeed, fare : to move quickly : to hurry : to drive at high, or at dangerously, unduly, or illegally high, speed.— *v.t.* to give or bring success to : to further : to send forth with good wishes : to bring to an end or finished state : to bring to a sorry plight, to do for (in *passive*) : to send swiftly : to push forward : to haste : to betake with speed : to urge to high speed : to set or regulate the speed of :—*pa.t.* and *pa.p.* **sped** (also **speed'ed**).—*ns.* **speed'boat,** a swift motor-boat; **speed'boating; speed'cop,** (*slang*) a policeman who observes the speed of motorists; **speed'er,** one who, or that which, speeds or promotes speed.—*adj.* **speed'ful.**— *advs.* **speed'fully; speed'ily.**—*ns.* **speed'iness,** quickness; **speed'ing,** success : promotion, furtherance : progressive increase of speed (often with *up*) : motoring at excessive speed.—Also *adj.* —*adj.* **speed'less.**—*ns.* **speedom'eter,** an instrument for measuring speed of vehicles; **speed'ster,** a speedboat : one who speeds; **speed'-up,** an acceleration, esp. in work; **speed'way,** a road for fast traffic : a motor-cycle racing track; **speed'- well,** any species of the scrophulariaceous genus *Veronica,* typically blue-flowered, posterior petals united, posterior sepal wanting.—*adj.* **speed'y,** swift : prompt : soon achieved.—**speed up,** to quicken the rate of working; **speedy cut, cutting,** injury to a horse's fore-leg by the opposite shoe. [O.E. *spéd*; Du. *spoed*.]

(ii) **speed** (spiːd) *n.* **1.** the act or quality of acting or moving fast; rapidity. **2.** the rate at which something moves, is done, or acts. **3.** *Physics.* **a.** a scalar measure of the rate of movement of a body expressed either as the distance travelled divided by the time taken (**average speed**) or the rate of change of position with respect to time at a particular point (**instantaneous speed**). It is measured in metres per second, miles per hour, etc. **b.** another word for **velocity** (sense 2). **4.** a rate of rotation, usually expressed in revolutions per unit time. **5. a.** a gear ratio in a motor vehicle, bicycle, etc. **b.** (*in combination*): *a three- speed gear.* **6.** *Photog.* a numerical expression of the sensitivity .o light of a particular type of film, paper, or plate. See also **ASA/BS, DIN. 7.** *Photog.* a measure of the ability of a lens to pass light from an object to the image position, determined by the aperture and also the transmitting power of the lens. It increases as the f-number is decreased and vice versa. **8.** a slang word for **amphetamine. 9.** *Archaic.* prosperity or success. ~*vb.* **speeds, speed·ing; sped** *or* **speed·ed. 10.** to move up and go or cause to move or go quickly. **11.** (*intr.*) to drive (a motor vehicle) at a high speed, esp. above legal limits. **12.** (*tr.*) to help further the success or completion of. **13.** (*intr.*) *Slang.* to take or be under the influence of amphetamines. **14.** (*intr.*) to operate or run at a high speed. **15.** *Archaic.* **a.** (*intr.*) to prosper or succeed. **b.** (*tr.*) to wish success to. [Old English *spéd* (originally in the sense: success); related to *spówan* to succeed, Latin *spés* hope, Old Slavonic *spêti* to be lucky] —**'speed· er** *n.*

speed·ball *n. Slang.* a mixture of cocaine with morphine or heroin.

speed·boat (ʹspiːd,bəʊt) *n.* a high-speed motorboat having either an inboard or outboard motor.

speed lim·it *n.* the maximum permitted speed at which a vehicle may travel on certain roads.

speed·o (ʹspiːdəʊ) *n., pl.* ·**os.** an informal name for **speedometer.**

speed·om·e·ter (spɪʹdɒmɪtə) *n.* a device fitted to a vehicle to measure and display the speed of travel. See also **mileometer.**

speed·ster (ʹspiːdstə) *n.* a fast car, esp. a sports model.

speed trap *n.* a section of road on which the police check the speed of vehicles, often using radar.

speed up *vb.* (*adv.*) **1.** to increase or cause to increase in speed or rate; accelerate. ~*n.* **speed-up. 2.** an instance of this; acceleration.

speed·way (ʹspiːd,weɪ) *n.* **1. a.** the sport of racing on light powerful motorcycles round cinder tracks. **b.** (*as modifier*): *a speedway track.* **2.** the track or stadium where such races are held. **3.** *U.S.* **a.** a racetrack for cars. **b.** a road on which fast driving is allowed.

speed·well (ʹspiːd,wɛl) *n.* any of various temperate scrophu- lariaceous plants of the genus *Veronica,* such as *V. officinalis* (**common speedwell**) and *V. chamaedrys* (**germander speed- well**), having small blue or pinkish-white flowers.

Speed·writ·ing (ʹspiːd,raɪtɪŋ) *n. Trademark.* a form of short- hand in which alphabetic combinations are used to represent groups of sounds or short common words.

speed·y (ʹspiːdɪ) *adj.* **speed·i·er, speed·i·est. 1.** characterized by speed of motion. **2.** done or decided without delay; quick. —**'speed·i·ly** *adv.* —**'speed·i·ness** *n.*

(c) Find entries for 'speed' from a number of dictionaries, and discuss what the entry indicates about the type of reader for whom the dictionary is intended.

(d) Now imagine that you are compiling a dictionary. Prepare your entries for the following words:

      range   smart   trace

Exercise 30

The following is taken from a modern edition of *Roget's Thesaurus* which groups words and phrases similar in meaning.

(a) Discuss what you find interesting in the grouping of the following words under their headings.

(i)

685. **Leisure** – N. leisure; spare -time, – moments; time, – to spare, – on one's hands; holiday &c. 687; ease.

V. have -leisure &c. *n.*; take one's -time, – leisure, – ease; repose &c. 687; move slowly &c. 275; while away the time &c. 681; be -master of one's time, – an idle man.

Adj. leisurely; slow &c. 275; deliberate, quiet, calm, undisturbed; at -leisure, – one's ease, – a loose end.

(ii)   *

686. **Exertion** – N. exertion, effort, strain, tug, pull, stress, force, pressure, stretch, struggle, spell, spurt.

heft; gymnastics, sports; exercise; wear and tear; ado; toil and trouble; uphill –, hard –, warm- work; harvest time.

labour, work, toil, travail, manual labour, sweat of one's brow, drudgery, slavery, fagging, hammering.

trouble, pains, duty; resolution &c. 604; energy &c. 171.

V. exert oneself; exert –, tax- one's energies.

labour, work, toil, moil, sweat, fag, drudge, slave, wade through, strive, strain; stretch a long arm; pull, tug, ply; do the work.

bestir oneself 682; take trouble, trouble oneself.

work hard; rough it; put forth one's strength; fall to work, bend the bow; buckle to, set one's shoulder to the wheel &c. 604; work like a galley-slave; labour –, work- day and night; redouble one's efforts; do double duty; sit up, burn the -midnight oil, – candle at both ends; stick to &c. 604*a*; fight one's way; lay about one, hammer at.

take pains; do one's -best, – level best, – utmost; do -the best one can, – all in one's power, – as much as in one lies; use one's best endeavour; try one's -best, – utmost; put one's best leg foremost; put all one's strength into, strain every nerve; spare no -efforts, – pains; go all lengths; go through fire and water &c. 604; move heaven and earth, leave no stone unturned.

Adj. labouring &c. *v.*

laborious; strained; toil-, trouble-, burden-, weari-some; uphill; herculean, gymnastic, athletic.

hardworking, painstaking, strenuous, energetic.

hard at work, on the stretch.

Adv. laboriously &c. *adj.*; lustily; with -might and main, – all one's might, – a strong hand, – a sledge-hammer, – much ado; to the best of one's abilities, tooth and nail, hammer and tongs, heart and soul; through thick and thin &c. 604*a*.

by the sweat of one's brow.

(iii)

687. Repose – N. repose, rest; sleep &c. 683.

relaxation, breathing time; halt, pause &c. 142; respite.

day of rest, dies non, Sabbath, Lord's day, holiday, red-letter day, vacation, recess.

V. repose; rest, – and be thankful; take -rest, – one's ease.

relax, unbend, slacken; take breath &c. 689; rest upon one's oars; pause &c. 142; stay one's hand.

lie down; recline; go to -rest, – bed, – sleep &c. 683

take a holiday, shut up shop; lie fallow &c. 681.

Adj. reposing &c. *v.*; unstrained.

Adv. at rest.

(iv)   *

688. Fatigue – N. fatigue; weariness &c. 841; yawning, drowsiness &c. 683; lassitude, tiredness, exhaustion; sweat.

shortness of breath, panting; faintness; collapse, prostration, swoon, fainting, syncope.

V. be -fatigued &c. *adj.*; yawn &c. 683; droop, sink, flag; lose -breath, – wind; gasp, pant, puff, blow. drop, swoon, faint, succumb.

fatigue, tire, weary, bore, irk, fag, jade, harass, exhaust, knock up, wear out, prostrate.

tax, task, strain; over-task, -work, -burden, -tax, -strain.

Adj. fatigued &c. *v.*; weary &c. 841; drowsy &c. 683; drooping &c. *v.*; haggard; toil-, way-worn; footsore, weather-beaten; faint; done –, used –, knocked- up; exhausted, prostrate, spent; over-tired, -spent, -fatigued; forspent.

worn out; battered, shattered, pulled down, seedy, altered.

breath-, wind-less; short of –, out of -breath, – wind; blown, puffing and blowing; short-breathed; broken-, short-winded.

ready to drop, more dead than alive, dog tired, walked off one's legs, tired to death, on one's last legs, played out, hors de combat.

(v)   fatiguing &c. *v.*; tire-, irk-, weari-some; weary; trying.

689. Refreshment – N. bracing &c. *v.*; recovery of -strength &c. 159; restoration, revival &c. 660; repair, refection, refreshment, regalement, bait; relief &c. 834.

V. brace &c. 159; reinvigorate; air, freshen up, refresh, recruit; repair &c. 660; fan.

breathe, respire; draw –, take –, gather –, take a long –, regain –, recover- breath; get better; recover –, regain –, renew- one's strength &c. 159; perk up.

come to oneself &c. 660; feel like a giant refreshed.

Adj. refreshing &c. *v.*; recuperative &c. 660.

refreshed &c. *v.*; un-tired, -wearied.

(b) Now compile entries for a Thesaurus for the following:

Beauty   Ugliness

Comment briefly on some of the words and phrases you have included and why.

Exercise 31

The following composition on the topic 'A summer storm' was written by a student for whom English is probably a second language. Imagine that you are this student's teacher and wish to improve the performance.

(a) Identify the different types of errors which the student's work reveals and suggest ways in which each might be eliminated.

(b) Write a detailed comment for the student pointing out the limitations and indicating how improvement might be achieved.

> A summer storm
>
>   It was a cool and sunny morning, during August, when everything had looked so blooming and bright. The wind was blowing sweetly and the birds were chirping sweetly, that no one could ever tell what would have happened later in the day. Everything seemed to be in its full spring, when the weather forecast people said that there were watching a storm, which is heading in the east and it could pass through Barbados.
>
>   During the early morning hours of seven to ten o'clock, although this storm was being forecast, it still wasn't any changes to say that it would strike us. Work was going along as usual, people were still coming and going to the city, schools were still open for children, and lots of other creativities were still avail.
>
>   As you were coming and going places you could hear persons talking about, the forecast and for the way the atmosphere, it don't even looked as though it would rain, but as the old people often say, the rain don't tell it is going to come down, but it rains.
>
>   Anyhow as the day crept on, there wasn't any signs not even from the sea, so then others say how the men at the met office don't even know what type of clouds are in the sky today. But I as an individual said "What ain't meet you haven't pass you." Some of my friends were there when I made that phrase and said I was old timeage. I said to them you don't see that sometimes when you get up on morning the sun is shining brightly and later in the it rains. These friends of mine tried to convince

me by saying that their would be some dark clouds, that was a fact to a point.

As the day proceeded seemed even longer too, there was a slight change, that was when the sea began to pick up this force. There was also a change in the wind, it become a little cold. Now persons were thinking differently, and saying it like it is going to be a storm for true because all of a sudden outside made a little change. But at this point now the sea pick it up even worse and started getting rough. This now cause the fishermen to pull in their nets and head for shore.

This wasn't easy but there tried their best, and there all came in too. But the winds became stronger the sea became rougher and that is when it all started, the sky became darken, the rain started drizzling, then became harder, lighting and thundering were in protest and no one was looking for this. Lots of low-lined areas became flooded, trees blow down, pen, sty and kennels rock with the toss of the wind, radio stations were off the air, telephones not working properly and electricity off. This was so for hours, then after the storm had pass, it left lots of rain behind, but not much wind, so lots of things were still safe except for the flooding in many areas, person had to evacuated until it was safe for them.

Exercise 32

The following extract is taken from a textbook used with ten year old children in schools 100 years ago.

(a) Comment on the instructions about the uses of the comma, and discuss what is presupposed about the understanding of the pupils.

(b) Examine and comment on what is being tested in the exercise.

(c) Write your own set of instructions about the uses of the comma which can be understood by ten year old pupils at present in school.

(d) Discuss how you would test the understanding of the uses of the comma in a primary school classroom, considering in particular what you would expect of pupils and what form your test would take.

THE COMMA

The comma is one of the points used to separate the different parts of a sentence. There is not an unvarying rule for the insertion of the comma; for in many cases it may be either inserted or omitted with propriety. A few hints will enable you to use this point without difficulty:-

1. When several parts of speech follow each other in the same sentence, they are divided by commas; as, Fire, air, earth, and water were formerly called the four elements; Children should love, honour, and obey their parents.

2. The comma is used to divide the members of a sentence that are closely connected in sense and structure; as, Labour drives the plough, scatters the seed, reaps the harvest, grinds the corn, and converts it into bread; If leaves are disturbed, they will turn again to their former position; The wind being favourable, the vessel set sail.

3. The comma is also used to separate words in apposition; as, James Watt, the improver of the steam engine, was a native of Greenock.

4. Some adverbial and prepositional phrases are enclosed by commas; as, The climate, on the whole, is healthy.

5. Commas are also put before and after words denoting persons or objects addressed; as, This, my lords, is a perilous and tremendous moment.

INSERT COMMAS IN THE FOLLOWING SENTENCES WHERE REQUIRED.
EXERCISE.

Norway was conquered by Canute king of Denmark. Consider for example the various parts of a flower. Rocks waves and winds delay the shattered bark. Taking all the circumstances into account his conduct cannot be blamed. Besides those who work for their living there are others who do not live on their labour at all. Raisins figs oranges and nuts are exported from Spain. Birds fly and fishes swim dogs run frogs leap and serpents creep. When victory was announced the people shouted. If it rain to-morrow we shall not go to the country. Helen can play sing dance draw and embroider. Reflect my friends upon the importance of the undertaking. Having finished dinner he walked into the garden.

CHAPTER 9

Exercise 33

The following is an episode from *Great Expectations* in which Charles Dickens presents a conversation between Pip, his central character, and Joe Gargery, the brother-in-law blacksmith who is only too well aware of his lack of education. Discuss the features of the language which seem to be of interest to Dickens and the ways in which he presents them through the observations of his characters.

One night, I was sitting in the chimney-corner with my slate, expending great efforts on the production of a letter to Joe. I think it must have been a full year after our hunt upon the marshes, for it was a long time after, and it was winter and a hard frost. With an alphabet on the hearth at my feet for reference, I contrived in an hour or two to print and smear this epistle:

'mI deEr JO i opE U r krWitE wEll i opE i shAl soN B haBelL 42 teeDge UJO aN theN wE shOrlbsO glOdd aN wEni M preNgtD 2 u JO woT larX an blEvE ME inF xn PiP.'

There was no indispensable necessity for my communicating with Joe by letter, inasmuch as he sat beside me and we were alone. But, I delivered this written communication (slate and all) with my own hand, and Joe received it, as a miracle of erudition.

'I say, Pip, old chap!' cried Joe, opening his blue eyes wide, 'what a scholar you are! Ain't you?'

'I should like to be,' said I, glancing at the slate as he held it: with a misgiving that the writing was rather hilly.

'Why, here's a J,' said Joe, 'and a O equal to anythink! Here's a J and a O, Pip, and a J-O, Joe.'

I had never heard Joe read aloud to any greater extent than this monosyllable, and I had observed at church last Sunday, when I accidentally held our Prayer-book upside down, that it seemed to suit his convenience quite as well as if it had been all right. Wishing to embrace the present occasion of finding out whether in teaching Joe, I should have to begin quite at the beginning, I said: 'Ah! But read the rest, Joe.'

'The rest, eh, Pip?' said Joe, looking at it with a slowly searching eye. 'One, two, three. Why, here's three Js, and three Os, and three J-O, Joes, in it, Pip!'

I leaned over Joe, and, with the aid of my forefinger, read him the whole letter.

'Astonishing!' said Joe, when I had finished. 'You ARE a scholar.'

'How do you spell Gargery, Joe?' I asked him, with a modest patronage.

'I don't spell it at all,' said Joe.

'But supposing you did?'

'It *can't* be supposed,' said Joe. 'Tho' I'm oncommon fond of reading, too.'

'Are you, Joe?'

'On-common. Give me,' said Joe, 'a good book, or a good newspaper, and sit me down afore a good fire, and I ask no better. Lord!' he continued, after rubbing his knees a little, 'when you *do* come to a J and a O, and says you: "Here, at last, is a J-O, Joe," how interesting reading is!'

Exercise 34

The following episode is from *Moll Flanders* by Daniel Defoe and the use of language is intended to represent the actions and thoughts of the central character. Comment on the features of the language that are of interest to you and discuss what they reveal about the way Moll Flanders is presented.

I went out now by Day-light, and wandred about I knew not whither, and in search of I knew not what, when the Devil put a Snare in my way of a dreadful Nature indeed, and such a one as I have never had before or since; going thro' *Aldersgate-street* there was a pretty little Child had been at a Dancing-School, and was going home, all alone, and my Prompter, like a true Devil, set me upon this innocent Creature; I talk'd to it, and it prattl'd to me again, and I took it by the Hand and led it a long till I came to a pav'd Alley that goes into *Bartholomew Close*, and I led it in there; the Child said that was not its way home; I said, yes, my Dear it is, I'll show you the way home; the Child had a little Necklace on of Gold Beads, and I had my Eye upon that, and in the dark of the Alley I stoop'd, pretending to mend the Child's Clog that was loose, and took off her Necklace and the Child never felt it, and so led the Child on again: Here, I say, the Devil put me upon killing the Child in the dark Alley, that it might not Cry; but the very thought frighted me so that I was ready to drop down, but I turn'd the Child about and bad it go back again, for that was not its way home; the Child said so she would, and I went thro' into *Bartholomew Close*, and then turn'd round to another Passage that goes into *Long-lane*, so away into *Charterhouse-Yard* and out into *St. John's-street*, then crossing into *Smithfield*, went down *Chick-lane* and into *Field-lane* to *Holbourn-bridge*, when mixing with the Crowd of People usually passing there, it was not possible to have been found out; and thus I enterpriz'd my second Sally into the World.

The thoughts of this Booty put out all the thoughts of the first, and the Reflections I had made wore quickly off; Poverty, as I have said, harden'd my Heart, and my own Necessities made me regardless of any thing: The last Affair left no great Concern upon me, for as I did the poor Child no harm, I only said to my self, I had given the Parents a just Reproof for their Negligence in leaving the poor little Lamb to come home by it self, and it would teach them to take more Care of it another time.

This String of Beads was worth about Twelve or Fourteen Pounds, I suppose it might have been formerly the Mother's, for it was too big for the

Child's wear, but that, perhaps, the Vanity of the Mother to have her Child look Fine at the Dancing School, had made her let the Child wear it, and no doubt the Child had a Maid sent to take care of it, but she, like a careless Jade, was taken up perhaps with some Fellow that had met her by the way, and so the poor Baby wandred till it fell into my Hands.

However, I did the Child no harm, I did not so much as fright it, for I had a great many tender Thoughts about me yet, and did nothing but what, as I may say, meer Necessity drove me to.

Exercise 35

The following text is taken from an advertisement for a new sound system. Point to and comment on features of interest to you in its use of language.

There's a bit of a storm about to break on the nation's hi-fi market.

It's called the JVC EX-3 Midi System.

This is a collection of hi-fi components that will deliver sound of exceptional realism and power.

And when we say power, we mean it.

The direct source selector amplifier will generate a sofa-shaking 30 watts RMS output per channel (yes, that's right, *thirty* watts).

No wonder those twin-driver speaker units look as though they mean business.

As well as being fully detached, you'll notice that they employ the latest 'flat woofer' technology.

This, we've discovered, enables compact speakers to produce just as wide a frequency range as any of our conventional-sized rivals.

The rest of the EX-3's specification can't be accused of being conventional, either.

The tape deck boasts a computer track search system, Dolby B noise reduction and soft touch logic controls.

The belt driven turntable features push-button automation and a high quality moving magnet cartridge.

Whilst the quartz-locked digital tuner electronically stores any 12 FM, MW or LW stations you care to choose.

There's even a 10-band graphic equaliser that lets you tailor the sound output to suit the acoustics of your own living room.

May we offer just one word of warning, however?

The EX-3 isn't the only storm that JVC has let loose on the market.

There's the mighty EX-5 and the more compact E22 to be reckoned with, too.

So we have just one thing to say to all our competitors out there.

Head for cover. **JVC**

Exercise 36

The following text is part of an article in a Hotel Group's in-house magazine setting out major improvements in one of its hotels. Discuss the features of the language, commenting in particular on the choice of vocabulary and the structure of sentences.

Why do people choose one hotel over another? Once a price range and geographical considerations are established, what is it that prompts, say, a businessman to stay in one particular hotel? The answer, though extremely elusive, is probably a complicated mix of emotive factors encompassing the hotel's appearance, atmosphere and facilities. It's also very much a subjective problem. What may be chic and sophisticated to one person may appear unsettling and uncomfortable to another. A case, indeed, of one man's meat being another man's *poisson*.

This question of what motivates customers is, of course, a perennial one for hoteliers. One answer is to 'play it safe', to utilise tried and trusted formulae with traditional facilities and certain minimum standards of comfort and service. Their goal would simply be not to disappoint rather than attempting to stimulate.

But there is another approach; a course of action that blends imagination and innovation; an approach which looks beyond traditional solutions. And that's the approach you'll find at the newly refurbished King James Thistle Hotel.

While it may well be true that other four-star hotels in Edinburgh could claim to be among the Capital's best, it is certain that the King James now presents a special character which is unmatched in the city.

Exercise 37

All the following are taken from accident claims forms received by car insurance companies.

(a) Comment on the ways in which the use of language affects the sense of what is stated.

(b) Rewrite each to make the sense of what is intended clearer, and comment on the changes you have had to make.

'To avoid a collision, I ran into the other car.'

'There was no damage to the car as the gatepost will testify.'

'The other man altered his mind so I had to run into him.'

'Dog on road applied brakes causing skid.'

'I can give no details of the accident as I was somewhat concussed at the time.'

'**Wilful damage was done to the upholstery by rats.**'

'A pedestrian hit me and went under my car.'

'**I blew my horn but it would not work as it was stolen.**'

'I unfortunately ran over a pedestrian and the old gentleman was taken to hospital much regretting the circumstances.'

'**I remember nothing after passing the Crown Hotel until I came to and saw Police Constable Brown.**'

'I knocked over a man. He admitted it was his fault as he had been run over before.'

'**Coming home, I drove into the wrong house and collided with a tree I have not got.**'

'I consider that neither vehicle was to blame, but if either was to blame, it was the other one.'

'**Turning into the garage, rear mudguard caught front bumper.**'

'One wheel went into the ditch, my feet jumped from brake to accelerator pedal, leapt across to the other side and jumped into the trunk of a tree.'

'**The accident was due to the other car narrowly missing me.**'

'I collided with a stationary car coming the other way.'

'**If the other driver had stopped a few yards behind himself, the accident would have been avoided.**'

'I thought the side window was down, but it was up as I found when I put my head through it.'

'**I ran into a shop window and sustained injuries to my wife.**'

'My car had to turn sharper than necessary owing to an invisible lorry.'

'**She saw me suddenly, lost her head and we met.**'

'I bumped into a lamp-post obscured by pedestrians.'

'**I was driving down the main road with my husband at the wheel.**'

'I know I was only doing 30 mph because there was a police car behind me.'

'**Cow wandered into my car. I was afterwards informed that the cow was half-witted.**'

'Three women were talking to one another and when one stepped backwards and one stepped forward I had to have an accident.'

Exercise 38

The following episode is from *Tess of the D'Urbervilles* by Thomas Hardy. It occurs early in the novel and presents not only the heroine of the novel, Tess, and how she appears and how she speaks, but also the way Tess's father and the girls of the area speak.

Comment on the varieties of uses of language in the episode, what effect they are intended to give, and how successful they are for you.

They came round by The Pure Drop Inn, and were turning out of the high road to pass through a wicket-gate into the meadows, when one of the women said—

'The Lord-a-Lord! Why, Tess Durbeyfield, if there isn't thy father riding hwome in a carriage!'

A young member of the band turned her head at the exclamation. She was a fine and handsome girl—not handsomer than some others, possibly—but her mobile peony mouth and large innocent eyes added eloquence to colour and shape. She wore a red ribbon in her hair, and was the only one of the white company who could boast of such a pronounced adornment. As she looked round Durbeyfield was seen moving along the road in a chaise belonging to The Pure Drop, driven by a frizzle-headed brawny damsel with her gown-sleeves rolled above her elbows. This was the cheerful servant of that establishment, who, in her part of factotum, turned groom and ostler at times. Durbeyfield, leaning back, and with his eyes closed luxuriously, was waving his hand above his head, and singing in a slow recitative—

'I've-got-a-gr't-family-vault-at-Kingsbere—and knighted forefathers-in-lead-coffins-there!'

The clubbists tittered, except the girl called Tess—in whom a slow heat seemed to rise at the sense that her father was making himself foolish in their eyes.

'He's tired, that's all,' she said hastily, 'and he has got a lift home, because our own horse has to rest today.'

'Bless thy simplicity, Tess,' said her companions. 'He's got his market-nitch. Haw-haw!'

'Look here; I won't walk another inch with you, if you say any jokes about him!' Tess cried, and the colour upon her cheeks spread over her face and neck. In a moment her eyes grew moist, and her glance drooped to the ground. Perceiving that they had really pained her they said no more, and order again prevailed. Tess's pride would not allow her to turn her head again, to learn what her father's meaning was, if he had any; and thus she moved on with the whole body to the enclosure where there was to be dancing on the green. By the time the spot was reached she had recovered her equanimity, and tapped her neighbour with her wand and talked as usual.

Tess Durbeyfield at this time of her life was a mere vessel of emotion untinctured by experience. The dialect was on her tongue to some extent, despite the village school: the characteristic intonation of that dialect for this district being the voicing approximately rendered by the syllable UR, probably as rich an utterance as any to be found in human speech. The pouted-up deep red mouth to which this syllable was native had hardly as yet settled into its definite shape, and her lower lip had a way of thrusting the middle of her top one upward, when they closed together after a word.

Phases of her childhood lurked in her aspect still. As she walked along to-day, for all her bouncing handsome womanliness, you could sometimes see her twelfth year in her cheeks, or her ninth sparkling from her eyes; and even her fifth would flit over the curves of her mouth now and then.

Yet few knew, and still fewer considered this. A small minority, mainly strangers, would look long at her in casually passing by, and grow momentarily fascinated by her freshness, and wonder if they would ever see her again: but to almost everybody she was a fine and picturesque girl, and no more.

Exercise 39

The following is part of a leaflet encouraging short holidays in Europe.

(a) Discuss the uses of language in the extract, considering, in particular, the type of reader for whom it is intended.

(b) What changes would you wish to make in the expression of the leaflet if it were to be specifically aimed at people of your age group?

THE PRICE IS RIGHT...

You'll find European Savers among the most attractive travel bargains to the Continent. London to Paris or Amsterdam and return – just £33, Brussels £32, and there are many, many more to choose from. InterCity Europe services are comfortable and convenient. Whether you travel

Fancy a few days away from it all? Here's the answer. "European Savers" are the ideal way to enjoy a short break on the Continent. And with InterCity Europe it's so easy and economical by rail and sea. Just imagine, within a few short hours from London you could be sipping an evening cocktail in romantic Paris, or taking in the exciting atmosphere of Amsterdam. Only five hours from London by rail and Jetfoil, and you're admiring the architectural splendour of Brussels.

by Jetfoil, Hovercraft or ship you will be sure of a relaxing journey with plenty of room to stretch your legs. Take in a breath of sea air and enjoy a drink or a meal on the way. Fast rail services speed you to and from the Continental ports. When you travel InterCity Europe the journey is part of the fun, especially for families.

Take a look through this leaflet and you'll find that InterCity Europe's European Savers open up a whole range of travel opportunities.

And remember, you can buy your European Saver ticket to travel from London or any British Rail station. Ask for details at your nearest British Rail travel centre or European Rail appointed travel agent. Advice about hotel accommodation at your destination can be obtained from the appropriate national tourist office or your local travel agent.

Whether it's a short break holiday or business trip, European Savers offer a wide range of destinations in France, Belgium, Luxembourg, Holland, Germany and Switzerland – allowing up to 4 nights away, perfect for that long weekend break!

InterCity Europe

Exercise 40

The following advertisement for the Welsh Tourist Board emphasises the inspiration and creativity that the Welsh landscape can arouse. With close reference to details of the text, discuss how the effect is achieved through the choice of vocabulary, the grammatical structures, and the layout of the text, as well as the organisation of the information.

What Dylan Thomas saw in Wales.

As well as the bars he's more commonly associated with, it was the sand bars of the Afon Taf which inspired Dylan Marlais Thomas.

It's his Georgian boathouse, built into the side of a cliff below the town of Laugharne, that overlooks the estuary.

The estuary of three rivers, in fact, which escape to distant Carmarthen Bay on Wales' south coast.

"Under Milk Wood" was written here and, although he travelled widely abroad, it was his native country in which he worked best.

"On high ground," says his biographer, Paul Ferris, "looking down on things: usually the sea, usually in Wales."

No wonder he was so prolific. The coastline in that part of the world is almost overcrowded with the sort of seascape so beloved of the poet.

Within easy reach of Laugharne, to the east, he could stroll the thirty unspoilt miles of bays and dunes around the Gower Peninsula.

Or, to the west, take his pick of the rugged sea cliffs and sheltered sandy coves of Pembrokeshire's St. Brides Bay.

Further up the coast, there's another, earlier, Thomas residence.

A cliff top bungalow which overlooks the tiny herring and lobster port of New Quay and some of the finest beaches in Britain.

Elsewhere other, perhaps more serene, shores beckoned.

Like the stunning Mawddach estuary in Gwynedd where, in another age, Wordsworth was a frequent visitor.

Or the rural calm of the Lleyn Peninsula where Shelley wrote "Queen Mab."

But if the Welsh coastline has attracted some of our finest writers, it has also attracted the angler, the sailor, and the hiker.

And even, dare we say it, the sunbather.

Bringing them back year upon year.

For details, send for our '84 Summer Brochure and don't lose the pen.

If you come to Wales, you never know, you just may need it.

For FREE 132 page colour brochure write to: Wales Tourist Board, Department H9, P.O. Box 1, Cardiff CF1 2XN.

Name _____

Address _____

_____ Postcode _____

24 hour answering service 0222-494473. Also available at Travel Agents. In London call at our Information Centre, 2/4 Maddox Street (off Regent St.) Tel: 01-409 0969.

Exercise 41

The following piece of writing by William Golding makes considerable use of variations in choice of vocabulary, grammatical forms, and sentence structures. Discuss, with precise reference, those features of the language that are of most interest to you and say what they contribute to the overall tone of the writing.

East Coast blanked out from North Carolina right up to the Canadian border; a half-continent under a pat of fog; nothing visible but the extreme tip of the Empire State Building; planes grounded. Fog, the airman's common cold; all the resources of science are squeaking and gibbering under it; lights blink unseen, radar echoes quiver and ping; the gigantic aircraft lumber round the ramps and aprons like death's-head moths in cold weather; money leaks away. We, the privileged, sit in a sort of underground air-raid shelter, racked by public-address systems and blasts of furious air-conditioning. Evening drags into night. Everything is astonishingly dirty, and time itself is stale. We sit.

Most passengers drift away, to go by train, or try a night's sleep in the airport hotel. But I am going too far to get there any way but by jet. Tomorrow I give the first of three lectures in Los Angeles, on the other side of America. Here it is midnight, or past midnight, or feels like midnight. I am late already, and must go by what flight I can. I cannot telegraph anyone, even though I shall land at the wrong airport.

A loudspeaker honks and burbles. Incredibly, and for the next hour, we have take-off and landing limits. Our plane is getting through; and sure enough, presently it bumbles out of the fog from the runway. I go with our group to Gate Nine, shudder into a freezing night with a dull grey roof. The jet crawls towards us, howling and whistling with rage, perhaps at the fog or perhaps at the human bondage which keeps it only just under control. For a moment or two, it faces us—no, is end-on to us; for here there is no touch of human, or animal, or insect, no face—only four holes that scream like nothing else in creation. Then it huddles round and is still. Doors open and two streams of passengers ooze out. Their faces are haggard. They ignore the night that has caught up with them. They stagger, or walk with the stiff gait of stage sleep-walkers. One or two look stunned, as if they know it is midnight more or less but cannot remember if it is today or tomorrow midnight and why or what. Strange vehicles flashing all over with red lights come out of the darkness, not for the passengers, but to tend the jet. They crouch under the wings and the front end, attach themselves by tubes while all their lights flash, and lights on the jet flash, and the engines sink from a wail to a moan—a note, one might think, of resignation, as if the machine now recognizes that it is caught and will have to do the whole thing over again. But for half an hour they feed it well, while it sucks or they blow, and we stand, imprisoned by the freezing cold and our own need to be somewhere else. Jet travel is a great convenience.

Exercise 42

The wording of the following advertisement is based on a well-known nursery rhyme.

(a) Discuss the ways in which language is used in the advertisement.

(b) Compose your own advertisement for a real or imaginary product using the format of another nursery rhyme.

This is the girl
that watched the TV
that drowned the sound
that came from the tap
that filled the bath
that overflowed
onto the landing
down the stairs
soaking the sitting room
drenching the dining room
and flooding the floors
of the home that Jack
had insured with
Sun Alliance.

Would you be so lucky?

I would like to know more about the advantages of insuring my home contents. Plus options to include Accidental Damage Cover; "All Risks" on personal valuables; money and credit cards; pedal cycles; food in the freezer; domestic pets and buildings.
Post the coupon now for our free information pack with details of our convenient monthly instalment scheme — at a low service charge of 6% (**APR 13.7%**) or contact your insurance adviser.
To: Home Insurance, DMD, Sun Alliance Insurance Group, FREEPOST, Horsham, West Sussex RH12 1ZA. No stamp required. No obligation. No Salesman will call.
Please send me full facts about Sun Alliance Home Insurance.

Name_____

Address_____

_____ Postcode_____

My present insurance policy
expires on_____

BIOR

 **SUN ALLIANCE**
HOME INSURANCE

Exercise 43

1. The following is taken from *The Young Visiters*, a story about society life
   written by Daisy Ashford when she was nine.

   (a) Comment on the features of the language which for you indicate
       the age of the writer.

   (b) Comment on the features of the language which for you indicate a
       maturity greatly in advance of the writer's age. What can you
       deduce from these about the writer?

A PROPOSALE

Next morning while imbibing his morning tea beneath his pink silken quilt
Bernard decided he must marry Ethel with no more delay. I love the girl he
said to himself and she must be mine but I somehow feel I can not propose in
London it would not be seemly in the city of London. We must go for a day
in the country and when surrounded by the gay twittering of the birds and
the smell of the cows I will lay my suit at her feet and he waved his arm
wildly at the gay thought. Then he sprang from bed and gave a rat-tat at
Ethel's door.

Are you up my dear he called.

Well not quite said Ethel hastilly jumping from her downy nest.

Be quick cried Bernard I have a plan to spend a day near Windsor Castle
and we will take our lunch and spend a happy day.

Oh Hurrah shouted Ethel I shall soon be ready as I had my bath last night
so wont wash very much now.

No dont said Bernard and added in a rather fervent tone through the
chink of the door you are fresher than the rose my dear no soap could make
you fairer.

Then he dashed off very embarrased to dress. Ethel blushed and felt a bit
excited as she heard the words and she put on a new white muslin dress in a
fit of high spirits. She looked very beautifull with some red roses in her hat
and the dainty red ruge in her cheeks looked quite the thing. Bernard heaved
a sigh and his eyes flashed as he beheld her and Ethel thorght to herself what
a fine type of manhood he reprisented with his nice thin legs in pale broun
trousers and well fitting spats and a red rose in his button hole and rather a
sporting cap which gave him a great air with its quaint check and little flaps
to pull down if necessary. Off they started the envy of all the waiters.

They arrived at Windsor very hot from the jorney and Bernard at once
hired a boat to row his beloved up the river. Ethel could not row but she
much enjoyed seeing the tough sunburnt arms of Bernard tugging at the oars
as she lay among the rich cushons of the dainty boat. She had a rarther lazy
nature but Bernard did not know of this. However he soon got dog tired and
sugested lunch by the mossy bank.

Oh yes said Ethel quickly opening the sparkling champaigne.

Dont spill any cried Bernard as he carved some chicken.

They eat and drank deeply of the charming viands ending up with
merangs and choclates.

Let us now bask under the spreading trees said Bernard in a passiunate tone.

Oh yes lets said Ethel and she opened her dainty parasole and sank down upon the long green grass. She closed her eyes but she was far from asleep. Bernard sat beside her in profound silence gazing at her pink face and long wavy eye lashes. He puffed at his pipe for some moments while the larks gaily caroled in the blue sky. Then he edged a trifle closer to Ethels form.

Ethel he murmered in a trembly voice.

Oh what is it said Ethel hastily sitting up.

Words fail me ejaculated Bernard horsly my passion for you is intense he added fervently. It has grown day and night since I first beheld you.

Oh said Ethel in supprise I am not prepared for this and she lent back against the trunk of the tree.

Bernard placed one arm tightly round her. When will you marry me Ethel he uttered you must be my wife it has come to that I love you so intensly that if you say no I shall perforce dash my body to the brink of yon muddy river he panted wildly.

Oh dont do that implored Ethel breathing rarther hard.

Then say you love me he cried.

Oh Bernard she sighed fervently I certinly love you madly you are to me like a Heathen god she cried looking at his manly form and handsome flashing face I will indeed marry you.

How soon gasped Bernard gazing at her intensly.

As soon as possible said Ethel gently closing her eyes.

My Darling whispered Bernard and he seiezed her in his arms we will be marrid next week.

Oh Bernard muttered Ethel this is so sudden.

No no cried Bernard and taking the bull by both horns he kissed her violently on her dainty face. My bride to be he murmered several times.

Ethel trembled with joy as she heard the mistick words.

Oh Bernard she said little did I ever dream of such as this and she suddenly fainted into his out stretched arms.

Oh I say gasped Bernard and laying the dainty burden on the grass he dashed to the waters edge and got a cup full of the fragrant river to pour on his true loves pallid brow.

She soon came to and looked up with a sickly smile. Take me back to the Gaierty hotel she whispered faintly.

With pleasure my darling said Bernard I will just pack up our viands ere I unloose the boat.

Ethel felt better after a few drops of champagne and began to tidy her hair while Bernard packed the remains of the food. Then arm in arm they tottered to the boat.

I trust you have not got an illness my darling murmered Bernard as he helped her in.

Oh no I am very strong said Ethel I fainted from joy she added to explain matters.

Oh I see said Bernard handing her a cushon well some people do he added kindly and so saying they rowed down the dark stream now flowing silently beneath a golden moon. All was silent as the lovers glided home with joy in

their hearts and radiunce on their faces only the sound of the mystearious
water lapping against the frail vessel broke the monotony of the night.
So I will end my chapter.

2 The following texts were written by two children on the same topic,
"Me". Make as close a grammatical analysis of them as you can, and
comment on some of the linguistic features revealed by such an analysis:

(a) my hobbie is collecting stamps and my age is 8 years of age and my
favourite subject is topic and maths they are very good I think and the
colour of my eyes are blue and for pets I have goldfish and a tortoies
and the colour of my hair is bloned and I like school very much because
sometimes we stay in at last play and do our yoned up writing and I
like yoned up writing very much the people who sit next to me are
Gina and Aled and the child who sits next to Aled is Robert.

(b) Now that I'm eleven, and although it doesn't seem very long ago since
I was ten when I was in Mr Jones class, I'm now in Mrs Smith's class. I
have very dark brown hair and I like drawing very much indeed. In
the mornings I have to get up early because I am a milk boy and on
Friday I have a very hard job because I have to get up in the morning
and do the milk and then I have to do the banking system. My features
are brown eyes dark brown hair and a round face. I live quite near the
school which is very handy because I have to get to school pretty early.

3 Comment on the main features of the following two passages written by
girls of nine. (The diagonal strokes indicate the ends of lines.)

(a)   HOW I LEARNT TO CYCLE
I really learnt to cycle through/Andrew's birthday, because he got a/
bicycle then from Mummy and Daddy./When we got down, we found it
and/pushed it out into the garden/straight after breakfast. Andrew/let
me have a go first, but no/sooner had I got on, than I fell/off. So I asked
Andrew to have/a go, and he got right round the/first time.

The next morning I fell off/once into the flower bed, but went/right
round the garden.

By this time Andrew could ride/beautifully, and I was improving./That
week-end I found that/I could cycle round the garden/twice, but when
it came to/getting of I couldn't, so I had/to go round and round until/I
fell off.

Now I can ride round about/fifty times without falling off, and/I can
manover the bicycle in/and out of the flower beds.

Our neighbours little girl, Angela, has/a bicycle as well, and we often/
play racing round our gardens/with her.

Andrew likes to go fast, but when/he is cycling round the corner/by the
wall, he usually crashes/headlong into it, or scaps the/bicycle on it.

Andrew has a passion for/standing in your way, and once/he was lying down where I I/was going to stop. I nearly ran/over him, but I just managed/to brake in time, almost going over/the handlebars myself.

(b)   A FUNNY THING THAT HAPPENED TO ME.
A funny thing that happed to me/was when I was walking down the/ road one day when I saw some/men opening a window and/climbing in it so I went to inves-/tigate I went behind a bush and/hid I was going to sneze so I held/my nose with my finger but I/could not hold it and I snezed/so hard that the men came out/to see what it was, they saw me/ hideing and they grabed me and/me up. and pushed me into the/van that was parked outside./the shut the van door and locked/the door and I was locked in/soon they came and shoved some/boxes into the van and I thought/they were thieves I tried to get/out and tell the police but/ they had locked the door again so/I could'nt. Soon they got in the/cab and drove off they went about/three miles away to a farm and then/they left me. I went into the/farm house and told the farmer/he asked me what the number of/the van, and I said it was KMO/613. The farmer said thank you/very much and the farmer's/wife gave me some thing to/ eat. I went with the farmer to/the police and they asked the/farmer lots of questions. Soon/he had finished talked so we/went with the police man/to the farm and we picked/up the tracks from there. We/ discovered the we we we van 4 miles/from the farm the bandits/were in the van and they were not/expecting the police. and they jumped/upon the Bandits. Your under arest/yelled one of the policemen so the/robers went to the police and I was/rewarded ten pound from the/police.

Exercise 44

The following four letters were written by people for whom English is a foreign language. The sincerity of the contents is readily apparent but the expression is not what would be expected of a native writer of English.

(a) Write out each letter in Standard English spelling, vocabulary and grammar.

(b) Comment on any difficulties you found in rewriting the letters.

(c) List and discuss details of the writing in each letter which do not conform to Standard English. With precise reference to information provided in Parts II–V, suggest 'rules' which each writer would need to grasp.

(i) **Letter 1** (from China)

Dear Sir,
    Mr. Cheung and I arrived at Beijing 17th December 1984, on schedule.
    During our staying in England, your energetic collaboration and kindly caring of us enable to gain successes of the disassembling work, I would like to take the liberty to express my heartfelt thanks.

Hoping you have a Merry Christmas and Happy New Year.

Cordial Yours, L. J. Wang, Gen, Eng.

(ii) **Letter 2** (from China)

Dear Sir,

I have the honour to inform you that Mr Yeung, was promoted from an engineer to a Director (Executive) of our works and had been approved and authorized by the higher organization which came into effect January 1st, 1986.

As you had been contacted with him twice in the year of 1985, and have a good understanding of him by practical work. He is more competent leading person in this works with a 4000 employees, and has a sound knowledge not only in metallurgical fields but also well educated intellectual to exercise for his new post. Moreover, his relatively younger age and enthusiusm makes him meeting the requirements of leadership in the process of building up modern industrialization of our country.

It is advicable that contact with him and any problem will be solved reasonablly. Your telex and letters referring to him will be in the first priority to conduct.

I remain,

Yours faithfully,

W. H. Lee

W. H. Lee, Consultant.

Letter 3 (from Japan)

Dear Dr Brown,

How are you getting along? I should have written to you earlier. Don't think ill of me for not writing for a long time. I had a nice time in two days at Chipping Campden. That Robert Dover's Game, Wake and beautiful sunset was given violent impression for me. I don't forget that nice days.

That night I took many photoes. I sent photoes, if you please, you should hand your friends.

I hope to go to anywhere in England last three months. If I have a time, will visit to you.

Hoping you will have a very nice days.

Very respectfully yours,
Keiichi Mitsubishi

Letter 4 (from France)

Dear Sir,

It is much times I do recherches on the old sports of combat and I have visited, it is 15 days, the actual exhibition in British Museum and I have readed in the catalogue, writted by Mr Paul Goldman the institution in the games of 1612 by Captain Robert Dover . . . 'shin-kicking'.

I have seen in British Library the Caulfield's book of 1818 in reference, but it haven't bibliography of Robert Dover.

Mr Paul Goldman have writted to me; in fact he has finded this information in H. L. Bennett's book 'Chipping-Campden – a short history and guide' an he has sent to me your adress for precise information.

At the British exhibition it is a print of (circa 1699) watching two *wrestlers*; I hope it is not this print only witch has had a no good interpretation for the subject of 'Shin-kicking'.

Please, could you give me information or photocopy for to said me, when the type of match has begun in England and what are the documents for that.

Sincerely yours,

Paul Duparc

Please scuse very much my bad English.

Exercise 45

The following episode is from *Pride and Prejudice* (1813) by Jane Austen.

(a) Comment on the varieties of language, particularly the dialogue and exchanges between Catherine and Isabella.

(b) Write out the first twenty-five lines as you imagine the conversation might be expressed if it occurred between two of your friends. Keep in mind the tone of the writing. Then give your comments on the changes you felt were necessary and why.

'But, my dearest Catherine, have you settled what to wear on your head to-night? I am determined at all events to be dressed exactly like you. The men take notice of *that* sometimes, you know.'

'But it does not signify, if they do,' said Catherine, very innocently.

5　'Signify! Oh heavens! I make it a rule never to mind what they say. They are very often amazingly impertinent if you do not treat them with spirit, and make them keep their distance.'

'Are they?—Well, I never observed *that*. They always behave very well to me.'

10　'Oh! they give themselves such airs. They are the most conceited creatures in the world, and think themselves of so much importance! By the bye, though I have thought of it a hundred times, I have always forgot to ask you what is your favourite complexion in a man. Do you like them best dark or fair?'

15　'I hardly know. I never much thought about it. Something between both, I think, Brown—not fair, and not very dark.'

'Very well, Catherine. That is exactly he. I have not forgot your description of Mr. Tilney;—"a brown skin, with dark eyes, and rather dark hair."—Well, my taste is different. I prefer light eyes, and as to

20 complexion—do you know—I like a sallow better than any other. You
must not betray me, if you should ever meet with one of your
acquaintance answering that description.'

'Betray you!—What do you mean?'

'Nay, do not distress me. I believe I have said too much. Let us drop the
25 subject.'

Catherine, in some amazement, complied; and after remaining a few
moments silent, was on the point of reverting to what interested her at
that time rather more than any thing else in the world, Laurentina's
skeleton; when her friend prevented her, by saying—'For Heaven's sake!
30 let us move away from this end of the room. Do you know, there are two
odious young men who have been staring at me this half hour. They
really put me quite out of countenance. Let us go and look at the arrivals.
They will hardly follow us there.'

Away they walked to the book; and while Isabella examined the
35 names, it was Catherine's employment to watch the proceedings of these
alarming young men.

'They are not coming this way, are they? I hope they are not so
impertinent as to follow us. Pray let me know if they are coming. I am
determined I will not look up.'

40 In a few moments Catherine, with unaffected pleasure, assured her
that she need not be longer uneasy, as the gentlemen had just left the
Pump-room.

'And which way are they gone?' said Isabella, turning hastily round.
'One was a very good-looking young man.'

45 'They went towards the churchyard.'

'Well, I am amazingly glad I have got rid of them! And now, what say
you to going to Edgar's Buildings with me, and looking at my new hat?
You said you should like to see it.'

Catherine readily agreed. 'Only,' she added, 'perhaps we may
50 overtake the two young men.'

'Oh! never mind that. If we make haste, we shall pass by them
presently, and I am dying to shew you my hat.'

'But if we only wait a few minutes, there will be no danger of our seeing
them at all.'

55 'I shall not pay them any such compliment, I assure you. I have no
notion of treating men with such respect. *That* is the way to spoil them.'

Catherine had nothing to oppose against such reasoning; and
therefore, to shew the independence of Miss Thorpe, and her resolution of
humbling the sex, they set off immediately as fast as they could walk, in
60 pursuit of the two young men.

Exercise 46

Read the following advertisement.

(a) Comment on its uses of language to make its appeal, in particular the choice of vocabulary, the structure of sentences, and the use of images.

(b) Compose an advertisement, using similar strategies, for a building you know well.

Identikit housing means boring housing. Little boxes packed in rows. But here's an interesting alternative. Salvesen. A wider range of house types, more variety in design and more thought in planning and layout. At Salvesen we give you more choice, so that your home and your surroundings suit you, not someone else. Individual homes, built to the highest specifications, yet still representing value for money. Surprising the difference a little imagination makes. Although by now you'd think everyone would have realised. Only shoes should live in boxes.

What House
Best Value for
Money Builder
1985

Exercise 47

Here is an episode from *Headlong Hall* (1816), a novel by Thomas Love Peacock, which pokes fun at several fashions of his age.

Mr. Milestone is a 'landscape gardener' who believes he can 'improve' the scenery of Squire Headlong's estate in North Wales. The squire, as his name indicates, takes up Miles Milestone's suggestions enthusiastically. Mr Cranium and Mr Panscope are two 'philosophers' who tend to take themselves seriously.

With close reference to details of the text, discuss how Peacock's uses of language, particularly his choice of vocabulary and grammatical structures, contribute to the humour of the episode.

The squire and Mr Milestone, as we have already said, had set out immediately after breakfast to examine the capabilities of the scenery. The object that most attracted Mr Milestone's admiration was a ruined tower on a projecting point of rock almost totally overgrown with ivy. This ivy, Mr Milestone observed, required trimming and clearing in various parts: a little pointing and polishing was also necessary for the dilapidated walls: and the whole effect would be materially increased by a plantation of spruce fir, interspersed with cypress and juniper, the present rugged and broken ascent from the land side being first converted into a beautiful slope, which might be easily effected by blowing up a part of the rock with gunpowder, laying on a quantity of fine mold, and covering the whole with an elegant stratum of turf.

Squire Headlong caught with avidity at this suggestion; and, as he had always a store of gunpowder in the house, for the accommodation of himself and his shooting visitors, and for the supply of a small battery of cannon, which he kept for his private amusement, he insisted on commencing operations immediately. Accordingly, he bounded back to the house, and very speedily returned, accompanied by the little butler, and half a dozen servants and labourers, with pickaxes and gunpowder, a hanging stove and a poker, together with a basket of cold meat and two or three bottles of Madeira: for the Squire thought, with many others, that a copious supply of provision is a very necessary ingredient in all rural amusements.

Mr Milestone superintended the proceedings. The rock was excavated, the powder introduced, the apertures strongly blockaded with fragments of stone: a long train was laid to a spot which Mr Milestone fixed on as sufficiently remote from the possibility of harm: the Squire seized the poker, and, after flourishing it in the air with a degree of dexterity which induced the rest of the party to leave him in solitary possession of an extensive circumference, applied the end of it to the train; and the rapidly communicated ignition ran hissing along the surface of the soil.

At this critical moment, Mr Cranium and Mr Panscope appeared at the top of the tower, which, unseeing and unseen, they had ascended on the opposite side to that where the Squire and Mr Milestone were conducting their operations. Their sudden appearance a little dismayed the Squire, who, however, comforted himself with the reflection, that the tower was perfectly safe, or at least was intended to be so, and that his friends were in no probable danger but of a knock on the head from a flying fragment of stone.

The succession of these thoughts in the mind of the Squire was commensurate in rapidity to the progress of the ignition, which having reached its extremity, the explosion took place, and the shattered rock was hurled into the air in the midst of fire and smoke.

Mr Milestone had properly calculated the force of the explosion, for the tower remained untouched: but the Squire, in his consolatory reflections, had omitted the consideration of the influence of sudden fear, which had so violent an effect on Mr Cranium, who was just commencing a speech concerning the very fine prospect from the top of the tower, that, cutting short the thread of his observations, he bounded, under the elastic influence of terror, several feet into the air. His ascent being unluckily a little out of the perpendicular, he descended with a proportionate curve from the apex of his projection, and alighted, not on the wall of the tower, but in an ivy-bush by its side, which, giving way beneath him, transferred him to a tuft of hazel at its base, which, after upholding him an instant, consigned him to the boughs of an ash that had rooted itself in a fissure about half way down the rock, which finally transmitted him to the waters below.

Squire Headlong anxiously watched the tower as the smoke which at first enveloped it rolled away; but when this shadowy curtain was withdrawn, and Mr Panscope was discovered, *solus* in a tragical attitude, his apprehensions became boundless, and he concluded that the unlucky collision of a flying fragment of rock had indeed emancipated the spirit of the craniologist from its terrestrial bondage.

Exercise 48

(a) Here is a poem by Roy Fisher about a fountain in a public park. Refer in detail to the different uses of language, in particular the choice of vocabulary, the grammatical structures, and the layout of the text, and discuss their impact on the effectiveness of the poem.

THE MEMORIAL FOUNTAIN

The fountain plays
            through summer dusk in gaunt shadows,
black constructions
            against a late clear sky,
water in the basin
            where the column falls
        shaking,
rapid and wild,
            in cross-waves, in back-waves,
        the light glinting and blue,
as in a wind
            though there is none.
                                    Harsh
skyline!

        Far-off scaffolding
bitten against the air.

           Sombre mood
in the presence of things,
        no matter what things;
respectful sepia.

        This scene:
        people on the public seats
        embedded in it, darkening
        intelligences of what's visible;
        private, given over, all of them—

Many scenes.

Still sombre.

As for the fountain:
        nothing in the describing
beyond what shows
        for anyone;
    above all
no 'atmosphere'.
        It's like this often—
I don't exaggerate.

        And the scene?
        a thirty-five-year-old man,
        poet,
           by temper, realist,
        watching a fountain
        and the figures round it
        in garish twilight,
             working
        to distinguish an event
        from an opinion;
           this man,
        intent and comfortable—

Romantic notion.

(b) Comment on the special qualities of the language and the stylistic
    features of this poem:

THE WINDHOVER
To Christ our Lord

I caught this morning morning's minion, King-
    dom of daylight's dauphin, dapple-dawn-drawn Falcon, in his riding
    Of the rolling level underneath him steady air, and striding

High there, how he rung upon the rein of a wimpling wing
In his ecstasy! then off, off forth on swing,
   As a skate's heel sweeps smooth on a bow-bend: the hurl and gliding
   Rebuffed the big wind. My heart in hiding
Stirred for a bird,—the achieve of, the mastery of the thing!

Brute beauty and valour and act, oh, air, pride, plume, here
   Buckle! AND the fire that breaks from thee then, a billion
Times told lovelier, more dangerous, O my chevalier!

   No wonder of it: sheer plod makes plough down sillion
Shine and blue-beak embers, ah my dear,
   Fall, gall themselves, and gash gold-vermilion.

G.M. Hopkins

Exercise 49

Here are the opening scenes of a play called *Marty* by Paddy Chayefsky.
Discuss the varieties of language used by the writer to set his scene,
introduce his characters, represent the ways they speak, and provide
guidance for a director of the play.

ACT I

   FADE IN: *A butcher shop in the Italian district of New York City. Actually, we
fade in on a close-up of a butcher's saw being carefully worked through a side of beef,
and we dolly back to show the butcher at work, and then the whole shop. The butcher
is a mild-mannered, stout, short, balding young man of thirty-six. His charm lies in
an almost indestructible good-natured amiability.*
   *The shop contains three women customers. One is a young mother with a baby
carriage. She is chatting with a second woman of about forty at the door. The
customer being waited on at the moment is a stout, elderly Italian woman who is
standing on tiptoe, peering over the white display counter, checking the butcher as he
saws away.*
ITALIAN WOMAN: Your kid brother got married last Sunday, eh, Marty?
MARTY: [*Absorbed in his work*] That's right, Missus Fusari. It was a very nice
affair.
ITALIAN WOMAN: That's the big tall one, the fellow with the mustache.
MARTY: [*Sawing away*] No, that's my other brother Freddie. My other
brother Freddie, he's been married four years already. He lives down on
Quincy Street. The one who got married Sunday, that was my little brother
Nickie.
ITALIAN WOMAN: I thought he was a big, tall, fat fellow. Didn't I meet him
here one time? Big, tall, fat fellow, he tried to sell me life insurance?
MARTY: [*Sets the cut of meat on the scale, watches its weight register*] No, that's my
sister Margaret's husband Frank. My sister Margaret, she's married to the
insurance salesman. My sister Rose, she married a contractor. They moved
to Detroit last year. And my other sister, Frances, she got married about two
and a half years ago in Saint John's Church on Adams Boulevard. Oh, that

was a big affair. Well, Missus Fusari, that'll be three dollars, ninetyfour cents. How's that with you?

The Italian woman produces an old leather change purse from her pocketbook and painfully extracts three single dollar bills and ninety-four cents to the penny and lays the money piece by piece on the counter.

YOUNG MOTHER: [*Calling from the door*] Hey, Marty, I'm inna hurry.

MARTY: [*Wrapping the meat, calls amiably back*] You're next right now, Missus Canduso.

The old Italian lady has been regarding Marty with a baleful scowl.

ITALIAN WOMAN: Well, Marty, when you gonna get married? You should be ashamed. All your brothers and sisters, they all younger than you, and they married, and they got children. I just saw your mother inna fruit shop, and she says to me: "Hey, you know a nice girl for my boy Marty?" Watsa matter with you? That's no way. Watsa matter with you? Now, you get married, you hear me what I say?

MARTY: [*Amiably*] I hear you, Missus Fusari.

The old lady takes her parcel of meat, but apparently feels she still hasn't quite made her point.

ITALIAN WOMAN: My son Frank he was married when he was nineteen years old. Watsa matter with you?

MARTY: Missus Fusari, Missus Canduso over there, she's inna big hurry, and . . .

ITALIAN WOMAN: You be ashamed of yourself.

She takes her package of meat, turns, and shuffles to the door and exits. Marty gathers up the money on the counter, turns to the cash register behind him to ring up the sale.

YOUNG MOTHER: Marty, I want a nice big fat pullet, about four pounds. I hear your kid brother got married last Sunday.

MARTY: Yeah, it was a very nice affair, Missus Canduso.

YOUNG MOTHER: Marty, you oughtta be ashamed. All your kid brothers and sisters, married and have children. When you gonna get married?

CLOSE-UP: *Marty. He sends a glance of weary exasperation up to the ceiling. With a gesture of mild irritation, he pushes the plunger of the cash register. It makes a sharp ping.*

DISSOLVE TO: *Close-up of television set. A baseball game is in progress. Camera pulls back to show we are in a typical neighborhood bar—red leatherette booths—a jukebox, some phone booths. About half the bar stools are occupied by neighborhood folk. Marty enters, pads amiably to one of the booths where a young man of about thirty-odd already sits. This is Angie. Marty slides into the booth across from Angie. Angie is a little wasp of a fellow. He has a newspaper spread out before him to the sports pages. Marty reaches over and pulls one of the pages over for himself to read. For a moment the two friends sit across from each other, reading the sports pages. Then Angie, without looking up, speaks.*

ANGIE: Well, what do you feel like doing tonight?

MARTY: I don't know, Angie. What do you feel like doing?

ANGIE: Well, we oughtta do something. It's Saturday night. I don't wanna go bowling like last Saturday. How about calling up that big girl we picked up inna movies about a month ago in the RKO Chester?

MARTY: [*Not very interested*] Which one was that?

ANGIE: That big girl that was sitting in front of us with the skinny friend.

MARTY: Oh, yeah.

ANGIE: We took them home alla way out in Brooklyn. Her name was Mary Feeney. What do you say? You think I oughtta give her a ring? I'll take the skinny one.

MARTY: It's five o'clock already, Angie. She's probably got a date by now.

ANGIE: Well, Let's call her up. What can we lose?

Exercise 50

Here are the opening scenes of a television play, *Jobs for the Boys* by Alan Bleasdale, about a number of unemployed men in Liverpool. The text includes a variety of language uses to provide the setting, indicate the camera shots, add comments by the writer, and present dialogue between different pairs of characters.

(a) With close reference to the text, comment in detail on the different uses of language and how they are recognisable.

(b) The dialogue includes speakers using different registers, incorporating colloquialisms or dialect, giving indirect responses, and being evasive or witty. Consider the different speech strategies evident in the dialogue, and comment on their effectiveness.

1. Exterior. Department of Employment Building. Day.
We establish the Department building. A series of shots: two workmen; a girl in white talking to a man; a man with bucket; the girl in white and the man; a Rastafarian. We see the DOE building. We hear the traffic going past.

2. Interior. Department of Employment Building. Day.
We see the interior of the DOE. Two general points of view show clerks at work. We see Chrissie, and we are aware of the counter clerk who is behind a wire mesh grille. We see Chrissie and the others in turn through this grille. Like caged animals.

CLERK. Name.

CHRISSIE. (*Misses a beat.*) Christopher Todd.

CLERK. Full name. (*Takes out a file.*)

CHRISSIE. (*Quietly.*) Christopher Robin Todd. (*Shrugs.*) It was me Mam. (*Turns head.*)

> *Freeze.*

> *We see Loggo. He is looking at his gold watch, and is expensively and well dressed.*

LOGGO. Wha'? Course I want a job. I'm desperate. But look, no offence meant like, but we've been through all this before an' well, y' have already made me miss me golf lessons.

CLERK. Look, these matters take time . . .

LOGGO. What I'm sayin' is, get a move on, will y', cos I'm supposed t'be at the Haydock races for half-past two. There's a good boy.

Freeze.

We see Yosser with his three children. He is leaning forward.

CLERK. The procedure of a test check is just a formality, Mr Hughes. However, I'm afraid—
YOSSER. Afraid? Y'll be terrified in a minute. (*Leans in.*) Now sort me soddin' Giro check out before I knock y' into the disability department.

Freeze.

We see George, who appears to be dressed in working clothes, but we can only see the top half of him.

CLERK. If you could just wait there, Mr Malone . . .

She goes to a filing cabinet.

GEORGE. Come on, girl. I should've been on site half an hour ago.

CLERK. (*Hesitant.*) Yeah. (*Opens filing cabinet.*)

GEORGE. (*Backing away.*) I don't like to let the boys down, you know. I mean, there'll be ten ton of the black stuff on the deck by now, waitin' for me.

We see the clerk, then George. He is wearing pyjama bottoms and slippers.

Freeze.

A row of men are waiting on a bench. Another row of men are waiting at the counter. We see Dixie.

CLERK. Dependants, Mr Dean?

DIXIE. Yeah, a wife and four kids. Two at school and two on the dole.

CLERK. Ah yes, but unfortunately the two on the dole don't count for—

DIXIE. No one on the dole counts, friend.

Freeze.

Two men peer through a barely open door leading to the interior offices of the Department. The door has a sign—'UNEMPLOYMENT OFFICE'—which is the euphemism for the fraud section. Both men are in their thirties and are wearing stock fashionless office suits. The younger of the two who will emerge as the driver (Lawton) mutters to the other one, his passenger (Moss). They come out.

LAWTON. (*Driver.*) Hey, there's one of them. Todd.

We see Lawton's point of view of Chrissie. He focuses on Chrissie. Moss joins him at the door, then walks off. We come back to Chrissie.

CLERK. It seems from your files, Mr Todd, that one of our inspectors has visited your house on two separate occasions during the past ten days without receiving any answer.

We see Moss watching Chrissie.

CHRISSIE. Ah what a shame.

CLERK. You were out?

CHRISSIE. Looks that way, doesn't it?

CLERK. Can you tell me where you were?

CHRISSIE. I might be able to if you tell me when you called.

CLERK. It's the . . . morning of Tuesday the third, and . . . the afternoon of Thursday the twelfth.

There is a pause.

CHRISSIE. Haven't a clue.

CLERK. Were you employed during those two days?

CHRISSIE. Who me?

CLERK. Look, have you got a job, Mr Todd?

CHRISSIE. Oh yeah, I just come here f'the company and the pleasant surroundings.

CLERK. (*Patiently, and not without sympathy.*) You haven't answered the question.

CHRISSIE. (*Looking away.*) I haven't worked in over a year.

CLERK. Right, Mr Todd, that's all.

Chrissie stands.

We will, however, be making further visits to your house in due course.

CHRISSIE. I'll bake a cake.

Chrissie walks away. We hear the clerk call the next contestant.

CLERK. Next.

We see the DOE hall at work. Chrissie walks towards the entrance.

3. Interior. Entrance hall of DOE Building. Day.
A man, Arthur, is waiting. Chrissie comes from the hall into the doorway of the building, and sees Arthur with his back turned, facing a window ledge. He is looking down at the racing section of The Daily Mirror, marking off some horses with a pen. Chrissie approaches him, and stands beside him. He looks over his shoulder at the paper.

CHRISSIE. Carnations are red in Albania this winter. Comrade.
(*He winks at Arthur.*)

ARTHUR. Say that again, Chrissie.

CHRISSIE. Ah, y'alright. You got anythin' for me? (*He puts his arm around Arthur's shoulder, and stares down at the paper.*)

ARTHUR. Malloy's been askin' after you. (*Looks at Chrissie.*)

CHRISSIE. That's nice of him. Go on.

ARTHUR. Bricks and wheels.

Chrissie nods.

Fourteen notes.

CHRISSIE. You're on.

Chrissie nods again. Arthur looks behind him for a second, then gets an envelope out of his pocket as Chrissie looks behind himself as well.

ARTHUR. The van'll be at the end of your road in the mornin'. The keys'll be in the teapot on the dashboard.

Arthur gives Chrissie the envelope. Chrissie puts it in his inside pocket. They focus on the racing section. Chrissie points at the paper. He moves round.

CHRISSIE. Teacher's Pet in the 3.15.

ARTHUR. Ah, well, I don't follow the horses, Chrissie. I only look at this so that . . . (*He looks behind again.*)

CHRISSIE. I'd bet my life on it. In fact I'd go so far as to say it was an absolute certainty.

Arthur looks at him, then at the paper, then back at Chrissie.

ARTHUR. How do you know that?

CHRISSIE. It's yesterday's paper. (*He half turns, then turns back.*) Y'd never make a spy, Arthur.

Chrissie pushes Arthur and goes out. Arthur leaves too.

Exercise 51

Here is an extract from *Oxbridge Blues* by Frederic Raphael about two men who first met as students at Oxford and who are now in their thirties.

(a) Comment on the uses of language which indicate that this extract is part of a play.

(b) The first speech by Victor gives one side of a telephone conversation. Provide your version of what you imagine was said by the person with whom he was talking.

(c) What impression does the writer give of the character of Victor? Refer in detail to different features of Victor's uses of language.

(d) Comment on the language used by Victor and Philip in their dialogue and the ways this creates a witty effect.

(e) Now compare the uses of language in this extract with those in the extract from Alan Bleasdale's play (Exercise 50)

Interior. Victor's office. Day.

Philip comes in. Victor is now a high-grade civil servant. At thirty-two, he remains handsome, but unsmiling. He wears his Hawk's club tie and a sound suit and a clean shirt and he sits behind the kind of desk appropriate to a candidate member of the mandarinate. He has a tea-tray with upper echelon china on it by his elbow.

VICTOR. (*On telephone.*) All I actually said about the think-tank was that I saw no objection to getting rid of the tank, but that we probably ought to hesitate about getting rid of the think. (*Smiles faintly.*) Well, if it went down well, I see no reason to deny authorship! (*On a new topic.*)

We had a very good time ourselves, sir, as I think my wife . . . Ah, well, Baudelaire *was* her special subject, you know. I'll certainly convey that to her. If I can find a purple cushion, I shall of course use it. Indeed.

Phillip, looks round as Victor hangs up.

PHILIP. This seems to be a step in the right direction. Well, that's the only direction you ever take them in, isn't it, old boy? Next stop the roof presumably.

VICTOR. You're rather lucky.

PHILIP. Am I? Aren't you?

VICTOR. Finding me free. We got through our weekly *tour d'horizon* rather earlier than usual. The Chancellor's jet developed a cough so he's stranded in Caracas.

PHILIP. (*Taking a biscuit.*) Graduated to cream sandwich, have you? It'll be a knighthood next. What are *tours d'horizon* in simple English?

VICTOR. Don't play the peasant, Pip.

PHILIP. Look, I dropped by your shop because I've got a bit of news I thought you might care to hear.

VICTOR. If you have beans, pray spill them.

PHILIP. (*Stares at him.*) I remember you in nappies.

VICTOR. That's not news.

PHILIP. It would be to some people. You look as though you were born in a suit. I'm going to get married.

VICTOR. Are you so? Whatever for?

PHILIP. To live happily ever after, of course.

VICTOR. Do I know her?

PHILIP. (*Shakes head.*) Unless you remember the Dimmages.

VICTOR. Pass.

PHILIP. They lived down the Maldon Road. She happens to be their niece. Her name is Max. Well, actually it's Maxine, but I call her Max. I hope you won't disapprove.

VICTOR. Marriage is an honourable estate.

PHILIP. I've told her all about you. Victor Geary. The man and the Mandarin. She's scared stiff. You will be nice to her, won't you?

VICTOR. What sort of girl is she?

PHILIP. She didn't go to university, if that's what you mean.

VICTOR. Millions of people don't go to university.

PHILIP. Yes, but you don't know any of them do you?

Exercise 52

The following text is taken from a car advertisement.

(a) List and comment on the variety of uses of language. You may wish to note, in particular, the paragraphing, the structures of sentences, the range and choice of vocabulary, the presentation of the contents, and the sense of audience or reader.

(b) Compose the text of an advertisement, using 200 words, for your ideal form of transport. The details may be real or imagined, and you may adopt a serious or a humorous tone.

With gloves or without, there can be few cars more rewarding to drive than the Porsche 924.

It is, after all, the most responsive of road-going machines. The sort of car to drive even when your only destination is driving enjoyment.

From the outset, the 924 was designed to be a superior handling sports coupé, with generous 2 + 2 accommodation.

The key to its performance: the Trans-axle system.

By locating the engine block to the front of the car and the gearbox to the rear, the 924 achieves perfect poise and balance. Even at high cornering speeds, steering is wonderfully precise.

It is virtually unaffected by cross winds. Grip is limpet-like even in the wet. And every curve in the road becomes a source of satisfaction to the performance-minded driver.

Once behind the wheel of a 924, you discover motoring has other dimensions.

For it's not just the roadholding that makes this such an exciting car to drive. It's the precision built, two litre 125 bhp engine. The Bosch K-Jetronic fuel injection. The dual circuit servo-assisted brakes. The silky 5-speed manual transmission. The anatomically designed seats. The layout of the instruments. The inherent safety features.

Self-indulgence alone should dictate.

But a Porsche becomes a much more rational choice than that.

There is the loadspace to consider.

Open the rear hatch, fold down the rear seats and you have additional carrying capacity that's most unsportscar-like. Consequently, luggage consumption is massive.

Yet, astonishingly, fuel consumption is meagre.

Your Porsche 924 can happily return over 30 mpg even though it is capable of 127 mph.

Uniquely, the bodyshell also carries the Porsche Longlife 7-year anti-corrosion warranty that is routine maintenance free. The major benefit from a double-sided galvanised bodyshell that has undergone an unsurpassed and painstakingly thorough paint process.

And there is an unlimited mileage, two year mechanical warranty that is second to none.

Twelve thousand mile inspection service intervals, of course.

And last, but by no means least, the price. From £12,260.

Happily, the experience still outweighs the expense.

Endorsed by excellent resale values.

When does the fun start?

The moment you test drive one at your nearest Official Porsche Centre.

Their enthusiasm for the Porsche 924 is limitless.

CHAPTER 10

Exercise 53

The following comments were made by students in secondary schools about the subjects they studied and the work that they had to do. Discuss
(a) the contents of their observations; and
(b) the features of the language used to express their opinions.

MY VIEWS ON WRITTEN WORK DONE IN SCHOOL

(i) I think that written work in some leassons is more difficult than any other leasons e.g. in some leassons teatures dictated to us and then after the teacher has dictated and then starts talking the pubiles start asking what he/she said last. Or when the teachers are talking they then say suddenly to write out what they had just said and then the publes don't right much because they forget what they started.

(ii) I think we should not have as much writeing in school. But in other ways it will come in handy in the way of exams.

(iii) I think you should do a lot of writing in History because you can't remember all the dates of History for when a test occurs. But I think that teachers should n't push you on so much or pur you in detention for just a little talk e.g. I will not name who I'm talking about but it gets to be a pain. But I can't really see History helping us in a job??

(iv) I think we do to much writing in school and less talking about things. We do too much of writing a story by our selves. In subjects like woodwork, metalwork and vehicle mechanics we should do more practical work than written work. I think there should be less written work in school.

(v) In some lessons I think we do too much writing and we don't learn enough from it (the writing). Some of the written work done teaches you a lot, but some can be too hard to understand. I think some work won't help you when you leave school, but most of it will.

(vi) We seem to do a lot of literature more than the language. I think we get too many essays and sometimes we don't do much writing in class. I think some things done in class like punctuation are/is useful, especially if you didn't understand it at the juniors or further up this sort of school.

(vii) I think writing in English for stories is a good idea as you might need it later on in life to get a job as a author, poet etc. I think when you are filling missing words in a sentence it is not a good idea to write the whole sentence as it takes more time (by writing more and also as it is so boring it makes your mind wander) thus meaning you *don't* get so many questions answered. I don't think the *OCCASIONAL* writing practice is too bad.

(viii) In English I think that spelling and handwriting are the most important things, because if you cannot spell correctly you cannot pronnounce words as they should be spoken which you need to do to know English Language. Handwriting is very important because if you cannot write neatly your teacher will not be able to mark and read your work and therefore will not know what you have written. English is a very important subject because if you cannot read or write you will not get a job.

(ix) In English we do spelling I think it is important to learn to spell because if you can not spell then you can not pronnounce words propaly. In English we write storys, I dont think it is really important but it does give you an imagination. It is good to have a good imagination because when you grow up you might become a story writer. In English we do descriptions of things it is good to do descriptions because if some one wanted to know what something looked like then you can tell them.

Exercise 54

The following is a transcript of a conversation between three five-year -old boys discussing a tower they have made. J.T. is the adult who leads the discussion.

(a) Comment on the features of the spoken language used, focusing in particular on the language used by the young boys.

(b) Using this transcript as an example, make your own transcript of a discussion with young people, and comment on the linguistic features of the text.

1. J.T: Yes, what have you made? You tell me what you've made, Trevor?
2. Trevor: A tower.
3. J.T: A tower, What sort of a tower is it?
4. Trevor: Funny one.
5. J.T: It is a funny one, but why do you say it's funny? What do you think about it, Paul?
6. Trevor: 'Cos I put the car on top of it.
7. J.T.   Ah, can't we have cars on top of towers?
8. Trevor: I do, I put 'em on top.
9. J.T: Can we really have cars on top of towers? What do you think, Paul?

10.	Andrew:	You can't.
11.	Paul:	You can't.
12.	J.T:	You can't. Why wouldn't you have them on the top of towers?
13.	Paul:	Because . . .
14.	J.T.	What would be the problem?
15.	Paul:	If . . . if you drive forward and there's an edge, you'll fall down.
16.	J.T:	You would, you would soon be falling off the top of his towers, wouldn't it? Could we get a car onto the top of a tower? How would you get a car on top of a tower?
17.	Andrew:	Go by lift.
18.	J.T:	You could do it by lift, could you? Any other way? How else could you get something up high?
19.	Andrew:	Get a . . . no . . . get a aeroplane, couldn't you. Put the car inside and fly up.
20.	J.T:	So we could put the car inside an aeroplane and we could fly over the top of a tower. And could we put the car on top of the tower from the aeroplane?
21.	Andrew:	Yes.
22.	J.T:	What do you think, Paul?
23.	Andrew:	. . . because you open the door and then drive it out.
24.	J.T:	Could an aeroplane really dr . . . have a car in that would drive on the top of a tower?
25.	Andrew:	Yes.
26.	J.T:	No.
27.	Trevor:	Because the door's too little and, er . . . it could, it could, just.
28.	J.T:	You think you couldn't get the car out of the aeroplane?
29.	Trevor:	No.
30.	J.T:	What about the aeroplane? Could you get the —could you get the car out of the aeroplane on top of the tower?
31.	Trevor:	No.
32.	J.T:	Paul, what do you think? What would the problem be?
33.	Trevor:	No you couldn't.
34.	Paul:	No. Because the door's too little.
35.	J.T:	Well, the door's little but if you'd got it in you would have had to have a door that was big enough to get it in, wouldn't you? I think you could get a car into an aeroplane.
37.	Andrew:	But you can't get it back out.
38.	J.T:	You couldn't get it to the top of the tower. Paul, why not?
39.	Andrew:	If they go too fast, they might go past it.
40.	J.T:	Yes, well, that is a problem isn't it? Is it possible to get a car onto the top of a tower, then? Or into a tower, or onto the top of a high building? How would you do it? Let's think again, shall we?
41.	Andrew:	By going not too fast and they'd have to go sideways instead of frontwards.
42.	J.T:	So we go not too fast.

43. Andrew: There must be two people.
44. J.T: There must be two people, where?
45. Andrew: Two at the back and one at the front.
46. J.T: Of the aeroplane, you mean?
47. Andrew: Because them two can have a look and see where the edge of the tower is.
48. J.T: I see, but you'd think if the aeroplane went very slowly that the car would drive out onto the top of the building.
49. Andrew: No.
50. J.T: No, you don't think it could, What do you think?
51. Trevor: If you . . . if you . . . if you'd a right long . . . a right long thingy . . .
52. J.T: Mm?
53. Trevor: . . . you could get it in.
54. J.T: A right long thingy, what's that?
55. Trevor: A long door.
56. J.T: A long door, yes. What's the problem about an aeroplane flying and trying to get a car onto a building? Can an aeroplane really go slowly enough for a car to drive out?
56. Andrew: No.
58. J.T: What would you have to have, then? There is something you could have.
59. Trevor: A brake.
60. J.T: You could have a brake, but what would happen to the aeroplane if you stopped it in the middle of the air?
61. Andrew: It'd fall down and break,
62. J.T: It would, wouldn't it? But there is some kind of an aeroplane that would do it.
63. J.T: If it were too, um, if it were too heavy, you might just go down.
64. J.T: You would. Yes, yes. But aeroplanes really don't stand still, out in the air, do they? They have to go flying on. Well, what do you know that can fly and can stay, stays?
65. Andrew: A bird.
66. J.T: That stays still in the air, or stays vertical?
67. Andrew: A bird.
68. J.T: Well, a bird can't carry a car up, can it?
69. Andrew: I don't mean a—to carry a car up.
70. J.T: No, well, I'm still thinking how we could put a car onto the top of a building.
71. Trevor: Or you could get some ladders.
72. J.T: You might.
73. Andrew: You can't drive it up ladders.
74. J.T: Well, what else how else would you do it?
75. Trevor: If you had a . . . if you had a strong man, he could.
76. J.T: You think a strong man could take a car up to the top of a building?
77. Andrew: Can't. Even a strong man can't do it.

78. J.T:	Why not?
79. Trevor:	With ladders, he could.
80. J.T:	Why not, a big car, why not, Andrew?
81. Andrew:	Because the car would be too heavy.
82. J.T:	Too heavy and too . . .
83. Andrew:	Too big.
84. J.T:	And too big. Well, you were right in the first place, if we had a strong enough lift we could take it up, couldn't we?

Exercise 55

Here are some extracts from package holiday brochures about the Spanish seaside resort of Benidorm and its surroundings. There are interesting differences in the description of the place, reflecting the age group for which each brochure is intended and the time of the year to which each brochure applies.

(a) Discuss these differences and how they are presented through the writers' choice of vocabulary and grammar.

(i) Benidorm is one of the liveliest resorts in the whole of Spain: cosmopolitan and friendly, big and bustling and absolutely packed with attractions. It is at the very heart of the Costa Blanca, which boasts mile after mile of glorious coastline protected by the wild mountains of Alicante and the mild, garden-like region of Murcia.

But the Mediterranean shore is only part of the attraction of a holiday in Benidorm. Inland, there are many ancient cities and towns which are well worth seeing, including Elche with its palm groves, the Baroque city of Lorca, and Aledo, which is surrounded by a wall dating from medieval times.

The Greeks, Phoenicians, Carthaginians and Romans all founded cities and established prosperous colonies in this part of Spain and their diverse cultures are reflected in local architecture and the many festivals which are a feature of life in the Costa Blanca.

The old village of Benidorm stands on a small hill which separates the beaches of Poniente and Levante. At the top of the hill stands the 18th century Baroque church of San Jaime and nearby there is Castillo, an area providing magnificent views over the whole of Benidorm. There are lots of seats here for you to sit in the sun and watch the ever changing panorama of the coast.

Benidorm normally only has about 20 days of rain a year, which means you can count on the weather being kind whenever you are there.

Excursion opportunities abound. The Altea Market, where the locals go shopping at open air stalls on Albir beach, and the full-day trip to Alicante, the provincial capital, are two of the most popular.

Another popular outing is to Guadalest right up in the mountains, where on the terraced hillside you can see almond trees, olive groves and oranges and lemons growing.

Our representatives in Benidorm can arrange for you to hire a car if you would like to, and they will tell you about the local transport system, which includes the unique Lemon Express, a super old train.

(ii) You will thoroughly enjoy shopping for food in Benidorm. There are plenty of excellent shops and supermarkets, stocking imported as well as local produce.

The local fruit and vegetables are of excellent quality and value, and the Spanish wines are a must. It is also comforting to know that most of the brands of canned and packaged goods we are familiar with at home can also be purchased.

(iii) The Costa Blanca—Spain's White Coast is renowned as a sun-worshippers paradise—the area orginally got its name from the way the white village houses shimmer in the brilliant sunshine. From Denia in the north down to the beaches of Torrevieja in the south the Costa Blanca has lots to offer—as well as lively resorts like Benidorm, you'll still discover quaint fishing villages, tranquil coves, rugged mountains, vineyards and the orange and lemon groves that first gave the people their livelihood. Now of course there are a host of up-to-the-minute resorts along the coast and Benidorm leads the way.

If you're looking forward to a lazy, do-nothing holiday, keep well away from Benidorm. There are few places in all of Europe which can rival the round-the-clock attractions of this amazing resort—it's in a league of its own. Benidorm's action never flags—people are out and about at all hours making the most of the staggering choice of bars, restaurants and nightspots.

(iv) Benidorm has two superb sandy beaches—the Levante (sunrise) and the Poniente (sunset)—where you can relax, soak up the sun and recharge the batteries for the long night ahead. But would't you know it, even during the day Benidorm has plenty to distract you from taking it easy! Water-skiing, windsurfing, sailing and snorkelling are all available, and for landlubbers there's tennis, ten-pin bowling, crazy-golf, horse-riding plus go-karting on one of Europe's largest circuits.

It's at night though, that Benidorm really jumps into top gear. There are literally hundreds of bars catering for every possible taste—among the Club's favourites are Rumples, Viking and Blinkers all of which keep a special welcome for 18–30s. Benidorm's discos are justly famous—you could go to a different one every night, and find new people, new music, and new styles in each one. The White Horse and the Bacchus Garden are just two of the nightspots that are well worth a visit.

(v) The 170-mile-long "White coast" has long been a favourite sunspot for young holidaymakers from all over Europe—and with its sheltering mountains, its miles of beautiful silvery-white beaches, its refreshing azure sea and its exciting nightlife, it's not hard to understand why!

Outside the major resorts, of which Benidorm is the most popular, you can find simple mountain villages, old fortresses, little whitewashed communities sloping down green hillsides to the sea. Even on this highly-developed coastline there are places hardly touched by tourism, where you can soak in the atmosphere of old Spain and enjoy a tranquillity that seems incredibly remote from the disco dance-floor!

But it's the constant sunshine and non-stop action by day and night that really gives the Costa Blanca its reputation as one of Europe's holiday hotspots—and we've chosen Benidorm for its superb nightlife and free-and-easy style.

(vi) As one of Europe's most popular summer resorts, Benidorm offers everything. It's a resort where holiday enjoyment is the name of the game—and for TWENTYS that makes it a must!

It's our first season here, but it won't be our last . . . we've fallen in love with it! Benidorm's superb beaches, reliable weather and non-stop nightlife excitement will make sure you never have a dull moment. And with all the fun and laughter of TWENTYS added in, your holiday here will be unforgettable!

The modern town has an informal, cosmopolitan atmosphere that defies you not to enjoy yourself—and our hotel, the Mayor, is right in the heart of the picturesque, bustling old town, once a fishing village.

This famous resort offers outstanding holiday value—and with TWENTYS you'll be enjoying it at its very best!

(vii) Apart from being the most popular single resort in Spain (or anywhere else, for that matter) with British holidaymakers. Benidorm has another very good reason why you should consider it as your 'Home' for a few weeks or even three months in the winter—the climate. Sheltered as it is by the distant mountains, its weather record is superb, with lots of sunny days and very rarely more than a gently cooling breeze to bother you.

Having catered so long for British visitors, you won't be surprised to find plenty of 'British' pubs run by people who have permanently left our shores—you've a good chance of even finding your favourite beer.

The old village of Benidorm, from which the resort has spread out along its two fabulous, huge beaches, is a delightful place to wander, with a wide choice of shops and very inexpensive eating places.

And entertainment here is equally wide and varied, as befits a year-round resort.

(b) Now choose a holiday resort you know well and compose entries for brochures advertising holidays there for:
  (i) young people of your age;
  (ii) families with young children; and
  (iii) retired people.

Exercise 56

The following is taken from the *Birmingham Daily Mail* for 9 October 1916 in the middle of the First World War. It was published at the time of the Battle of the Somme, when casualties were high on all sides.

(a) Comment on the observations attributed to an NCO and the various uses of language to sustain the morale of people at home.

WAR-BATTERED WARWICKS

PUT THROUGH THE MILL IN SOMME BATTLE

WHAT " ANY CHRISTIAN MIGHT HAVE ENJOYED. "

Wounded men of the Warwickshire Regiment who have returned home speak with pride of the achievements of the regiment on the Somme during recent fighting.

'We have been nicknamed the war-battered Warwicks, ' said a non-commissioned officer, 'and it's the truth, for the battalion I am in has been put through the mill and no mistake. We bumped up against as rough a lot of Germans as I want to meet any day. They were dug in for all they were worth, and they started to rain bullets on us when we showed ourselves. Our chaps were wonderfully game. They know it isn't the least use arguing with a machine-gun; so when the beauties got slapping out death in the wholesale line our boys just got up and went straight for Brother Boche and his whole bag of tricks. It was warmish work. It meant being mown down all the time, but once our boys got at it they got right slap up against the German trench. Then they got to business with the bayonet, and the Huns had a lively time.

'Don't you believe these fancy tales about the Huns being unable to fight. There may be Huns that can't or won't fight. I've never struck the breed yet. These chaps could, and did fight. It took up all we knew to get the upper hand. They were wonderfully determined, and fought their corner so long as it was possible. Every time we flung them back they were on to us again as lively as ever, and we had to fight hard for every square inch of

ground we took from them. We had an absolutely topping bomb fight that any Christian might have enjoyed. We fairly emptied bombs on the devils, and they got blown to bits. Then they took to their heels, those who were left I mean, and sought shelter in their dug-outs.

GERMANS WHO REFUSED QUARTER.

'They had dug deep, and no mistake—so deep that one would think that there were no Huns anywhere. But we came on them before long, and we started blasting them out. Some of them couldn't stand it, and came rushing up shivering all over to surrender. Others were as game as they make them, and died where they were without a whine. One body of chaps got right down into some deep shelters. They had fought very hard, and we didn't want to be too rough, so we offered them quarter if they would come out without further trouble. They refused, all but one chap, who said he wanted to see his old mother again. He won't, as a matter of fact, for his mates were so incensed at his funking it that they shot him dead before he could be taken away. Then they defied us to do our worst. So we had to do it. We blew the whole place to bits, and buried the lot in the grave of their own choosing. The more I think of what ours boys went through, the prouder I am of belonging to the Warwicks. Nothing could have been finer than their cool daring when the moment came for driving the Huns out. Hell couldn't have been a patch on what they had to go through in carrying out their orders, but they carried them out all the same, and made the Huns feel very sick before the day was done. Our boys didn't show the white feather once. They don't know what fear means, and I think they are equal to anything that may be allotted them out there. That's good for the Allies, but bad for the Huns.'

(b) Imagine that you are one of the soldiers who took part in the action. You have just read a copy of the newspaper with this account, and you want to give your parents your own version of what happened and your feelings at the time. You do not want to alarm them unduly, but you do want them to have a clearer idea of what the fighting was like.

Write them a letter about your part in the battle. Base the details of your letter on what is included in the newspaper report and use an appropriate style.

Then comment briefly but precisely on features of the language you have used and why.

(c) Read the following poem by Isaac Rosenberg about a similar action during the First World War. Comment in detail on the features of the language used in the poem and the effect they have on its tone.

Dead Man's Dump

The plunging limbers over the shattered track
Racketed with their rusty freight,
Stuck out like many crowns of thorns,
And the rusty stakes like sceptres sold
To stay the flood of brutish men
Upon our brothers dear.

The wheels lurched over sprawled dead
But pained them not, though their bones crunched;
Their shut mouths made no moan.
They lie there huddled, friend and foeman,
Man born of man, and born of woman;
And shells go crying over them
From night till night and now.

Earth has waited for them
All the time of their growth
Fretting for their decay:
Now she has them at last!
In the strength of their strength
Suspended—stopped and held.

What fierce imaginings their dark souls lit?
Earth! Have they gone into you?
Somewhere they must have gone,
And flung on your hard back

Is their souls' sack,
Emptied of God-ancestralled essences.
Who hurled them out? Who hurled?

None saw their spirits' shadow shake the grass,
Or stood aside for the half used life to pass
Out of those doomed nostrils and the doomed mouth,
When the swift iron burning bee
Drained the wild honey of their youth.

What of us who, flung on the shrieking pyre,
Walk, our usual thoughts untouched,
Our lucky limbs as on ichor fed,
Immortal seeming ever?
Perhaps when the flames beat loud on us,
A fear may choke in our veins
And the startled blood may stop.
The air is loud with death,
The dark air spurts with fire,
The explosions ceaseless are.
Timelessly now, some minutes past,
These dead strode time with vigorous life,
Till the shrapnel called 'An end!'
But not to all. In bleeding pangs
Some borne on stretchers dreamed of home,
Dear things, war-blotted from their hearts.

A man's brains splattered on
A stretcher-bearer's face:
His shook shoulders slipped their load,
But when they bent to look again
The drowning soul was sunk too deep
For human tenderness.

They left this dead with the older dead,
Stretched at the cross roads.

Burnt black by strange decay
Their sinister faces lie,
The lid over each eye;
The grass and coloured clay
More motion have than they,
Joined to the great sunk silences.

Here is one not long dead.
His dark hearing caught our far wheels,
And the choked soul stretched weak hands
To reach the living world the far wheels said;
The blood-dazed intelligence beating for light,
Crying through the suspense of the far-torturing wheels
Swift for the end to break
Or the wheels to break,

Cried as the tick of the world broke over his sight,
'Will they come? Will they ever come?'
Even as the mixed hoofs of the mules,
The quivering-bellied mules,
And the rushing wheels all mixed
With his tortured upturned sight.

So we crashed round the bend,
We heard his weak scream,
We heard his very last sound,
And our wheels grazed his dead face.

Isaac Rosenberg

Exercise 57

In 1930 Bruno Richard Hauptmann was tried for the kidnapping and murder three years previously of the baby son of Charles Lindbergh, famous for his solo flight from New York to Paris. Hauptmann was found to have part of the ransom money paid at the time of the kidnapping. His explanation was that he had been given a box to look after by a business friend, Isidor Fisch, who had gone to Germany and subsequently died. By chance Hauptmann discovered that the box contained money.

The following is an extract from Hauptmann's cross-examination by David Wilentz, prosecuting counsel. Comment on Wilentz's use of language in his questions and Hauptmann's responses. Hauptmann was found guilty and electrocuted, but his conviction is still a matter of debate.

Q: When you found fourteen thousand dollars or more in gold, how did you feel? Did you cry? Did you laugh? Were you happy or were you sad?
A: I was excited.
Q: Did you say anything? Did you holler out 'Anna, look what I found!'?
A: No.
Q: Did you tell your wife?
A: I did not.
Q: You didn't tell your wife?
A: No!
Q: Was this your way of being honest with her? A woman who slaved for you all hours in a bakery, who handed over her earnings and savings to you, given you every dollar she had in the world?
A: Why should I make my wife excited about it?
Q: How much money was in that box? You counted it many times. How much?
A: I find out later it was close to fifteen thousand dollars.

Q: You don't know the exact amount?

A: Not exactly.

Q: When you found that money and took it to the garage to dry and put it into a basket you didn't count it, did you?

A: No.

Q: You let it lie in a basket all night and you didn't count it?

A: That is right.

Q: You let it lie another night and you didn't count it?

A: That is right.

Q: The reason you didn't count it was because you knew, didn't you?

A: I didn't know anything.

Q: It took two weeks for you to count the money?

A: Yes.

Q: For two weeks you left gold lying in the basket and didn't know how much was there!

A: That is right.

Q: Fisch was your best friend, wasn't he?

A: Not my best friend.

Q: You knew he was sick?

A: Yes.

Q: Here was your sick friend going home, and he asked you to keep this box in a dry place?

A: Yes.

Q: You knew from the day you moved into that house that that closet was a wet place; you had complained about it. But even though you knew it was a wet closet, even though Fisch told you to keep the box in a dry place, you put it in the closet?

A: Because I couldn't go into the front room and I couldn't go into the middle room either when Fisch gave me this package.

Q: Who was going to stop you? Weren't you the boss of the house?

A: Yes, but I got somebody in the front room, and my wife was in the baby's room, and so I put it in this closet, and I forgot all about it.

Smilingly Wilentz sneered, 'So you forgot all about it?' Then he changed tack.

Q: During your so called partnership with Fisch you had given him 5,500 dollars in cash.

A: No. I didn't.

Q: You didn't?

A: No.

Q: But this letter . . . After Fisch's death you wrote to his family in Germany and asked about the estate?

A: Yes.

Q: In this letter you say you had given Fisch 5,500 dollars in cash from your private bank account.

A: Yes.

Q: Was that true?

A: No.

Q: My God, don't you tell *anybody* the truth?

Exercise 58

Poets frequently work on first drafts or texts of their poems in order to 'improve' them. Here are examples which indicate methods of composition.

For each,

(a) describe and comment on the original draft or text, particularly the poet's choice of rhyme and rhythm;
(b) describe the changes made to the text and comment on the effects of the revisions.

(i) The following episode occurs in Alexander Pope's poem *The Rape of the Lock*. It describes in mock-heroic terms the cutting of a lock of the heroine's hair. The first version is from the text of 1712, Canto I, lines 105–124; the second from the text of 1714, Canto III, lines 125–160.

But when to Mischief Mortals bend their Mind,
How soon fit Instruments of Ill they find?
Just then, *Clarissa* drew with tempting Grace
A two-edg'd Weapon from her shining Case;
So Ladies in Romance assist their Knight,
Present the Spear, and arm him for the Fight.
He takes the Gift with rev'rence, and extends
The little Engine on his Finger's Ends,
This just behind *Belinda*'s Neck he spread,
As o'er the fragrant Steams she bends her Head;
He first expands the glitt'ring *Forfex* wide
T'inclose the Lock; then joins it, to divide;
One fatal stroke the sacred Hair does sever
From the fair Head, for ever, and for ever!
The living Fires come flashing from her Eyes,
And Screams of Horrow rend th'affrighted Skies.
Not louder Shrieks by Dames to Heav'n are cast,
When Husbands die, or *Lap-dogs* breath their last,
Or when rich *China* Vessels fal'n from high,
in Glittring Dust and painted Fragments lie!

But when to Mischief Mortals bend their Will,
How soon they find fit Instruments of Ill!
Just then, *Clarissa* drew with tempting Grace
A two-edg'd Weapon from her shining Case;
So Ladies in Romance assist their Knight,
Present the Spear, and arm him for the Fight.
He takes the Gift with rev'rence, and extends
The little Engine on his Fingers' Ends,
This just behind *Belinda*'s Neck he spread,
As o'er the fragrant Steams she bends her Head:

Swift to the Lock a thousand Sprights repair,
A thousand Wings, by turns, blow back the Hair,
And thrice they twitch'd the Diamond in her Ear,
Thrice she look'd back, and thrice the Foe drew near.
Just in that instant, anxious *Ariel* sought
The close Recesses of the Virgin's Thought;
As on the Nosegay in her Breast reclin'd,
He watch'd th'Ideas rising in her Mind,

Sudden he view'd, in spite of all her Art,
An Earthly Lover lurking at her Heart.
Amaz'd, confus'd, he found his Pow'r expir'd,
Resign'd to Fate, and with a Sigh retir'd.
  The Peer now spread the glitt'ring *Forfex* wide,
T'inclose the Lock; now joins it, to divide.
Ev'n then, before the fatal Engine clos'd,
A wretched *Sylph* too fondly interpos'd;
Fate urg'd the Sheers, and cut the *Sylph* in twain,
(But Airy Substance soon unites again)
The meeting Points the sacred Hair dissever
From the fair Head, for ever and for ever!
  Then flash'd the living Lightnings from her Eyes,
And Screams of Horror rend th' affrighted Skies.
Not louder Shrieks to pitying Heav'n are cast,
When Husbands or when Lap-dogs breathe their last,
Or when rich *China* Vessels, fal'n from high,
In glittring Dust and painted Fragments lie!

(ii) Here is the text of William Blake's poem 'London' published in his
    Songs of Experience (1793), with the changes from the draft written in his
    Notebook (*MS*) given beneath.

I wander thro' each charter'd street,
Near where the charter'd Thames does flow
And mark in every face I meet
Marks of weakness, marks of woe.

In every cry of every Man,
In every Infants cry of fear,
In every voice; in every ban,
The mind-forg'd manacles I hear

How the Chimney-sweepers cry
Every blackning Church appalls,
And the hapless Soldiers sigh
Runs in blood down Palace walls

But most thro' midnight streets I hear
How the youthful Harlots curse
Blasts the new born Infants tear
And blights with plagues the Marriage hearse

1,2 charter'd] dirty *MS*.   3 mark] see *MS*.

6 In every voice of every child *MS.*
8 The german forgd links I hear *MS.*
9,10   But most the chimney sweepers cry
       blackens oer the churches walls *MS.*
13–16 read in *MS.*
       But most the midnight harlots curse
       From every dismal street I hear
       Weaves around the marriage hearse
       And blasts the new born infants tear

Exercise 59

The following is taken from the beginning of *Pygmalion* by George Bernard Shaw.

(a) Comment on the features of the text which show that this is part of a play.

(b) Discuss the features of the dialogue which are used to indicate that Freddy, his mother and sister are of a different class from the others who speak.

(c) Transcribe the remarks of Eliza Dolittle, the flower girl, into standard English. Discuss, with detailed reference to the text, the way in which Shaw represents the way in which Eliza pronounces words.

(d) The play is concerned principally with the way Professor Higgins, the man with the notebook, teaches Eliza to speak in a way which makes her acceptable to the society of Freddy's mother.
    Refer to a copy of the play and discuss one more of the later scenes which centre on Eliza's use of language.

(e) In his Preface to the play, Shaw discusses the nature of spoken language and its acceptability. Take one or more of Shaw's assertions and discuss the implications.

London at 11.15 p.m. Torrents of heavy summer rain. Cab whistles blowing frantically in all directions. Pedestrians running for shelter into the portico of St Paul's church (not Wren's cathedral but Inigo Jones's church in Covent Garden vegetable market), among them a lady and her daughter in evening dress. All are peering out gloomily at the rain, except one man with his back turned to the rest, wholly preoccupied with a notebook in which he is writing.

The church clock strikes the first quarter.

THE DAUGHTER (*in the space between the central pillars, close to the one on her left*) I'm getting chilled to the bone. What can Freddy be doing all this time? He's been gone twenty minutes.

THE MOTHER (*on her daughter's right*) Not so long. But he ought to have got us a cab by this.

A BYSTANDER (*on the lady's right*) He wont get no cab not until half-past eleven, missus, when they come back after dropping their theatre fares.

THE MOTHER. But we must have a cab. We cant stand here until half-past eleven. It's too bad.

THE BYSTANDER. Well, it aint my fault, missus.

THE DAUGHTER. If Freddy had a bit of gumption, he would have got one at the theatre door.

THE MOTHER. What could he have done, poor boy?

THE DAUGHTER. Other people got cabs. Why couldnt he?

Freddy rushes in out of the rain from the Southampton Street side, and comes between them closing a dripping umbrella. He is a young man of twenty, in evening dress, very wet around the ankles.

THE DAUGHTER. Well, havnt you got a cab?

FREDDY. Theres not one to be had for love or money.

THE MOTHER. Oh, Freddy, there must be one. You cant have tried.

THE DAUGHTER. It's too tiresome. Do you expect us to go and get one ourselves?

FREDDY. I tell you theyre all engaged. The rain was so sudden: nobody was prepared; and everybody had to take a cab. Ive been to Charing Cross one way and early to Ludgate Circus the other; and they were all engaged.

THE MOTHER. Did you try Trafalgar Square?

FREDDY. There wasnt one at Trafalgar Square.

THE DAUGHTER. Did you try?

FREDDY. I tried as far as Charing Cross Station. Did you expect me to walk to Hammersmith?

THE DAUGHTER. You havnt tried at all.

THE MOTHER. You really are very helpless, Freddy. Go again; and dont come back until you have found a cab.

FREDDY. I shall simply get soaked for nothing.

THE DAUGHTER. And what about us? Are we to stay here all night in this draught, with next to nothing on? You selfish pig—

FREDDY. Oh, very well: I'll go, I'll go. (*He opens his umbrella and dashes off Strandwards, but comes into collision with a flower girl who is hurrying in for shelter, knocking her basket out of her hands. A blinding flash of lightning, followed instantly by a rattling peal of thunder, orchestrates the incident.*)

THE FLOWER GIRL. Nah then, Freddy: look wh' y' gowin, deah.

FREDDY. Sorry (*he rushes off*).

THE FLOWER GIRL (*picking up her scattered flowers and replacing them in the basket*) Theres menners f' yer! Te-oo banches o voylets trod into the mad. (*She sits down on the plinth of the column, sorting her flowers, on the lady's right. She is not at all a romantic figure. She is perhaps eighteen, perhaps twenty, hardly older. She wears a little sailor hat of black straw that has long been exposed to the dust and soot of London and has seldom if ever been brushed. Her hair needs washing rather badly: its mousy color can hardly be natural. She wears a shoddy black coat that reaches nearly to her knees and is shaped to her waist. She has a brown skirt with a coarse apron. Her boots are much the worse for wear. She is no doubt as clean as she can afford to be; but compared to the ladies she is very dirty. Her features are no worse than theirs; but their condition leaves something to be desired; and she needs the services of a dentist*).

THE MOTHER. How do you know that my son's name is Freddy, pray?

THE FLOWER GIRL. Ow, eez ye-ooa san, is e? Wal, fewd dan y' do-ooty bawmz a mather should, eed now bettern to spawl a pore gel's flahrzn than ran awy athaht pyin. Will ye-oo py me f'them? (*Here, with apologies, this desperate attempt to represent her dialect without a phonetic alphabet must be abandoned as unintelligible outside London*).

Exercise 60

The following extract is taken from *Ulysses* by James Joyce. The setting is a public house in Dublin on a June morning in 1904. The central character is Stephen Dedalus who, with his drinking friends, is discussing the genius of Shakespeare.

Part of the text is dialogue between characters; part is imaginative recreation of a performance of *Hamlet* in Shakespeare's time; part is 'interior monologue', telling us what Stephen is thinking; part is narrative. By close reference to the text show how we can recognise the difference between these parts of the text, and comment on any other interesting features of the writer's use of language.

You may find it helpful to refer to the text of *Hamlet* and also to gather information about Shakespeare's life and the performance of his plays.

—He will have it that *Hamlet* is a ghoststory, John Eglinton said for Mr Best's behoof. Like the fat boy in Pickwick he wants to make our flesh creep.

List! List! O List!

My flesh hears him: creeping, hears.

If thou didst ever . . .

—What is a ghost? Stephen said with tingling energy. One who has faded into impalpability through death, through absence, through change of manners. Elizabethan London lay as far from Stratford as corrupt Paris lies from virgin Dublin. Who is the ghost from *limbo patrum*, returning to the world that has forgotten him? Who is king Hamlet?

John Eglinton shifted his spare body, leaning back to judge.

Lifted.

—It is this hour of a day in mid June, Stephen said, begging with a swift glance their hearing. The flag is up on the playhouse by the bankside. The bear Sackerson growls in the pit near it, Paris garden. Canvasclimbers who sailed with Drake chew their sausages among the groundlings.

Local colour. Work in all you know. Make them accomplices.

—Shakespeare has left the huguenot's house in Silver street and walks by the swanmews along the riverbank. But he does not stay to feed the pen chivying her game of cygnets towards the rushes. The swan of Avon has other thoughts.

Composition of place. Ignatius Loyola, make haste to help me!

—The play begins. A player comes on under the shadow, made up in the castoff mail of a court buck, a wellset man with a bass voice. It is the ghost, the king, a king and no king, and the player is Shakespeare who has studied *Hamlet* all the years of his life which were not vanity in order to play the part of the spectre. He speaks the words to Burbage, the young player who stands before him beyond the rack of cerecloth, calling him by a name:

Hamlet, I am thy father's spirit

bidding him list. To a son he speaks, the son of his soul, the prince, young Hamlet and to the son of his body, Hamnet Shakespeare, who has died in Stratford that his namesake may live for ever.

—Is it possible that that player Shakespeare, a ghost by absence, and in the vesture of buried Denmark, a ghost by death, speaking his own words to his own son's name (had Hamnet Shakespeare lived he would have been prince Hamlet's twin) is it possible, I want to know, or probable that he did not draw or foresee the logical conclusion of those premises: you are the dispossessed son: I am the murdered father: your mother is the guilty queen. Ann Shakespeare, born Hathaway?

—But this prying into the family life of a great man, Russell began impatiently.

Art thou there, truepenny?

—Interesting only to the parish clerk. I mean, we have the plays. I mean when we read the poetry of *King Lear* what is it to us how the poet lived? As for living, our servants can do that for us, Villiers de l'Isle has said. Peeping and prying into greenroom gossip of the day, the poet's drinking, the poet's debt. We have *King Lear*: and it is immortal.

Mr Best's face appealed to, agreed.

Exercise 61

Here are three versions of an episode in the life of Jesus to be found in the New Testament (Mark 6.30–46):

(i) is taken from the *Revised Standard Version of the Holy Bible* (1952), based on the *Authorised Version* of King James I's reign.

(ii) is taken from the *Jerusalem Bible* (1966).

(iii) is taken from *New World* (1967), a version of the New Testament by the Rev. Alan Dale intended originally for students in the lower forms of secondary schools.

(a) Comment, with detailed reference, on the features of the language of Text (i).

(b) Compare the features of the Text (ii) with those of Text (i), and comment on the differences.

(c) Text (iii) was drafted for a particular audience. Discuss the features of its language and layout, commenting in particular on how successfully it incorporates the details of Text (i) in a text that is simpler to read.

(d) You may find it of interest to get a copy of the text of this episode in the *Authorised Version*, and compare the language of the three texts here with the language of the early 17th century.

   (i) 30 The apostles returned to Jesus, and told him all that they had done and taught. [31]And he said to them, "Come away by yourselves to a lonely place, and rest a while." For many were coming and going, and they had no leisure even to eat. ³²And they went away in the boat to a lonely place by themselves. ³³Now many saw them going, and knew them, and they ran there on foot from all the towns, and got there ahead of them. ³⁴As he landed he saw a great throng, and he had compassion on them, because they were like sheep without a shepherd; and he began to teach them many things. ³⁵And when it grew late, his disciples came to him and said, "This is a lonely place, and the hour is now late; ³⁶send them away, to go into the country and villages round about and buy themselves something to eat." ³⁷But he answered them, "You give them something to eat." And they said to him, "Shall we go and buy two hundred denarii worth of bread, and give it to them to eat?"³⁸And he said to them, "How many loaves have you? Go and see." And when they had found out, they said, "Five, and two fish." ³⁹Then he commanded them all to sit down by companies upon the green grass. ⁴⁰So they sat down in groups, by hundreds and by fifties. ⁴¹And taking the five loaves and the two fish he looked up to heaven, and blessed, and broke the loaves, and gave them to the disciples to set before the people; and he divided the two fish among them all. ⁴²And they all ate and were satisfied. ⁴³And they took up twelve baskets full of broken pieces and of the fish. ⁴⁴And those who ate the loaves were five thousand men.

45 Immediately he made his disciples get into the boat and go before him to the other side, to Beth-Sa'ida, while he dismissed the crowd. ⁴⁶And after he had taken leave of them, he went into the hills to pray

(ii) **First miracle of the loaves**

30   The apostles rejoined Jesus and told him all they had done and
31   taught. Then he said to them, 'You must come away to some lonely place all by yourselves and rest for a while'; for there were so many
32   coming and going that the apostles had no time even to eat. • So they went off in a boat to a lonely place where they could be by
33   themselves. • But people saw them going, and many could guess where; and from every town they all hurried to the place on foot
34   and reached it before them. • So as he stepped ashore he saw a large crowd; and he took pity on them because they were like sheep without a shepherd, and he set himself to teach them at some
35   length. • By now it was getting very late, and his disciples came up
36   to him and said, 'This is a lonely place and it is getting very late, • so send them away, and they can go to the farms and villages round
37   about, to buy themselves something to eat'. • He replied, 'Give them something to eat yourselves'. They answered, 'Are we to go
38   and spend two hundred denarii on bread for them to eat?' • How many loaves have you?' he asked. 'Go and see.' And when they had
39   found out they said, 'Five, and two fish'. • Then he ordered them to
40   get all the people together in groups on the green grass, • and they
41   sat down on the ground in squares of hundreds and fifties. • Then he took the five loaves and the two fish, raised his eyes to heaven and said the blessing; then he broke the loaves and handed them to his disciples to distribute among the people. He also shared out the two

⁴²
⁴³   fish among them all. • They all ate as much as they wanted. • They
        collected twelve basketfuls of scraps of bread and pieces of fish.
44   • Those who had eaten the loaves numbered five thousand men.
45   Directly after this he made his disciples get into the boat and go
46   on ahead to Bethsaida, .while he himself sent the crowd away.
47   • After saying good-bye to them he went off into the hills to pray.

(iii) **The Desert Meal**
        Everybody seemed to be coming and going; there was not time even
to eat.
        'Come,' said Jesus to his friends, 'it's you who need a holiday, away
from the people, by yourselves.'
        So off they went in a boat right away from everybody. But a lot of
people saw them going away and recognized them; the crowds who
had come from near-by villages hurried along the shore and got ahead
of them.
        Jesus put the boat back to land and got out.
        He looked at the great crowd of people—5,000 men—and he was
very sorry for them. He remembered the words from the Bible: 'Like
sheep without a shepherd to look after them'. That's what this crowd
was like; they had no leader. Jesus talked to them for quite a long time.
        By now the afternoon was passing.
        'This is a very lonely place,' said his friends to Jesus, 'and it's getting
very late. Send the crowd off; they can find their way to the farms and
villages over there and get some food.'
        'You feed them,' said Jesus.
        'What!' they said. 'Do you want us to go and buy £50 worth of bread
to feed them?'
        'How many loaves have you got?' asked Jesus. 'Go and see.'
        They found out.
        'Five,' they said, 'and two fish!'
        Jesus told the men to sit down in groups on the green grass, and they
sat down in companies, some one hundred and some fifty strong.
        Jesus took the five loaves and the two fish, and looked up and said
Grace over them. He broke the loaves and gave the pieces to his friends
to give to the people; and he shared the fish with them all, too.
Everybody had enough to eat, and they gathered what was left of the
crumbs and the fish into twelve baskets.
        Then Jesus straight away made his friends get into the boat and go
ahead of him over to the far shore of the lake, near Bethsaida. He
stayed behind to get the crowd to go home. When he had said good-bye
to them he went away up into the hills to pray.

Exercise 62

A study of political speeches to large audiences noted the following
characteristics of the delivery of the speaker, devices which ensured the
appropriate response of those listening.

(a) Speeches use lists, the best form of list having three items, giving it a sense of unity and completeness. The items in the list may be identical, as in Hugh Gaitskell's: 'We shall fight, fight and fight again to save the party we love.' More frequently the items in the list have a cumulative effect, as in Abraham Lincoln's speech at Gettysburg which stressed 'government of the people, by the people, for the people' or Winston Churchill's call for 'blood, sweat and tears'.

The following illustrates an excellent sense of timing by Margaret Thatcher at a party conference (with pauses indicated by the times in brackets):

This week has demonstrated (0.4) that we are a *party*
*uni*ted in *pur*pose (0.4)
strategy (0.2)
and resolve (*Applause*)

Gather your own examples of the uses of lists in public speeches. Set these down, indicating where words were stressed and pauses occurred and showing the audience response.

(b) Similarly, speeches frequently use two-part contrasts, particularly between 'them' and 'us'. Find examples of the uses of this strategy and set down your transcript, indicating stressed words, pauses and the response of the audience.

(c) Speeches rely greatly on repetition for emphasis. Here is part of the memorable speech by Martin Luther King in Washington in 1963:

I have a dream that one day on the red hills of Georgia the sons of former slaves and the sons of former slave-owners will be able to sit down together at the table of brotherhood. I have a dream that one day even the state of Mississippi, a state sweltering with the heat of oppression, will be transformed into an oasis of freedom and justice . . . I have a dream that one day every valley shall be exalted, every hill and mountain shall be made low . . . This is the faith that I go back to the South with. With this faith we will be able to hew out of the mountains of despair the stone of hope. With this faith we will be able to work together, to pray together, to struggle together, to go to jail together, to stand up for freedom together, knowing we will be free one day.

Discuss the part played by repetition in this speech, and comment on other features of the choice and use of language which help to make the speech memorable.

(d) Speakers may make use of a range of rhetorical devices to influence their audience. A famous example of a speech which incorporates a variety of strategies is that by Mark Antony in Shakespeare's *Julius Caesar* shortly after the murder of Caesar. Comment on the uses of language in the speech, and then set out the speech as you would want to deliver it were you acting the part of Antony.

Ant. Friends, Romans, countrymen, lend me your ears;
I come to bury Cæsar, not to praise him.
The evil that men do lives after them,
The good is oft interred with their bones;
So let it be with Cæsar. The noble Brutus
Hath told you Cæsar was ambitious;
If it were so, it was a grievous fault,
And grievously hath Cæsar answer'd it.
Here, under leave of Brutus and the rest,—
For Brutus is an honourable man;
So are they all, all honourable men,—
Come I to speak in Cæsar's funeral,
He was my friend, faithful and just to me:
But Brutus says he was ambitious;
And Brutus is an honourable man.
He hath brought many captives home to Rome,
Whose ransoms did the general coffers fill:
Did this in Cæsar seem ambitious?
When that the poor have cried, Cæsar hath wept;
Ambition should be made of sterner stuff:
Yet Brutus says he was ambitious;
And Brutus is an honourable man.
You all did see that on the Lupercal
I thrice presented him a kingly crown,
Which he did thrice refuse: was this ambition?
Yet Brutus says he was ambitious;
And, sure, he is an honourable man.
I speak not to disprove what Brutus spoke,
But here I am to speak what I do know.
You all did love him once, not without cause:
What cause withholds you then to mourn for him?
O judgment! thou art fled to brutish beasts,
And men have lost their reason. Bear with me;
My heart is in the coffin there with Cæsar,
And I must pause till it come back to me.
    First Cit. Methinks there is much reason in
      his sayings.
    Sec. Cit. If thou consider rightly of the
      matter,
Cæsar has had great wrong.
    Third Cit.   Has he, masters?
I fear there will a worse come in his place.
    Fourth Cit. Mark'd ye his words? He would
      not take the crown;
Therefore 'tis certain he was not ambitious.
    First Cit. If it be found so, some will dear abide it.
    Sec. Cit. Poor soul! his eyes are red as fire with weeping.
    Third Cit. There's not a nobler man in Rome than Antony.
    Fourth Cit. Now mark him; he begins again to speak.
    Ant. But yesterday the word of Cæsar might

Have stood against the world; now lies he there,
And none so poor to do him reverence,
O masters! if I were dispos'd to stir
Your hearts and minds to mutiny and rage,
I should do Brutus wrong, and Cassius wrong,
Who, you all know, are honourable men.
I will not do them wrong; I rather choose
To wrong the dead, to wrong myself, and you,
Than I will wrong such honourable men.
But here's a parchment with the seal of Cæsar;
I found it in his closet, 'tis his will.
Let but the commons hear this testament—
Which, pardon me, I do not mean to read—
And they would go and kiss dead Cæsar's
      wounds,
And dip their napkins in his sacred blood,
Yea, beg a hair of him for memory,
And, dying, mention it within their wills,
Bequeathing it as a rich legacy
Unto their issue.
    Fourth Cit. We'll hear the will: read it, Mark Antony.
    Citizens. The will, the will! we will hear Cæsar's will.
    Ant. Have patience, gentle friends; I must not read it:
It is not meet you know how Cæsar lov'd you.
You are not wood, you are not stones, but men;
And, being men, hearing the will of Cæsar,
It will inflame you, it will make you mad.
'Tis good you know not that you are his heirs;
For if you should, O! what would come of it.
    Fourth Cit. Read the will! we'll hear it, Antony;
You shall read us the will, Cæsar's will.
    Ant. Will you be patient? Will you stay awhile?
I have o'ershot myself to tell you of it.
I fear I wrong the honourable men
Whose daggers have stabb'd Cæsar; I do fear it.
    Fourth Cit. They were traitors: honourable men!
    Citizens. The will! the testament!
    Sec. Cit. They were villains, murderers. The will! read the will.
    *Ant.*You will compel me then to read the will?
Then make a ring about the corpse of Cæsar,
And let me show you him that made the will.
Shall I descend? and will you give me leave?
    Citizens. Come down.
    Sec.Cit. Descend.   [ANTONY *comes down.*
    Third Cit. You shall have leave.
    Fourth Cit. A ring; stand round.
    First Cit. Stand from the hearse; stand from the body.
    Sec. Cit. Room for Antony; most noble Antony.
    Ant. Nay, press not so upon me; stand far off.
    Citizens. Stand back! room! bear back!

Ant. If you have tears, prepare to shed them now.
You all do know this mantle: I remember
The first time ever Cæsar put it on;
'Twas on a summer's evening, in his tent,
That day he overcame the Nervii.
Look! in this place ran Cassius' dagger through:
See what a rent the envious Casca made:
Through this the well-beloved Brutus stabb'd;
And, as he pluck'd his cursed steel away,
Mark how the blood of Cæsar follow'd it,
As rushing out of doors, to be resolv'd
If Brutus so unkindly knock'd or no;
For Brutus, as you know, was Cæsar's angel:
Judge, O you gods! how dearly Cæsar lov'd him.
This was the most unkindest cut of all;
For when the noble Cæsar saw him stab,
Ingratitude, more strong than traitors' arms,
Quite vanquish'd him; then burst his mighty heart;
And, in his mantle muffling up his face,
Even at the base of Pompey's statua,
Which all the while ran blood, great Cæsar fell.
O! what a fall was there, my countrymen;
Then I, and you, and all of us fell down,
Whilst bloody treason flourish'd over us.
O! now you weep, and I perceive you feel
The dint of pity; these are gracious drops.
Kind souls, what! weep you when you but behold
Our Cæsar's vesture wounded? Look you here,
Here is himself, marr'd, as you see, with traitors.
  First Cit. O piteous spectacle!
  Sec. Cit. O noble Cæsar!
  Third Cit. O woeful day!
  Fourth Cit. O traitors! villains!
  First Cit. O most bloody sight!
  Sec. Cit. We will be revenged.
  Citizens. Revenge!—About!—Seek!—Burn!
Fire!—Kill!—Slay! Let not a traitor live.
  Ant. Stay, countrymen!
  First Citizen. Peace there! Hear the noble Antony.
  Sec. Cit. We'll hear him, we'll follow him, we'll die with him.
  Ant. Good friends, sweet friends, let me not stir you up
To such a sudden flood of mutiny.
They that have done this deed are honourable:
What private griefs they have, alas! I know not,
That made them do it; they are wise and honourable,
And will, no doubt, with reasons answer you.
I come not, friends to steal away your hearts:
I am no orator, as Brutus is;
But, as you know me all, a plain blunt man,
That love my friend; and that they know full well

That gave me public leave to speak of him.
For I have neither wit, nor words, nor worth,
Action, nor utterance, nor the power of speech,
To stir men's blood: I only speak right on;
I tell you that which you yourselves do know,
Show you sweet Cæsar's wounds, poor poor dumb mouths,
And bid them speak for me: but were I Brutus,
And Brutus Antony, there were an Antony
Would ruffle up your spirits, and put a tongue
In every wound of Cæsar, that should move
The stones of Rome to rise and mutiny.
    Citizens. We'll mutiny.
    First Cit. We'll burn the house of Brutus.
    Third Cit. Away, then! come, seek the conspirators.
    Ant. Yet hear me, countrymen; yet hear me speak.
    Citizens. Peace, ho!—Hear Antony,—most noble Antony.
    Ant. Why, friends, you go to do you know not what.
Wherein hath Cæsar thus deserv'd your loves?
Alas! you know not: I must tell you then.
You have forgot the will I told you of.
    Citizens. Most true. The will! let's stay and hear the will.
    Ant. Here is the will, and under Cæsar's seal,
To every Roman citizen he gives,
To every several man, seventy-five drachmas.
    Sec. Cit. Most noble Cæsar! we'll revenge his death.
    Third Cit. O royal Cæsar!
    Ant. Hear me with patience.
    Citizens. Peace, ho!
    Ant. Moreover, he hath left you all his walks,
His private arbours, and new-planted orchards,
On this side Tiber; he hath left them you,
And to your heirs for ever; common pleasures,
To walk abroad, and recreate yourselves.
Here was a Cæsar! when comes such another?
    First Cit. Never, never! Come, away, away!
We'll burn his body in the holy place,
And with the brands fire the traitors' houses.
Take up the body.
    Sec.Cit. Go fetch fire.
    Third Cit. Pluck down benches.
    Fourth Cit. Pluck down forms, windows, any thing.
    [*Exeunt* Citizens, *with the body.*
    Ant. Now let it work: mischief, thou art afoot,
Take thou what course thou wilt!

Exercise 63

Read the following short article by John Whale on ways of placing the emphasis in writing.

*He went into an Espresso bar and drank some coffee. No one turned round to look at him.
He was a failure, certainly. Failure, it occurred to him, was the secular equivalent of sin.
Modern secular man was born into a world whose moral framework was composed not
of laws and duties, but of tests and comparisons. There were no absolute outside
standards, so standards had to generate themselves from within, relativistically. One's
natural sense of inadequacy could be kept at bay only by pious acts of repeated
successfulness.* (Michael Frayn, *Towards the End of the Morning*, Collins, 1967;
chapter 6)

As you read through that passage (from a funny and truthful novel about
journalists), listen to the emphases—the places where the rhythm imposes
the principal stresses. Nearly all of them fall just before a pause, as marked
by punctuation: at the end of sentences, or of subordinate parts of sentences.
Borrow that device, if you don't use it already, and it will do more than any
other single change to make your writing tell.

It isn't automatic. End a sentence with weak words, and the emphasis is
driven forward; as in the second Frayn sentence, where it falls— by the
writer's wish— on the word 'look'. But most commonly the main emphasis
drops on to the word before the full stop. In the first Frayn sentence, it falls
unmistakably on 'coffee'—and so solidly as to remove a problem about
'some', often an unsafe word because readers cannot immediately tell
whether they are to hear it in its clipped pronunciation (the king's 'Give me
some light' in *Hamlet*) or as a whole sound (the king's 'How some have been
depos'd' in *Richard II*). Frayn clearly wants the former.

The emphasis goes to the end in more complicated sentences than that.
Consider this marvellous sentence from that great newspaper novel, Evelyn
Waugh's *Scoop* (1938): 'Mrs Earl Russell Jackson padded in stockinged feet
across the bare boards of the lounge looking for a sizeable cigar-end, found
one, screwed it into her pipe, and settled down in the office rocking-chair to
read her Bible.'

But besides the emphasis before a full stop, there are lesser emphases
before lesser punctuation marks: in the Waugh sentence, on 'cigar' and
'found' and 'pipe'. And you can use this convenient fact to emphasise a word
that is nowhere near the end of a sentence or a part of one. Look at 'Failure'
in Frayn's fourth sentence. It suffers from a double weakness: it is at the very
beginning of a sentence, and it repeats a word we have just had. But Frayn's
interpolation of 'it occurred to him' just afterwards, between commas,
secures the pause that bestows the emphasis he wants.

You can do the same thing with the smallest word, a 'so', a 'but'. Just to
shove in a comma, though, lacks logic. You need an interpolation that takes
commas at both ends—like this 'after all' from Lytton Strachey, at the
famous close of his essay on Cardinal Manning in *Eminent Victorians* (1918):
'For whatever cause, the minds of the people had been impressed; and yet,
after all, the impression was more acute than lasting. The Cardinal's
memory is a dim thing today. And he who descends into the crypt . . .''

No room, sadly, to quote it all. You very seldom need to read a Lytton
Strachey sentence twice: he gets the pauses, and therefore the emphases,
dead right. Yet a reader wrote to me lately: 'In the grammar school I went
to, we were taught never to punctuate before "and". A comma is needless

before "and"; a semicolon makes "and" itself superfluous; a full stop before "and" is a sin!'

I find that a melancholy example of the way we make writing more difficult, for writer and reader, than it need be. I prefer the liberating example of writers like Lytton Strachey and Waugh (and Frayn, and countless others).

(a) Make notes of what the article has to say about the position of words, the importance of punctuation marks, and the uses of interpolations.

(b) Find illustrations from your own reading of each of the points that is made. Set these down and comment on where the emphasis lies and how it is achieved.

(c) Compose your own illustrations of emphasis in writing and comment on what effects you have tried to achieve and how.

(d) Late in the article there is a comment on the use of a punctuation mark with 'and'. Give your views on the uses of 'and', with supporting illustrations.

Exercise 64

(a) Describe some of the features of the language of the following text and make some stylistic comment based on your description:

Most people have just one thought when they receive a cassette recorder. Unlimited music.

'Just wait for this number by Iron Jelly,' they'll say excitedly. Or 'Listen to the magical flute on this version of Kolkov's Fifth'.

So in the first rush of enthusiasm, they sometimes overlook another aspect of these remarkable machines.

Unlimited recordings.

And that can be a pity.

With the whole family enjoying the Christmas spirit, you can pick up quite a few good ones.

There's an automatic recording level and a built-in electric microphone. So they don't even have to know they're making a live appearance. (Which can cause a riot when you play it back.)

And the built-in loudspeaker even reproduces their whispers.

You can record all kinds of other things too.

From a radio, record player or second recorder.

And then just play them back through the same internal speaker.

Or, if you've got them, external speakers, headphones or amplifier.

Both models shown here come with a direct recording lead.

And a blank C-60 cassette to start you off.

They'll also run off either mains or batteries. So you can even take them with you when you go visiting on Boxing Day.

You're bound to get a good recording there.
Even if it's only Dad's remark when Aunt Edna hands him yet another pair
of socks.

(b)   The following are answers to this question written by students under
      examination conditions. Imagine that you are the teacher of these
      students. Discuss the relative merits of each answer, and add comments
      on the ways in which aspects of the answers might be improved.

(i)   **First Answer**

This text is an advertisement for a cassette recorder aimed at the Christmas buyer. There is a lot of information contained within the passage regarding the recorder and its attributes, although the passage is divided into two sections, one dealing with the traditional first impressions of a recorder, the second emphasising the other things, such as recordings, which the buyer can do with it.

The text itself could be on a tape playing to the customer to give a good impression of the machine. The vocabulary in the text is relatively simple and straightforward, not going into too much technical detail for the prospective buyer. If it became to technical, talking about all the various things which it had in detail, the customer would probably not be interested or be put off because they do not understand it. It is aimed at the Christmas shopper, since the main idea is for recordings to be taken "with the whole family enjoying the Christmas spirit" as well as on Boxing day.

This theme of recording is the main one running through the last twenty four lines or so. Everything is geared towards selling the machine on this attribute.

The sentence structures, like the vocabulary, is short and to the point, thus making it easy to read or listen to. It also makes it easy to keep track of what is being said, relating things to the customers own experiences.

The first two sentences start off with a great wave of enthusiasm, attempting to capture the audience's attention almost straight away and then keep it; one feature of advertising language.

With the sentences being relatively short it makes listening or reading easier and quicker, that is designed to capture the imagination and get as much information across in a short as time as possible.

The sounds of the words used help to bring across a tone of lightheartedness and happiness which is around at the time of year. Words and phrases such as "Christmas spirit", "visiting on Boxing day" or even the final joke "when Aunt Edna hands him yet another pair of socks." All the time these little puns are put in to keep the attention of the prospective buyer, always with this tone of lightheartedness to detract from the technicalities of the machine, if they were getting too much.

Even this technical data is kept to a minimum, emphasising the recording aspect of the cassette and the fun which that can cause over Christmas.

Towards the end of the passage there are three short sentences with which to leave a final impression on the mind of the buyer. They are short, to the point, giving a final touch to what could be the deciding factor on the part of the buyer:

"Both models have come with a direct recording lead.

And a blank c60 cassette to start you off.

They'll also run off either mains or batteries."

Again straight straight after is a reference back to the family and Boxing day, keeping the attention but not detracting from the main idea of the passage.

To conclude, we can see that this piece of

advertising is fairly typical of this kind of writing, that is, short sentences written to the point, not containing too much information. There are small jokes or references put in to keep the reader's attention, but not detracting from the obviously great attributes of this machine. Vocabulary is also very limited, again simple, since if it was too difficult the audience would rapidly loose interest and possibly not buy the machine. It is even printed in such a way to make it easy to read, that is, each sentence printed in a separate line.

(ii) Second Answer

The text seems to be an advertisment which may well be found in a newspaper, magazine or indeed in a brochure, and it seems to portray the idea that there are many reasons for buying a cassette recorder, other than just for playing music. Aimed at the new buyer, the advertisement is typically persuasive and appeals in a familiar way, yet, hand in hand with this idea, the nature of the language used in the text often adapts a poetic quality which further aims at persuading the buyer by enticing his sense of sound.

The way in which the text is set out on the page clearly illustrates the nature of the passage as an advertisment. The sentences are of irregular length — the largest of seventeen words but the shortest only of two. — "Unlimited music". This seems to indicate that a space of a certain size has been allocated to the writer for the advertisment and, because of this, his prose takes on the appearance of a poem — narrow in form as sentence length becomes controlled by space and breakages conform likewise :—

" With the whole family enjoying the Christmas spirit, you can pick up quite a few good ones."

The advertisment is obviously written with an aim to sell, and therefore needs an opening with relative impact to capture the attention of the reader. "Most people"... is a colloquial way of beginning an advertisment as it implies the "majority" and is therefore of relevance to those reading it. Similarly, the term "have just one thought..." is equally familiar — "just" implying "only" — therefore assuming a casual air. The opening phrase is persuasive also in that it propells the reader to continue reading as the initial line, challenging a common idea, is in the form of a question, or a part-finished phrase which necessitates a continuation to the next line to find out the answer. The answer, being short and brief,^(and having a line of its own,) obviously shows the impact this is intended to have on the reader while also posing the question; "Well, what thought SHOULD we have in mind, therefore, when buying a cassette recorder?"

The colloquial, casualness of the piece continues implying that the advertisment is really intended more for the unaware 'new' buyer, freshly introduced to electronics, rather than the expert. The author uses "oft quoted" phrases in line 3 to appeal to the layman with abbreviations such as "they'll"; and later "they're" in line 15, in an attempt to make the passage read more like the spoken word than a formal, written document.

Line nine is particularly interesting in that it sees a definite repetition of line 3 — "Unlimited recordings." which aids a completion or a rounding off of the paragraph, and, aswell as achieving this

neat, compact, orderly flow, also serves to reflect
back to the initial idea portrayed by the opening.
This time, however, the author continues to portray
this strongly felt idea with another line on its own
"And that can be a pity," using a type of sentence
structure, which, although is colloquial and
effective, is a type which we would discourage
children from using— beginning sentences with
"And" is commonly challenged, yet it is interesting
how it is used to great effect in passages such as
these.

An advertisement, particularly of this type in
wanting to appeal to the new, unaware buyer so
wanting to stimulate curiosity and interest, must
also be simple to read. This writer achieves this in
the easy flow of his sentences in which he uses not
long, complex words, but, short, simple, snappy words
which facilitates reading and also maintains interest
with its ease. ie. "...you can pick up quite a few
good ones." — and again, the "you" creates a
familiarity which is further a persuasive implement
as it is used casually not in a dogmatic way

The advertisement moves easily and towards
its end seems almost to seduce the reader into
familiarising himself with relative jargon. Having,
in line 17, achieved an almost comical air with
including an afterthought in parenthesis :

"(which can cause a riot when you play it
                                          back.) "
further appealed to the readers personality — as
everyone knows what it is like to ff hear your

own voice on tape – the writer begins to use his real
selling power. With poetic alliteration, again,
appealing to sense of sound, and achieving a "listing" quality, the writer injects
some jargon (although not too complex) into his passage

"From a radio, _re_cord player or _re_cord recorder."

foll03ed by terms like "internal speaker"; "external
speakers,""headphones","amplifier"; "direct recording
lead." Yet by using familiar, speech-like terms
as a context for such jargon softens their impact
as sentences again begin with "And" and the
word "just" appears once more.

Phrases like "if you've got them," similarly
colloquial, further seduce the reader, as indeed it
does imply "You would be better off if you bought
these too!" yet having captured the interest of the
reader this didactic approach is lightened.

The ending, draws more attention to detail,
the interested readers being those continuing to the
end, and so this is why the real selling power is
reserved until last. However, the passage further
ends on a colloquial, common footing for it is a
common joke that "socks" are likely presents for
Dad at Christmas and in drawing the readers attention
to this point, again with colloquial abbreviations
like . "Dad's" and "yet another." the author is
using the festive season as an excuse for why a
tape recorder should be purchased.

The type of language used in texts, therefore,
seems to have some bearing upon the nature of
these texts – this one, in being an advertisment,

chiefly bring to mind its soft reduction in poetic qualities and colloquial familiarity ~~whilst at t~~ to capture interest, whilst at the same time injecting sufficient information and power in order to sell the product.

Exercise 65

(a) Read the following transcriptions of a snatch of conversation between two ladies meeting in Cardiff. Point to differences in the way the texts are presented, and discuss what can be inferred from these differences.

    (i)   "Hullo, Glad, how nice to see you."

           "Hullo, Val, how are you—I'm surprised to see you down here!"

           "I came down for the sales with 'Trisha, we decided to come at the last minute."

           "How did it go?"

           "There were plenty of bargains, but what I was really looking for was a handbag to match my new suit, but I couldn't find anything suitable anywhere."

           "Did you get your dress in Howells' sale?"

           "No, I've had this for some years—a real bargain—it washes so well— and still looks as good as new."

           "I bought a lovely one last year, but I had to have it cleaned—and this was not a success—I hardly wear it now . . ."

    (ii)   "Hi-ya, Glad., there's nice to see you."

           " 'ullo there, Val., 'ow's tricks gul—fancy seein' you down by 'ere!"

           "Came down for the sales with ouer 'Trish—came on the 'op, we did!"

           " 'ow did you get on?"

           "Found a tidy few bargains—but I came down special for a new 'ambarg to go with my new rig-out—but there was nothing to suit in the whool place."

           "Did you get youer frock in Howellses sale?"

           "No, gul, I've 'ad this one this years—a real cop it was—it do wash like a rag—and there's still not a brack in it!"

           "I bought a bewty last year, but I atto 'ave it cleaned—and they made a real mess of it for me—I've got no looks on it at all now!"

(b) Record a conversation between two people in the area where you live. Provide two transcripts of the conversation, the first in Standard English and the second more closely indicating the spoken language of your area. Comment on the differences.

Exercise 66

Here are some language objectives for pupils, listed in a recent discussion document.

Take a number of specific objectives of interest to you, and comment on each, discussing the value and importance of the objective and the difficulties involved in achieving it.

Objectives for 11 year old pupils
About language

They should know:

The rules of spelling

The difference between vowels and consonants

The functions and names of the main parts of speech (noun, pronoun, verb, adjective and adverb), and be able to identify these in their own writing for the purpose of discussing what they have written

The difference between statements, questions, commands and exclamations

The terms 'subject' and 'object' and be able to identify them in their own writing

That a sentence has a subject and a verb, and that the two must agree

That word order determines meaning.

They should:

Be aware of differences between tenses, and recognise when the past, present, or future tense is being used

Know that language can be literal or figurative, and be aware of the difference when they use or respond to language

Be aware of some of the ways in which written language differs from spoken language.

Objectives for 16 year old pupils
About language

They should:

Know the functions and names of all the main parts of speech (noun, pronoun, adjective, article, verb, adverb, preposition, conjunction) and be able to identify them in their own writing or in what they read, for the purpose of discussing language

Be able to distinguish between sentence, clause and phrase in what they write or read

Be aware of differences in usage, eg between formal and informal modes

Recognise differences between standard and dialect forms of the language

Be aware that language embodies values, conveys attitudes and defines relationships; and that it is by no means always concerned with the objective transmission of information

Be aware of 'register' (the use of different styles of language for different purposes)

Be aware that meaning is not confined to the content of what one says or writes: it is determined by how one says or writes it. The 'how' will affect the listener's or reader's understanding and response

Recognise that language is a spectrum which ranges from simple factual statements to complex uses of the sound and texture of words, of rhythm, of imagery and of symbol; and that such effects are not confined to poetry but occur in daily life (e.g. in advertising)

Have a vocabulary for discussing stylistic effects, including 'simile', 'metaphor' and 'cliché'

Recognise that we constantly use figurative expressions; that alertly used they are a great help to expressing meaning; but that thoughtlessly used they impede meaning and indicate slovenly thinking.

Exercise 67

Comment on the following observations on (a) grammar and (b) punctuation, taken from a recent discussion document on the teaching of them. Provide your own illustrations for any views you express.

(a) There is much confusion over whether grammar should be explicitly taught. It has long been recognised that formal exercises in the analysis and classification of language contribute little or nothing to the ability to use it. One consequence of this, however, is that many pupils are taught nothing at all about how language works as a system, and consequently do not understand the nature of their mistakes or how to put them right. We suggest that if some attention is given to the examination and discussion of the structure of the language pupils speak, write, read, or listen to for real purposes, their awareness of its possibilities and pitfalls can be sharpened. In the course of this, it is reasonable that they should learn such grammatical terminology as is useful to them for the discussion of language. But what and how much terminology they should be taught at any given stage must depend on how much they can assimilate with understanding and apply to purposes they see to be meaningful and interesting. The least able at using language are the least likely to understand the terminology, let alone apply, it in any useful way. As the Bullock Report remarks:

Explicit rules and facts about language . . . have direct practical value to a pupil when

(a) they solve particular problems in the tasks he is engaged on, or
(b) he is able to reconstruct for himself the analysis that led to the rule.

(b) Punctuation needs more attention in English teaching than it some-times receives. It is a systematic aspect of the written language and essential to meaning, for it performs two vital functions. One is the grammatical function of making clear the relationship between parts of sentences and of paragraphs. The other is the rhetorical function of indicating tone, attitude, feeling and emphasis. In speech, both these functions are carried out by such means as pause, pitch, pace, intonation and volume, often accompanied by facial expression and gesture. In the written language, accurate punctuation is the necessary substitute for those resources.

Exercise 68

The following group of letters was published recently in *The Guardian*. The writers comment on different aspects of spelling and the teaching of it, the heading being supplied by a *Guardian* editor.

Choose one or more of the letters and write a letter in reply, taking up some of the views expressed.

Spelin rools OK—
but itsthe kers of the soshul klases

I FIND Veronica Tippetts' letter about spelling rules (Nov. 6) disturbing on three counts. First, what does she (or the DES) understand by "knowing the rules of spelling" by the age of eleven?

Rules for any activity may be stated theoretically or demonstrated practic-ally. Every day most of us practise skills such as cooking or driving for which we would be unable easily to state the rules unless we were cookery or driving in-structors. We all operate according to rules and precedents whenever we exer-cise a skill. Even children who are poor spellers often follow their own rules in consistently misspelling common words, for example "whent' (went), "frened" (friend) cf "when," "seemed." Abstract rules of the I before E variety are less useful than remembering that ceiling looks better than cieling.

This leads to my second point which is that spelling rules and even books of rules do exist. The most comprehensive are published for the benefit of dyslexics, or foreign students of English, but there are also many school spelling schemes which state simple rules of the "magic e" type. For those who wish to understand more complex rules, Fowler's Modern English Usage is perhaps the best known reference. In practice, however, most of us are not able without taking great thought to explain the rule about doubling con-sonants in fit-fitting: benefit-benefiting; or referee, referrable, referrable/ible. We know what looks right because we work by analogy or extrapolation. It is possible to learn or deduce rules, but most of us find that only a small number are necessary.

Thirdly, I question the implication that most children acquire language skills incidentally. In learning to talk, children do not simply imitate their elders. Parents teach by correcting grammar and explaining new expressions. In reading, all but a few children benefit from explicit instruction. As for spelling, it is common knowledge that not all journalists, doc-tors, teachers, lawyers, or writers of let-ters to newspapers have picked up the knack of being infallibly accurate.

A question which Ms Tippetts does not raise is whether accurate spelling is im-portant. Everyone I have asked thinks that it is. Gross spelling errors carry the risk that the message will be misinter-preted. Minor errors in spelling or gram-mar distract attention from the message; witness the number of letters to news-papers which criticise the way a writer expresses his ideas, and use this as a weapon to attack the substance of what he says.

For myself, I hope that the DES docu-

ment will ensure that children in primary schools are taught how to learn spellings, to classify words into spelling families, to know when a word looks wrong and how to check it in a dictionary, and to treasure oddities and exceptions. It will be unfortunate if the DES statement is interpreted as a directive to measure children's spelling competence by ability to state rules or write obscure words accurately, at eleven or any other age. Yours faithfully,
Rene Boote.
Head of the Reading
  and Language Service,
Stockport.

WHAT do we mean by "poor spelling'? asks Veronica Tippetts. Perhaps some recent examples will help her understand.
  These have appeared in shop windows or displays in Sunderland in the last two weeks: Saterday, novalties, definetely (corrected to definatley, wrougt iron, carcus (for carcase), duke box, canva s skirt's, resently, quaranted, overalling (for overhauling), chester draws.

Does Ms Tippetts really believe that this does not matter?—Yours faithfully,
George Patterson.
8 Humbledon View,
Sunderland.

AS a teacher, I have to teach that adequate spelling is necessary for communication, correct spelling for social advancement, and that the values implicit in each are very different.
Chris Nicholls.
The Practical
English Centre,
The Old School House,
School Gardens,
Shrewsbury.

Ile show you watt damige a week speler can wreek on the English langwedge, as sugested by Veronica Tippetts a confusing seeries of idiotecs wiv no comunicashun bitween any of them. Shurely if their were no standardised forms of werds, we mite as wel bee in 14th century england.
Ronnie Parker.
7 Bleachfield,
York University.

Exercise 69

The following is an extract from *Small World* (1984), a humorous novel by David Lodge. Morris Zapp is an American professor, here delivering a lecture at an English conference.

(a) Comment on the form of the lecture and its uses of language, discussing what is revealed about the character of Morris Zapp.

(b) During the lecture Morris Zapp, who is presented as a comic figure, makes a number of assertions about the meaning of texts, the nature of language, the form of discourse, and the characteristic of reading.
  Consider one or more of his assertions and discuss whether there is any validity in what he is made to say.

Morris Zapp delivered it striding up and down the platform with his notes in one hand and a fat cigar in the other. 'You see before you,' he began, 'a man who once believed in the possibility of interpretation. That is, I thought that the goal of reading was to establish the meaning of texts. I used to be a Jane Austen man. I think I can say in all modesty I was *the* Jane Austen man. I wrote five books on Jane Austen, every one of which was trying to establish what her novels meant—and, naturally, to prove that no one had properly understood what they meant before. Then I began a commentary on the works of Jane Austen, the aim of which was to be utterly exhaustive, to examine the novels from every conceivable angle—historical, biographical, rhetorical, mythical, structural, Freudian, Jungian, Marxist, existentialist, Christian, allegorical, ethical, phenomenological, archetypal, you name it. So that when each commentary was written, there would be *nothing further to say* about the novel in question.

Of course, I never finished it. The project was not so much Utopian as self-defeating. By that I don't just mean that if successful it would have eventually put us all out of business. I mean that it couldn't succeed because it isn't possible, and it isn't possible because of the nature of language itself, in which meaning is constantly being transferred from one signifier to another and can never be absolutely possessed.

'To understand a message is to decode it. Language is a code. *But every decoding is another encoding.* If you say something to me I check that I have understood your message by saying it back to you in my own words, that is, different words from the ones you used, for if I repeat your own words exactly you will doubt whether I have really understood you. But if I use *my* words it follows that I have changed *your* meaning, however slightly; and even if I were, deviantly, to indicate my comprehension by repeating back to you your own unaltered words, that is no guarantee that I have duplicated your meaning in my head, because I bring a different experience of language, literature, and non-verbal reality to those words, therefore they mean something different to me from what they mean to you. And if you think I have not understood the meaning of your message, you do not simply repeat it in the same words, you try to explain it in different words, different from the ones you used originally; but then the *it* is no longer the *it* that you started with. And for that matter, you are not the *you* that you started with. Time has moved on since you opened your mouth to speak, the molecules in your body have changed, what you intended to say has been superseded by what you did say, and that has already become part of your personal history, imperfectly remembered. Conversation is like playing tennis with a ball made of Krazy Putty that keeps coming back over the net in a different shape.

'Reading, of course, is different from conversation. It is more passive in the sense that we can't interact with the text, we can't affect the development of the text by our own words, since the text's words are already given. That is what perhaps encourages the quest for interpretation. If the words are fixed once and for all, on the page, may not their meaning be fixed also? Not so, because the same axiom, *every decoding is another encoding,* applies to literary criticism even more stringently than it does to ordinary spoken discourse. In ordinary spoken discourse, the endless cycle of encoding-decoding-encoding may be terminated by an action, as when for instance I say, 'The door is open,' and you say, 'Do you mean you would like me to shut it?' and I say, 'If you don't mind,' and you shut the door—we may be satisfied that at a certain level my meaning has been understood. But if the literary text says, 'The door was open,' I cannot ask the text what it means by saying that the door was open, I can only speculate about the significance of that door—opened by what agency, leading to what discovery, mystery, goal? The tennis analogy will not do for the activity of reading—it is not a to-and-fro process, but an endless, tantalising leading on.

Exercise 70

Read the following review of a book about the English language.

(a) Comment on the text as a review, taking note not only of the reviewer's opinions of the book but the way these are expressed.

The mongrel tongue

SURPRISINGLY little is known about the history of the English language – a fact which the abundant scholarship on the subject tends to obscure. Speech could not be recorded at all until Edison began experimenting with wax cylinders in the 1870s; and written English, a specialised, minority activity, tells us almost nothing about how the mass of people used language in any given period.

What must be still more frustrating for linguistic historians is that, though they can deduce from written records that English has always been in a state of change, the factors which cause its mutations, and how they operate, remain largely mysterious. In this respect English is quite as problematic as astro-physics, and much less likely to become clearer with time.

An attraction of Robert Burchfield's sturdy little book is that it has no qualms about admitting ignorance. When English first reached these shores, as part of the luggage of a few thousand illegal German immigrants in the fifth century, it had grammatical gender and case endings, rather like Latin. Why these disappeared is unclear. According to one theory, when the next wave of invaders, the Scandinavians, arrived, the Anglo-Saxons strove to converse with them in a simple "creolised" English, which put paid to niceties like gender. This picture of stumbling inter-racial dialogue has obvious charms, but Burchfield firmly squashes it. How the Anglo-Saxons lost their grammar is just another secret hidden in the pre-Edisonian silence.

Anyway, it was a lucky break for English, since a rigid grammatical structure might have cramped its talent for digesting other languages. Stylists used to revere "pure" English, but in reality English is about as pure as factory effluent, and has displayed its mongrel toughness over the centuries by cannibalising a picturesque array of foreign tongues from Greek to Polynesian. This absorption of loan words has slowed down, Burchfield notes, in the last 200 years, and there has been a huge increase in the outflow of English words to less successful languages, which are having to adapt themselves to the master speech-system.

Though linguists can identify loan words in English, they have no idea, apparently, why some foreign words get bor-

THE ENGLISH LANGUAGE by Robert Burchfield/ Oxford £9.50 pp194

John Carey

rowed and some not. An extremely complex cultural filter seems to function, which would be worth exploring. Burchfield remarks, for instance, that British English shows a resistance to Yiddish words in sch – *(schmuck, schnook),* common in the US.

Also unexplained is the facility some coinages have for making themselves at home in the language, while others pine unused. Shakespeare, Spenser and their contemporaries dreamed up hundreds of words which gained instant membership, but there is a pathetic graveyard of neologisms that have found no takers at all. Admittedly, the samples of these stillborn brainwaves Burchfield cites have every appearance of being non-starters: *commotrix* ("a maid that

makes ready her mistress"); *parentate* ("to celebrate one's parents' funerals"). But what about *neverness,* another 17th-century invention, which fills a gap in the language (as the opposite of *eternity* – a useful 20th century concept), and is also beautiful, but has been ignored by everyone except its originator, Bishop Wilkins, and his modern admirer, Borges?

Given all these aspects that linguists are at a loss to explain, it is no surprise that they cannot account for semantic change (why words develop new meanings) either. Words move up and down league tables of respectability in wholly unpredictable ways, and have no doubt been doing so since runic times. *Boy,* for example, originally meant "fettered person", then "male servant", and finally "male child", whereas *knave* drifted in the other direction, starting out as "male child", then "male servant", and

eventually "rascal". Linguists often proclaim that something Burchfield calls "the Mitford factor" controls such developments – which means that words or usages adopted by a dominant social class tend to prevail. But this only pushes the whole problem one step back, since you still have to explain why a word attracts a particular class. Burchfield's conclusion on the whole issue of shifting words, meanings and pronunciations is that these things "just happen", and cannot be explained, "any more than it is possible to say why rooks choose one tree rather than another." That comparison may be over-hopeful, since systematic rook-watching would probably yield a solution and systematic word-watching has not.

Although the one essential feature of English, to judge from its past record, is its rampant and chaotic changeability, there are always those who believe that it achieved its true, fragile perfection in the period of their own youth, and will be irretrievably damaged if the vulgar persist in using *like* for *as,* or misplacing the apostrophe. Burchfield cheerfully kills off various illusions of the "correct English" addicts. Infinitives have been split, he points out, since at least the 14th century; and purists who shudder over new words which mix up Greek, Latin and English elements *(helipad, breathalyser)* would have logically to renounce *ostrich* or *plainness,* which are similar hybrids.

The language swarms with "incorrect" formations. *Pea, burial* (and others) are mistaken shortenings of Old English singular forms *(pise, byrgels),* which were ignorantly assumed

to be plurals; yet even the most fastidious refiners seem happy with them now. Foes of "Americanisms" can rarely, if challenged, pick them out once they have been in the language for a few years. *Law-abiding,* for example, surely the most British of vocables, is American in origin.

These sound arguments for accepting the linguistic novelties that happen to surface during one's lifetime do not, of course, stop any of us from detesting a sizeable proportion of them. How can you respect someone who says "No way" – a sure mark of the semi-educated, now fortunately obsolescent? How can you repress a shiver at seeing the word *silo* ("a store for grain") hideously applied to underground missile sites? Since our personalities and memories are so largely composed of language, it is as difficult to feel objective about linguistic change as it is about ageing.

Burchfield's own conservatism shows through unashamedly. He has written a traditional, historically-based study, and has no patience with Chomskyan transformational grammar or other new-fangled tacks. The star-wars among the theorists have, he fears, blunted many fine minds and retarded real knowledge. Linguistics, which looked such a bright hope 10 years back, now appears addled, internecine and fruitless. His own determination to keep language study within the grasp of intelligent laypersons is healthy and democratic. But I wish he had allowed himself to be less routine at times. His sections on English dictionaries and the English Bible are commonplace, and a scholar of Burchfield's calibre could, you feel, have penned them while attending to something tricky on the gas stove.

I should have like, instead, some account of current relations between English and its users. The Oxford Dictionary contains 414,000 words, but how big is the vocabulary of the average English speaker? It used to be given as 4,000 – has that gone up or down in the last half century? How many words do you need to read The Times? The Sun? What correlation is there between vocabulary size and income? Vocabulary size and crime? Burchfield, reigning editor of the Oxford Dictionary, would be ideally placed to tell us. All that apart, this remains an expert, absorbing guidebook to the English-speaking world's biggest asset.

(b) The writer of the review makes use of the opportunity to remark on aspects of the English language, its development, its uses and its usage. Set down in a list a summary of the ideas expressed by the reviewer. Then take *two* of his observations and examine them more fully. You will need to consult the appropriate sections of Parts II–V of this book and to gather information and illustrations from other sources. For each of the areas chosen, write a short essay which shows clearly how far you agree or disagree with the reviewer.

(c) The writer of the review expresses criticism of a number of aspects of linguistics. Comment on this criticism.

Exercise 71

Write on the following:

(a) 'The English are socially divided by a common language.' Discuss.

(b) '. . . That which we call a rose
By any other name would smell as sweet' (*Romeo and Juliet*)
How important is the name of something to what it represents?

(c) 'True Americanisms are of two kinds: cultural and linguistic. Linguistic Americanisms are exemplified in such well-known pairs as *pants/trousers, dumb/stupid,* and *cabana/beach hut.* Cultural Americanisms are terms for which there is no British equivalent, because the thing denoted does not exist in Britain. Examples are *caucus, diner, dude ranch.*' Consider the language of Americans in the light of this comment.

(d) Comment on the following.

Black Londoners speak what linguists call London Jamaican, and while versions in other cities may have some differences, they are broadly similar. Characteristic features include 'mi kom' (I came), 'shi a go', (she's going) and 'dem mad' (they're mad).

Black youngsters speak perfectly normal London English, almost indistinguishable for their white peers. But they also switch into and out of London Jamaican.

It is part of a search for identity in a culture which some of them feel is rejecting them. It's mainly an in-group talk, which is sometimes used to white people, usually to put them in their place.

(e) Language varieties—by what criteria can they be identified?

(f) What is important about studying language in relation to the society which produces it?

(g)   'One of the most interesting aspects of studying a language is the knowledge that it will never stop developing and changing.' Discuss.

(h)   Consider, with examples, the differences between regional dialects and social dialects.

(i)   'The style of language to which children are exposed in their family and neighbourhood crucially affects the type of language they develop.' Discuss.

(j)   Do you believe that schools tend to inhibit rather than foster linguistic skills?

(k)   How helpful to you is the notion of 'Standard English'?

(l)   What do you see as the main differences between the formal and informal use of English?

(m)   Can it ever be determined how children acquire language? (You may like to reflect on your own experience and on what you have observed of others.)

(n)   'The young acquire their model of language from the uses they perceive in the language of older people.' Discuss.

(o)   How helpful to the study of language are notions of 'correctness' and 'appropriacy'?

(p)   How far does the term 'register' help in describing the use of language in different situations?

(q)   How important to a study of language is an understanding of non-verbal communication?

(r)   Should the English spelling system be changed to a phonemic one?

(s)   Discuss the relationship between play dialogue and real conversation.

(t)   'Indifference, indiscipline and ignorance are battering and destroying some of the best features of our language.' Discuss.

(u)   The following review of a book appeared in a local newspaper.
    (i) Comment on the way in which the review is expressed.
    (ii) Discuss the assumptions about spoken English which are set out and criticised in the review.

How one Speaks the Queen's English

A crash course in learning to speak the Queen's English is available from today in a tongue-in-cheek attempt to bring down the 'language barrier between the classes'.

To judge from their speech, millions of English people 'might as well be foreigners', according to one of the contributors to a book entitled *The Queen's English*, by Dorgan Ruston, published today.

It contains many useful tips from 'shiteing' for a 'wheateh' in a restaurant to singing 'Gawd Sieve Ah Grey Shahs Quin'.

The books sets out a series of field trips for readers, culminating with tips for attending a 'gordon potty' at Buckingham Palace.

Useful phrases to memorise in case of a meeting with Her Majesty are given, including 'Thing kew fah ianvating may,' 'Wart ay lawt awv kawghees' and 'Wart's ay nayce parson lake yaw doing ian ay pellarse lake these?'

The book purports to teach 'Upper class English' phonetically and is said to contain all you will ever need to say from the cradle to the grave.

Suggested sporting field trips to test your newly acquired speaking skills include visiting Asskit, Hinleach, Weemble-dawn and Kyes (Cowes).

Tips for 'general chat' include 'Gawd Lawd! Theh Lend Raver hairs rahn ava an gordon names' (garden gnomes) and 'Thah Weeng Cawmahn-dah's nior lig (new leg) hes bin ay greet sark-sis'.

The book observes that one of the greatest exponents of the 'modified language' is Prince Charles, who, it is said, after more than 30 years of 'correct speaking' has extremely well-developed jowl muscles.

PART VII

Language Projects

CHAPTER 11

Case Studies

The Language Project, or Case Study as it is sometimes called, is an important part of most language courses and may count for up to a third of the marks available at the assessment. It provides an opportunity for you to study in some detail an area of language of particular personal interest, and to relate practice and theory. Frequently the Project allows you to study an aspect of spoken language and to develop your ideas in a way not possible in a timed examination. It is therefore important that you make the most of the opportunity provided.

The syllabus

The first thing you should do is read what is stated in your syllabus about the Project or Case Study. The syllabus will give guidance about what is expected both in the subject matter and in the nature and length of the response. You may be required to produce a project reporting a personal investigation into a specified aspect of language use in everyday life, your project being 2000–4000 words in length. More exactly, you may be asked to make a practical study of the spoken language in a specific context, commenting on the implications of the chosen area of the spoken language and discussing interesting and significant features of the recorded material on which the project is based. Such a project would expect you to refer particularly to a selective description of the sounds and/or forms of the material transcribed. The length of such a study would normally, however, not exceed 3000 words with the transcription of the recorded material being additional to this limit.

Syllabuses frequently include guidance about areas of study that have been found to be profitable for individual students, and any lists should be read as a stimulus to your own ideas. They may suggest such areas as:
- analysis of conversations;
- the language of pre-school children or pupils in the early stages of language development;

- instances of talk—between customer and salesman; within a family; on the radio or on television; between people having an argument; at a formal meeting; as gossip;
- examples of everyday language in certain situations—giving instructions, making greetings—or by certain occupational groups—politicians, lawyers, news and sports commentators; entertainers.

Where the area does not have to be selected from a spoken use of language, the syllabus may point to the stylistic features of contrasted texts—for example, changes in style according to the readership or age group for whom a text is intended, or contrasts in the use of language because of the passage of time.

Whatever the requirement, the syllabus may give you some ideas, but the choice of area of study should be essentially yours. What interests you most about the uses of language? What would you like to know more about? What would hold your interest over a period of time and contain sufficient variety to allow you to make a range of observations and to draw conclusions which could be individual to you?

The choice of topic

The choice of topic is therefore of vital importance. It is essential that you discuss areas of interest and possibilities with your tutor who will know from experience which areas are capable of sustaining a study. If there is no particular area that springs to mind, you may find it helpful to ask yourself more specific questions about the form of your research. Do you see yourself as being active or passive? Do you want to create the uses of language, say in an interview, or do you prefer to be an observer, listening to the language uses of others, whether on the radio or at home or at college? Additionally, do you want to focus on one particular instance of language use, or would you prefer to make a comparative study, contrasting different uses of language by several people in a similar context or by the same person in different contexts?

It is easy to bombard you with a number of possibilities. The important thing is that you focus on an area of particular interest to you which will sustain your interest over six or more months.

Preparation

Once having decided on an area of study, you need to examine its possibilities and what you need to make the most of them. It is important that you sample in general the material of your chosen area first so that you come to recognise what is typical of the situation. Familiarity with an area in general will allow you to identify what is individual or particular to the extract you are focusing on for your study. To provide a brief example, consider what features of language use disc-jockeys have in common and what features are particular to the style of one named disc-jockey. In the same vein, you may need to assess how consistent a person is in the use of a style and how typical the extract you are studying is of that style.

In order to gather your material accurately in a study of spoken English, you will need a tape-recorder, and you may find a video-recorder invaluable. You should become so familiar with the controls of whatever instrument you use that you do not have to fuss with stopping, rewinding and playing back the tape or adjustments of the recording level in order to be sure of what you are doing. If you are recording using batteries away from a mains supply, it should become automatic for you to check the power of your batteries before beginning in order to ensure a consistent quality of recording.

Remember to preface any recording with a brief statement of the subject matter, the source and the date, the sort of information you would expect to put at the beginning of an essay.

Keep full notes of what you have recorded on a tape and where it occurs on the tape. You should always keep a record, possibly on a card, of the source of your recording, setting down the date, the time, the situation and the circumstances.

If you intend to gather original material for your recording, then you need to plan in detail in advance a structure for your recording. To take one typical area of study as an example, you may decide that you want to base your project on the interview of an old person in order to consider not only the reminiscences of that person but also the forms of language used. Two areas of preparation are essential for such an interview. First, you need to observe the art of interviewing as practised by a range of professionals on radio and television. Secondly, you need to prepare the ground for your specific interview, not only getting permission from the person concerned, but also thinking precisely about the questions you would want to ask.

The following groups of questions show the detail that may be helpful as a guide. You would not expect to ask all the questions set down, but they would serve to help you avoid too many irrelevant responses and would act as a prompt. People, particularly the old, become nervous in the presence of a tape-recorder, and gentle guidance, based on clear planning, helps to put a person at ease and hence to converse naturally.

Here are some examples of the kinds of questions you might ask in conducting an interview with someone who has left school or college long ago:

(a) Name, age, birthplace.

(b) As a child, whom did you play with? Brothers; sisters; neighbours. Did you have your own special group of friends? Did you play games against other groups? Where?

What games did you play? Were you allowed to get dirty when you played? Did boys and girls play the same games?

Were you free to play with anyone you pleased? Did your parents discourage you from playing with certain children? (*If yes:* Why?) What did they think about children fighting or gambling in the street? I should now like to ask about how you spent your free time when you were at school. Did you have any hobbies then? (Collecting—cigarette cards, etc.) Did you keep any pets? Gardening. Did you go fishing? Walks; bicycling. With whom?

Did you take part in any sports?

Did you belong to any youth organizations (Scouts, Guides)? Activities. Theatres; concerts; music halls; cinemas. Did your parents give you any pocket money? What did you spend the money on?

(c) Were you given lessons by anyone before going to school?

How old were you when you first went to school?

Type of school (board/private/church; day/boarding; boys/girls/ mixed)?

What did you think of school? How did you feel about the teachers? If you did something the teachers disapproved of, what would happen? Did the teachers emphasize certain things as important in life? Manners, how to treat the opposite sex; tidiness; punctuality; ways of speaking.

Did they encourage discussion? Was any science taught? Games.

What sort of homes did most of the other children come from? Were some worse dressed than others?

Were there any gangs or groups in the school?

Did you go on to another school afterwards? *If yes: repeat. If a secondary school:* a cadet corps; prefects.

How old were you when you left school? Would you have stayed longer if you had had the opportunity? Did you attend any part-time education afterwards? (e.g. evening classes).

If at university: Subjects; new friends; new attitudes; influence of tutors; intellectual discussion; religion; clubs and societies; other leisure. How were women regarded at university at that time?

(d) While you were at school, did you have a part-time job or any means of earning a little regular money? *If yes:* How did you get it? (Through parents?) What exactly did you have to do in this job? How did you learn? Were any practical jokes played on you? What hours did you work? (Saturday; Sunday; half-day). Were there any breaks for meals? Did you have any holidays with pay? What were you paid? Did you feel that was a fair wage, or not? (Did you give any of the money to your mother? What was it spent on?)

How did you get on with the other people you worked with? Did men and women work together? Could you talk or relax at all? (Could you play games in the breaks?) Was there a works club? A works outing? Any other entertainments for employees? Was there a presentation when a worker retired? Did any of the employers or wives visit workers and their wives at times of sickness or bereavement?

How did your employer treat you? How did you feel about him?

How did you feel about the work? Did you like or dislike it? How long did you do it for? When did you give it up? What did you do after that? *Repeat for any other part-time jobs while at school.*

Now I should like to ask you about your first full-time job. What was that? *Repeat questions above, for all jobs (including part-time) to retirement. These questions are schematic and much fuller questions and promptings are desirable for main occupations.*

Did you serve an apprenticeship or training period for any of your jobs?

The text

From whatever you have decided to examine you will establish a text, that is the evidence on which you wish to base your observations and speculations about the use of language in a particular context. The first prerequisite is that your text is accurate. In a study of recorded speech, you are required to transcribe your material. A syllabus may suggest the transcription of three to five minutes, according to the difficulty of the material. What is important is that you establish a consistent method of setting out your transcription to show that you have responded accurately to the sounds and expression of the language. You may use ordinary spelling but you need to be able to show aspects of speech such as stress and intonation, pauses and hesitations. It obviously helps if you are able to use phonemic or phonetic symbols, provided you are competent in their use. The most important thing, however, is that you provide a key with your transcription which makes the conventions you have adopted clear to the reader.

Allow yourself plenty of time to make your transcription. You will need to play parts of your material again and again before you are satisfied that you have heard sounds correctly.

Analysis

As you are producing your transcription, with the close attention to detail that it demands, you should find yourself thinking about its characteristics. You should note down separately items of interest to you—the choice of words, the emphasis given to them, the way they are pronounced, their uses with other words, the pattern which the words produce, the grammatical constructions which the order of words indicates, the characteristics which show that something is spoken rather than written. You will begin to identify how the language of your transcription differs from what you would consider 'normal' English, and you should begin to ask yourself why. Is it because of the speaker or the nature of the subject or the sense of audience or the relationship between the speaker and the audience?

From such questioning you will begin to think about the general linguistic implications of your observations, and you will find it helpful at this stage to turn to established works on linguistics to consider how far what you have discovered confirms what is stated by authorities and how far you have come across deviations from the norm. You could well think about reasons for such individual characteristics.

You should then be in a position to draft the results of your project.

Presentation

It is helpful to present the material for your project in the following sequence.

Introduction: This can be a general and brief discussion of what you have chosen to study, where your interest lay and why, and what approach you felt was necessary to make the most of the opportunity.

Description: This section, which can also be brief, would make clear what material you felt it important to collect and why, with some personal comments on the method of gathering the material and its benefits and limitations.

The material: Here you provide the material individual to you. In a project on spoken English this will be your transcription, with the principles on which it is based clearly established. You will be expected to provide the tape from which your transcription is taken.

Analysis: At this stage you begin to draw attention to features of your text which are of interest to you. Rather than working your way through a text from beginning to end, you should decide on certain characteristics of particular importance, place them in a logical order, and comment on them with particular reference to details in the text.

Evaluation: In this final section you should try to set your observations in a wider context, drawing inferences about the nature of language and its uses. Always support any general assertions with detailed reference to your text. If you do refer to general works on linguistics you should be sure to give the sources with page references.

Bibliography: Your project should conclude with a list of any works consulted, set out as in the bibliography to this book, namely author, title, publisher and year of publication, and you should also provide acknowledgments for the material in your project and for any help received.

Selected Bibliography

J. Aitchison, *Linguistics*, second edition, Hodder and Stoughton, 1978.

R. A. Banks, *Living English*, Hodder and Stoughton, 1983.

R. A. Banks, *Directed Writing and Reading*, Hodder and Stoughton, 1985.

L. Bloomfield, *Language*, Allen and Unwin (paperback), 1969 (first published 1933).

G. L. Brook, *English Dialects*, Blackwell, 1963.

G. L. Brook, *Varieties of English*, second edition, Macmillan, 1979.

A. C. Baugh and T. Cable, *A History of the English Language*, third edition, Routledge, 1978.

R. Chapman, *Linguistics and Literature*, Edward Arnold, 1973.

N. Chomsky, *Syntactic Structures*, Mouton Paperback Edition, 1978 (first published 1957).

N. Chomsky, *Aspects of the Theory of Syntax*, Massachussetts Institute of Technology, 1965.

N. Chomsky, *Topics in the Theory of Generative Grammar*, Mouton Paperback Edition, 1978 (first published 1966).

N. Chomsky, *Studies on Semantics in Generative Grammar*, Mouton Paperback Edition, 1972.

N. Chomsky, *Rules and Representations*, new edition, Blackwell (paperback), 1982.

R. A. Close, *A Reference Grammar for Students of English*, Longman, 1975.

D. Crystal, *Linguistics*, Penguin, 1971.

W. Empson, *Seven Types of Ambiguity*, second edition, Hogarth (paperback), 1984 (first published 1947).

D. Jones, *An Outline of English Phonetics*, ninth edition, Cambridge University Press (paperback), 1976 (first published 1962).

G. Kress, *Halliday: System and Function in Language*, Oxford University Press, 1976.

S. M. Lamb, *Outline of Stratificational Grammar*, Georgetown University Press, 1966.

G. N. Leech, *A Linguistic Guide to English Poetry*, Longman, 1973.

J. Lyons, *Semantics*, 2 vols, Cambridge University Press, 1977.

A. MacIntosh and M. A. K. Halliday, *Descriptive and Applied Linguistics*, Longman, 1966.

A.MacIntosh and M. A. K. Halliday, *Patterns of Language: Papers in General*, Longman, 1966.

W. R. O'Donnell and Loreto Todd, *Variety in Contemporary English*, Allen and Unwin, 1980.

H. E. Palmer and F. G. Blandford (revised by R. Kingdon), *A Grammar of Spoken English*, third edition, W. Heffer and Son, 1969.

H. E. Palmer, *Descriptive and Comparative Linguistics*, Faber (paperback), 1978.

R. Quirk. *The Use of English*, Longman, 1962.

R. Quirk, S. Greenbaum, G. Leech, J. Svartik, *A Grammar of Contemporary English*, Longman, 1972.

R. Quirk and S. Greenbaum, *A University Grammar of English*, Longman, 1973.

P. Trudgill, *Sociolinguistics*, Penguin, 1974.

P. Trudgill, *International English: A Guide to Varieties of Standard English*, Edward Arnold, 1985.

G. A. Vallins (revised by D. G. Scragg), *Spelling*, A. Deutsch, 1965.

M. F. Wakelin, *English Dialects: an Introduction*, Athlone Press, 1977.

Index